Democratization Without Representation

Democratization Without Representation

THE POLITICS OF SMALL INDUSTRY IN MEXICO

Kenneth C. Shadlen

THE PENNSYLVANIA STATE UNIVERSITY PRESS
UNIVERSITY PARK, PENNSYLVANIA

Library of Congress Cataloging-in-Publication Data

Shadlen, Kenneth C.
Democratization without representation : the politics of small
industry in Mexico / Kenneth C. Shadlen.
p.   cm.
Includes bibliographical references and index.
ISBN 0-271-02696-0 (alk. paper)
1. Trade associations—Mexico—Political activity.
2. Cámara Nacional de la Industria de Transformación (Mexico).
3. Industrial policy—Mexico.
4. Industrial promotion—Mexico.
5. Small business—Government policy—Mexico.
6. Democratization—Mexico.
I. Title: Democracy without representation. II. Title.

HD2429.M4S53 2004
322'.3'0972—dc22
2004006254

First paperback prniting, 2006

The Pennsylvania State University Press is a member of the
Association of American University Presses.

It is the policy of The Pennsylvania State University Press
to use acid-free paper. Publications on uncoated stock satisfy the
minimum requirements of American National Standard for
Information Sciences—Permanence of Paper for
Printed Library Material, ANSI Z39.48–1992.

CONTENTS

FIGURES AND TABLES

ACKNOWLEDGMENTS

This project has traveled with me to various institutions in a number of countries. I wish to thank some of the many people who have helped me along the way and with whom I have shared ideas. First and foremost, I thank Ruth Berins Collier for the tremendous guidance, support, and encouragement she has provided. Anyone familiar with Ruth's work will notice her influence on the pages that follow. Indeed, the central question at the heart of this book—how variation in regime characteristics affects political representation—was inspired by some of her work (e.g., R. B. Collier 1992), her graduate seminar, and the ongoing interaction we have had over many years. I also wish to thank David Collier, whose enthusiasm for this project has been unwavering. Both David and Ruth have offered me more than the customary advice that professors offer their students. They have been sounding boards for my ideas, and I've benefited enormously from the insightful observations and criticisms they have shared with me.

A number of people have read and commented on parts of the manuscript. Others have provided feedback on presentations at professional meetings and university colloquiums. And I've had countless conversations with friends and colleagues over coffee. All these interactions have contributed one way or another to the final project. In what is without doubt an incomplete list, let me express my thanks here to, among others, Vinod Aggarwal, Felipe Agüero, Carlos Alba, Giorgio Alberti, Jeff Anderson, Bruce Bagley, Melani Cammett, Patrick Cronin, Louise Davidson-Schmich, Jonathan DiJohn, Mahrukh Doctor, Vicente Donato, Enrique Dussel Peters, Peter Evans, Jean-Paul Faguet, Rosa María Garza, Geoff Gershenson, Miguel Glatzer, Jerry Haar, John Harriss, Peter Houtzager, Dave Kang, Tim Kessler, Peter Kingstone, Glen Kuecker, Marcus Kurtz, Jim Mahoney, Matt Marostica, Susan Martin, Kevin Middlebrook, Yemile Mizrahi, Pete Moore, Tim Power, James Putzel, Dennis Rodgers, Dietrich Rueschemeyer, Ben Schneider, Andrew Schrank, Jon Shefner, Rudy Sil, Eduardo Silva, Tom Skidmore, Bill Smith, Strom Thacker, Peter Uvin, Robert Wade, Van Whiting, and Alan Zuckerman.

A few people merit extra-special thanks. Marcus Kurtz read each and every chapter of this book more times than he probably cares to remember, yet even when reading something for the fifth or sixth time he never failed to provide fresh insights. By now I suspect Marcus knows this topic better than I do! Andrew Schrank has been a close friend since the day we met in the summer of 2000, as assistant professors at the University of Miami. Andrew is the colleague whom most people can only dream of having—a constant source of creative and perceptive ideas, coupled with unbridled enthusiasm and a boundless level of energy. I am lucky to have friends like Marcus and Andrew.

Robert Wade has provided steady and invaluable support since we met in Providence in 1998. His intellectual curiosity, his fervor for addressing not just the big but the *biggest* questions in political science and international relations, and his courage to leap fearlessly and boldly into unfamiliar territory are inspirational. Robert's path-breaking work on development and the politics of the global economy is no secret. What is perhaps less well known is his extraordinary capacity as mentor. I cannot sufficiently thank Robert for what his friendship, collegiality, and mentorship have meant for me. He instilled me with a renewed sense of enthusiasm for which I will remain forever indebted.

I received funding for this book from the Center for Latin American Studies at the University of California, Berkeley; the Center for Latin American and Caribbean Studies at the University of Connecticut; the School of Business Administration at the University of Miami; and the Crisis States Programme at the London School of Economics. Each of these institutions funded separate trips to Latin America, without which completion of this book would not have been possible. I am grateful for all of their support.

Portions of this book have appeared in "Neoliberalism, Corporatism, and Small Business Political Activism in Contemporary Mexico," *Latin American Research Review* 35, no. 2 (2000): 73–106, and "Orphaned by Democracy: Small Industry in Contemporary Mexico," *Comparative Politics* 35, no. 1 (2002): 43–62. I thank the journals for permission to use some of this material.

I also wish to take this opportunity to thank Sandy Thatcher, of Penn State Press, for his assistance in bringing this book to completion. Sandy took an early interest in the project, and he stayed interested even as I undertook additional research and, it might have seemed, disappeared. I also thank Romaine Perin for tremendously improving the final version of the book with her masterful copyediting (my adjective, not hers).

Susan Martin brings joy to my life on a daily basis. She goes above and beyond the call of duty in her encouragement, support, and patience (and tolerance). Having your closest friend, colleague, and soulmate also be your spouse has, in my case, been a magical formula. Thanks, Susan. I hope I can make the same contribution to her career as she makes to mine. Last, I wish to express my deepest thanks to my parents and brothers for their unlimited and unconditional support and encouragement, and to Susan's family as well.

ABBREVIATIONS

ABM	Asociación de Banqueros de Mexico (Mexican Bankers' Association)
ALAMPYME	Asociación Latinoamericana de la Micro, Pequeña y Mediana Empresa (Latin American Association of Micro, Small, and Medium Firms)
AMCB	Asociación Mexicana de Casas de Bolsa (Mexican Stockbrokers' Association)
AMIB	Asociación Mexicana de Instituciones Bursátiles (Mexican Association of Securities Institutions)
AMIS	Asociación Mexicana de Institutos de Seguro (Mexican Association of Insurance Institutions)
ANIERM	Asociación Nacional de Importadores y Exportadores de la República Mexicana (National Association of Mexican Importers and Exporters)
ANIQ	Asociación Nacional de la Industria Química (National Association of the Chemical Industry)
ANIT	Asociación Nacional de Industriales de Transformación (National Association of Manufacturing Industrialists)
APYME	Asamblea de Pequeños y Medianos Empresarios (Assembly of Small and Medium Business)
CADEMPI	Câmara de Desenvolvimento da Micro e Pequena Indústria (Chamber for the Development of Micro and Small Industry)
CAFI	Centro de Apoyo Financiero a la Industria (Center for Financial Support for Industry)
CAINTRA	Cámara de la Industria de Transformacón de Nuevo León (Chamber of Manufacturing Industry of Nuevo León)
CANIBICA	Cámara Nacional de Bienes de Capital (National Chamber of Capital Goods Industry)

CANACINTRA	Cámara Nacional de la Industria de la Transformación (National Chamber of Manufacturing Industry)
CAREINTRA	Cámara Regional de la Industria de Transformación (Regional Chamber of Manufacturing Industry)
CCE	Consejo Coordinador Empresarial (Business Coordinating Council)
CEMAI	Consejo Empresarial Mexicano para Asuntos Internacionales (Mexican Business Council for International Affairs)
CGE	Confederación General Económica (General Economic Confederation)
CIVES	Associação Brasileira de Empresários pela Cidadania (Brazilian Association of Business for Citizenship)
CGT	Confederación General de Trabajo (General Labor Confederation)
CLT	Consolidação das Leis do Trabalho (Consolidation of Labor Laws)
CMHN	Consejo Mexicano de Hombres de Negocio (Mexican Businessmen's Council)
CNA	Consejo Nacional Agropecuario (National Agricultural Council)
CNDH	Comisión Nacional de Derechos Humanos (National Human Rights Commission)
CNI	Confederação Nacional da Indústria (National Industrial Confederation)
COCAI	Consejor Coordinador de Asociaciones Industriales (Coordinating Council of Industrial Associations)
COECE	Coordinadora de Organismos Empresariales de Comercio Exterior (Coordinator of Foreign Trade Business Organizations)
CONACEX	Consejo Nacional de Comercio Exterior (National Foreign Trade Council)
CONCAMIN	Confederación de Cámaras Industriales (Confederation of Industrial Chambers)

CONCANACO	Confederación de Cámaras Nacionales de Comercio (Confederation of Chambers of Commerce)
CONCANACOMIN	Confederación de Cámaras Nacionales de Comercio y de la Industria (Confederation of Chambers of Commerce and Industry)
COPARMEX	Confederación Patronal de la República Mexicana (Mexican Employers' Confederation)
CTA	Confederación de Trabajadores Argentinos (Confederation of Argentine Workers)
CTM	Confederación de Trabajadores de México (Confederation of Mexican Workers)
FAA	Federación Agraria Argentina (Argentine Agrarian Federation)
FIESP	Federação das Indústrias do Estado de São Paulo (Federation of Industries of the State of São Paulo)
FOGAIN	Fondo de Garantía y Fomento a la Pequeña y Mediana Industria (Guarantee Fund for the Development of Medium and Small Industry)
FRENAPO	Frente Nacional contra la Pobreza (National Front Against Poverty)
FPP	Federación de Partidos Populares (Federation of Popular Parties)
GATT	General Agreement on Tariffs and Trade
LANFI	Laboratorios Nacionales de Fomento Industrial (National Industrial Development Laboratories)
LAP	Ley de Asociaciones Profesionales (Law of Professional Associations)
MONAMPE	Movimiento Nacional da Micro e Pequena Empresa (National Movement of Small and Medium Firms)
NAFIN	Nacional Financiera (National Development Bank)
NAFTA	North American Free Trade Agreement
PAN	Partido Acción Nacional (National Action Party)
PNBE	Pensamento Nacional das Bases Empresariais (National Thought of the Business Bases)

PRD	Partido de la Revolución Democrática (Party of the Democratic Revolution)
PRI	Partido Revolucionario Institucional (Institutional Revolutionary Party)
PSE	Pacto de Solidaridad Económica (Economic Solidarity Pact)
PRONAFICE	Programa Nacional de Fomento Industrial y Comercio Exterior (National Program for Industrial Development and Foreign Trade)
RMALC	Red Mexicana de Acción Frente al Libre Comercio (Mexican Free Trade Action Network)
SECOFI	Secretaría de Comercio y Fomento Industrial (Secretariat of Trade and Industrial Development)
SECON	Secretaría de Economía (Secretariat of the Economy)
SHCP	Secretaría de Hacienda y Crédito Público (Secretariat of the Treasury)
SIC	Secretaría de Industria y Comercio (Secretariat of Industry and Trade)
SIMPI	Sindicato da Micro e Pequena Indústria do Estado de São Paulo (Syndicate of Micro and Small Industry of the State of São Paulo)
SPP	Secretaría de Planeación y Presupuesto (Secretariat of Programming and Budget)
UCR	Unión Cívica Radical (Radical Civic Union)
UIA	Unión Industrial Argentina (Argentine Industrial Union)
UTT	Unidad de Transferencia Tecnológica (Technological Transfer Unit)

ONE

The Politics of Small Industry Representation

The close of the twentieth century witnessed a "third wave" of democratization, as countries throughout the developing world and Eastern Europe underwent transitions from authoritarian to democratic political regimes. There are sound reasons to expect democratization to enhance representation and improve the quality of political life. In democracies, political parties bid for voters' support. And in democracies, citizens generally can join, with minimal constraints from the state, the associations they care to join. Democratization, in sum, opens up new opportunities for social actors to participate in politics and to be represented. It comes as no surprise that people have fought so hard for so long to live in democracies, and that the spread of democracy is a celebrated event in world history.

Yet some actors are ill equipped to take advantage of these new opportunities, and this fact should change how we think about the phenomenon of democratization. In this book we shall see that small industry is such an actor. Small firms possess a set of core sociopolitical attributes that complicate the process of representation. The challenges to securing representation can be overcome—there is no iron law of underrepresentation—but these core attributes make it particularly difficult to take advantage of increased electoral competition and associational pluralism. Moreover, democratization can unleash conflicts that exacerbate the already difficult challenges of small industry representation. The result, then, is that democratization can *diminish* representation.

That democratization can lead to declining representation for some citizens and groups of citizens is not terribly surprising, in principle. After all, we would expect democratization to dilute the influence of privileged actors who had disproportionate influence and benefited from special treatment under the preceding regime. Yet small industrialists are typically not insiders who benefit from cronylike relations with the state; they are rarely part of the party nomenclature or ruling elite. Industry, yes, but not small industry. Small industry, the weak segment of local capital, is not among that set of actors that we would expect to be well represented under authoritarianism, or that we would expect to experience declining representation during the course of democratization.

Weak actors such as small industry need to devise strategies to secure representation. They cannot expect the state—neither authoritarian nor democratic—to look after their interests. Among the central points revealed in this book, however, is that democratization can foreclose some channels for representation, all the while creating new opportunities that weak actors can exploit only with great difficulty.

Representative decline in the case of small industry is particularly puzzling for another reason as well. Most countries undergoing democratization have simultaneously undergone equally significant economic transitions that should increase the importance of small enterprises. That is, the third wave of democratization has coincided with a global shift away from state-led strategies of economic development to neoliberalism, where private investors become primarily responsible for job creation and capital accumulation.[1] Countries adopting neoliberal models have relaxed restrictions on trade, investment, and capital flows; privatized many state industries; and adopted more orthodox fiscal and monetary positions.[2] While it is no secret that larger firms—national and transnational—with access to capital and technology play the leading developmental role, the capacity of small firms to integrate into global production chains has critical effects on economic outcomes under the new development model (Peres and Stumpo 2002). To the extent that small firms fail to adjust to international competition, developing countries suffer from higher levels of vulnerability to external shocks. Moreover, in the context of high levels of poverty and

---

1. The abundant literature on dual transitions includes Przeworski 1991; Smith, Acuña, and Gamarra 1994; Haggard and Kaufman 1995; Przeworski et al. 1995; and Oxhorn and Ducatenzeiler 1998.

2. The core dimensions of neoliberalism are similar to what J. Williamson (1990) identified as the "Washington Consensus."

inequality, and with the state reducing its role as employer, small industry's capacity to generate employment gains unprecedented urgency.[3]

Because representation affects public policy, the difficult challenges of small industry representation have profound developmental implications. To be sure, providing assistance to small firms is increasingly discussed as a critical dimension of "second-generation reform" in Latin America and the developing world (Pastor and Wise 1999). Yet while the potential developmental role of small firms is recognized, the importance of representation in developing policies to assist such firms is not. It is essential to consider not just the supply of policy but also the conditions under which the potential beneficiaries can articulate their needs and participate in the design and shaping of such policies. As we shall see, assisting small firms is not a technical choice, but rather a political choice, for doing so may create conflicts between small industrialists and other actors with different preferences. Thus, it is essential that we consider the capacity of small industrialists to construct durable mechanisms of representation.

Democratization Without Representation in Mexico

In the 1980s and 1990s, Mexico underwent a transition from authoritarianism to democracy, a transition that featured the removal of various legal impediments to representation. This transition occurred later and more slowly than in many countries in Latin America and elsewhere throughout the developing world.[4] Indeed, debates over how democratic Mexico was or was becoming raged throughout the period, as did debates over whether and when Mexico crossed a magic threshold and became a democracy. Did the election of Vicente Fox in 2000—the first time in modern Mexican history that the president would not be from the Institutional Revolutionary Party (PRI)—mean that Mexico was now a democracy? Or did this election mark the beginning of the transition? Similar questions were

---

3. This urgency is only furthered by the fact that in many developing countries the more competitive firms are, counterintuitively, in capital-intensive industries (e.g., automobiles, autoparts, electronics, and pharmaceuticals). For analyses of this phenomenon in Mexico, see Heath 1997; and Ruíz Duran and Kagami 1993.

4. Among the many volumes that provide country-by-country case studies of democratization throughout the region, see, for example, O'Donnell, Schmitter, and Whitehead 1986; Dominguez and Lowenthal 1996; and Diamond et al. 1999. For a concise political history of the Mexican case, see Levy and Bruhn 2001.

debated three years earlier, following the midterm elections of 1997, when the PRI lost control of the national legislature for the first time.

Resolving these debates about regime classification and the end point of Mexico's transition is not the point here. What is clear is that Mexico was undergoing a process of democratization in this period, that a wide range of legal impediments to participation and representation were eradicated. And, importantly, it is clear that the relaxation of state-imposed constraints on interest association created new space for civic engagement and that the emergence of an increasingly competitive electoral environment created new opportunities for political parties.

Yet during this same period, as Mexico became more democratic, small industry's capacity to participate in policy making diminished. As we shall see, small industry secured greater representation under decades of single-party authoritarian rule then in the more competitive political environment. This is an actor that throughout the post–World War II era gained representation through interest associations, but in the course of democratization the most important business organization for small industry representation lost its capacity to defend such firms' interests. Nor has democratization generated an environment for alternative business associations, civil society organizations (CSOs), or political parties to fill this vacated space and represent small industry.

Why has small industry's representation diminished in the context of democratization? Why, in a country plagued by high levels of unemployment and underemployment, might actors capable of providing jobs seem to diminish in political importance? To address these questions, and to explain the phenomenon of declining representation, in this book I analyze the mechanisms by which small industrialists' interests have been represented in Mexican politics. We will examine the challenges of representation through two basic channels, associations and parties. A set of inherent core attributes are identified, attributes that pose obstacles for securing representation through these two channels; and then actors' strategies for overcoming these obstacles in changing economic and political conditions are analyzed.

Transitions from authoritarianism to democracy, we shall see, can unleash conflicts and introduce institutional changes that exacerbate the complex challenges of representation. Removing authoritarian constraints on interest association and party competition presents new opportunities, but these are opportunities that small firms may have disproportionately greater difficulty exploiting. In short, small firms may find themselves handicapped by a set of attributes that make gaining representation exceedingly difficult.

The irony is that small industrialists may have greater ability to secure representation in an authoritarian context—they may be less able to aggregate and articulate their interests when "free" to do so in a democratic setting.[5]

Definitions and Clarifications

Before we proceed, some brief points of definition and clarification are in order. In Mexico, the definition of "small" firm changed throughout the twentieth century. In fact, at times different government agencies used different definitions. A 1990 regulation, which established a common system for all branches of government, is the basis for the classification system used in this book. Firms with up to 15 employees are defined as micro, those with 16–100 employees are small, those with 101–250 employees are medium, and those with more than 251 employees are large.[6] The 1990 regulation also classifies firms according to their level of sales. In conducting firm-level research, however, inquiring about and obtaining data on sales is rather complicated and intrusive. For that reason the classifications in this book are based only on the criterion of the number of employees.

In this book, the term *small* refers to micro, small, and medium-size businesses—the whole set of firms with up to 250 employees. Use of this broad category is a function of public policy. Since the 1950s, economic policies have generally distinguished between, on the one hand, firms defined as micro, small, and medium, and, on the other hand, firms defined as large; but policy has rarely distinguished within the former category, grouping micro, small, and medium firms together.[7] That said, because this broad twofold classification can obscure important differences between firms with fewer than 250 employees, relevant distinctions are made throughout the text among different sizes within the category "small."

Small firms account for greater than 99 percent of all manufacturing establishments, provide more than half of manufacturing employment, and contribute more than one-third of industrial production (Fig. 1). With regard to the sectoral distribution of small firms (Table 1), we see that small firms

5. Kurtz (forthcoming 2004) analyzes a similar phenomenon, showing the relative inabilities of peasants to gain representation even in the context of democratic regime change.

6. In 1999, a new regulation changed these definitions for industrial firms, increasing the upper limits of employees in "micro" and "medium" firms to thirty and five hundred employees, respectively. All discussion in this book is based on the 1990 definition.

7. Recently, following the proliferation of micro firms in the 1980s, this has begun to change, a phenomenon discussed in Chapter 6.

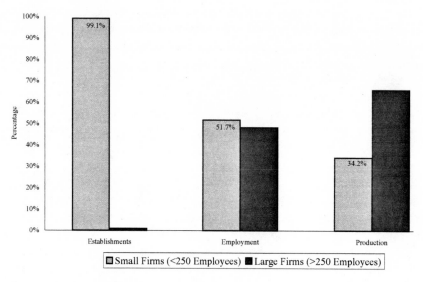

Fig. 1   Mexican manufacturing sector, 1998
Source: Author's calculations, based on INEGI 1999, table 2.

Table 1   Sectoral distribution of small manufacturing firms, 1998

	Number of Employees	
Subsector	0–250	16–250
Food, Beverages, and Tobacco	34.34%	16.01%
Textiles, Apparel, and Leather	15.99%	25.97%
Wood and Wood Products	12.67%	7.17%
Paper and Paper Products	5.68%	7.79%
Chemicals and Petrochemicals[#]	3.04%	14.49%
Nonmetallic Mineral Products[*]	8.86%	5.05%
Basic Metals	0.08%	0.61%
Metal Products and Machinery	17.34%	21.26%
Other	2.00%	1.65%

Source: Author's calculations, based on INEGI 1999, table 2

[#]   Includes rubber and plastics
[*]   Excluding petroleum and coal

are involved in most industrial activities, but with a minimal presence in the production of basic metals. Although more than one-third of all small firms are in the food, beverages, and tobacco subsector, this is owed to the concentration of tiny firms in this subsector. When micro firms are removed and we examine the distribution of "small" and "medium" firms (16–250 employees), we see that the two branches with highest concentration are textiles and apparel and metalworking and machinery.

It is also worth noting that while the present analysis focuses on small industrialists (or manufacturers), many of the political and economic attributes of small firms are not restricted to the industrial sector. At times, then, and also for the sake of varying and lightening the prose, the more general terms *small business* and *small firms* are used. The reader may interpret these more general labels as including small *industry,* but one should not extrapolate in the other direction—the term *small industry* does not refer to retail and service-sector firms. Again, distinctions are made throughout the text to avoid ambiguities.

Last, with regard to the outcome being explained, *representation* refers here to institutionalized input into policy making. Representation is not the same as power, and input into policy making is not to be equated with influence over policy outputs. As we shall see in Chapter 2, not even at the high point of small industry representation in the 1960s and 1970s did small firms drive economic policy. Small industrialists and their organizational advocates never sat anywhere near the head of the table, but they did have a seat at the table. What changes over time in Mexico is not small industrialists' dominance of or control over economic policy, but rather the sector's ability to participate regularly and reliably in the political forums where key economic policy decisions are made.

Democracy and Representation

The phenomenon of declining representation has profound implications for how scholars and students should think about democratization and democratic politics. Scholars working on the third wave of democratization, which began in southern Europe in the 1970s and spread to Latin America and Eastern Europe in the 1980s and 1990s, have responded to three related research agendas: democratic transitions, democratic stability, and democratic quality (see Munck 2001; Whitehead 1996). Among scholars who focus on the emergence of democratic regimes, some emphasize the strategic choices made by civilian political leaders to exploit intraregime divisions and the formal and informal arrangements made by political elites,[8]

---

8. O'Donnell and Schmitter (1986); di Palma (1990); Karl (1986); Rustow (1970). Hagopian (1990) offers a critical evaluation of pacts in democratic transitions.

while other scholars combine analysis of political agency with structural approaches that emphasize the configuration of class forces.[9]

Complementing analysis of democratic transitions, a related body of work focuses on the "consolidation" of democratic regimes.[10] Here the analytic center of attention moves from establishing democracy to retaining democracy—to constructing stable arrangements that are less susceptible to authoritarian reversal. The shift in democracy studies from analysis of regime change to analysis of regime stability gives greater prominence to the study of parties and political institutions.[11] Thus, for example, scholars analyze how political institutions manage conflict in societies with high levels of economic and social polarization.[12]

Although analyses of transition and consolidation have dominated the field of democracy studies, an increasing number of scholars have come to focus on the "quality" of contemporary democracies.[13] The unfortunate reality is that a good deal of the hope for the grand social and political change that would accompany democratization has been shattered; many economic, social, and political conditions have persisted throughout the processes of regime change. Indeed, according to a 2002 survey conducted by Latinobarómetro, fewer than 40 percent of Latin Americans were content with how democracy works in practice in their own countries (Hakim 2003).[14] The disappointment of many citizens has been matched by an interest among political analysts in explaining the conditions that make it so difficult for new democracies to fulfill the expectations that accompanied their emergence (Hershberg 1999; UNDP 2002). For example, Weyland (1996) shows how legacies of clientelism and patronage undermine the effectiveness of the new Brazilian democracy and its ability to undertake equity-enhancing

9. Rueschmeyer, Stephens, and Stephens (1992); R. B. Collier and Mahoney (1997); R. B. Collier (1999); Hollifield and Jillson (2000); Wood (2001).

10. For discussions of democratic consolidation, a problematic concept in its own right, see Schmitter 1995; O'Donnell 1996; Schedler 1998, 2001; and Munck 2001.

11. For an analysis of regime *change* that also emphasizes institutions, see Snyder and Mahoney 1999.

12. Mainwaring, O'Donnell, and Valenzuela (1992); Mainwaring and Scully (1995); Przeworski et al. (1995); Diamond et al. (1997); Linz and Stepan (1996); Power (2000); Siavelis (2000). In countries with extensive periods of military rule, a number of scholars concerned with democratic consolidation have analyzed civil-military relations in the new democracies. See, for example, Hunter 1996; Norden 1996; and Pion-Berlin 1997.

13. See Munck 2001, 2003 for a discussion of "democratic quality" as a third leg in the tripod of scholarship on democracy studies. Hagopian (1998) calls for a reorientation in democracy studies from analysis of regime change and democratic consolidation to analysis of democratic accountability.

14. See also "Democracy Clings on in a Cold Economic Climate," *Economist,* 15 August 2002.

reforms; and in a series of publications O'Donnell has lamented the failure of states in Latin American democracies to deliver basic rights of citizenship (1993a, 1993b) and the limited effective accountability of officials to the citizens that elect them (1994, 1998, 1999).

This book contributes to the study of democratic quality through its focus on representation.[15] Democracy makes representation more important, but regime change itself does not guarantee representation. As Hagopian (1998) cautions, Latin American democracies may be more formally inclusive and participatory than their authoritarian predecessors, yet they are not necessarily more representative. The extent to which democratization provides new opportunities for representation is an empirical question that needs to be analyzed. A key issue in the study of democratic quality is the extent to which emerging political arrangements provide social actors with the capacity to insert their interests and perspectives into national political debates. We have to examine how institutions and organizations—new, old, and refurbished—represent interests. Put another way, we seek to analyze how new democracies generate, or fail to generate, the conditions for interest representation.

The central task is to problematize the processes of representation and interest intermediation. Representation entails intermediation, because most social groups rely on some sort of agent to articulate and defend their interests in policy-making arenas. Political intermediaries, such as interest associations, civil society organizations, and political parties, aggregate interests and give voice to groups in society. In this book I analyze the particular challenges and difficulties that confront intermediaries representing small industry, and assess how the complex set of challenges change in the context of democratization.

The emphasis on a range of intermediaries—associations, CSOs, and parties—is derived from the observation that political regimes are constituted by multiple channels of representation. Stepan (1988, chapter 1), for example, emphasizes the importance of distinguishing "civil society," the arena where interest groups and social movements articulate their interests, from "political society," the arena that hosts formal contestation among parties over policy-making authority (see also Schmitter 1992; Hagopian 1998). Thus, while political parties and electoral

15. Two rich collections of essays on the quality of representation in contemporary Latin America are Agüero and Stark 1998 and Chalmers et al. 1997. See also Huber, Rueschemeyer, and Stephens 1997; and Hazan and Rahat 2000.

channels of representation obviously play an important role in contemporary democracies, and have captured the attention of analysts during the third wave (e.g., Przeworski, Stokes, and Manin 1999), they do not constitute the exclusive mechanism for interest intermediation. Competitive interparty dynamics notwithstanding, the aggregation and articulation of "basic interests" (Baumgartner and Leech 1998) through associations and movements remains a critically important aspect of democracy (see Putnam 1993). Indeed, in new democracies, where parties operate in less institutionalized party systems and typically structure competition and aggregate interests less effectively than parties in more developed countries, the continued importance of associations is particularly vital (Schmitter 1997). Scholars of democracy must continue to take seriously the issue of interest intermediation and consider how emerging institutional arrangements affect the representative capacity of associations, CSOs, and political parties.

Importantly, with regard to the analysis of democratic quality, the study of small industry in Mexico reorients our attention toward the problem of *declining* representation. Although an increasing number of scholars have highlighted the deficiencies of contemporary democracies, emphasis tends to be placed on actors that also experienced low-quality politics in the preceding authoritarian regime. Democratic quality is questioned, then, in the sense of unfulfilled expectations—the failure of democracy to resolve preexisting social and political problems. In this book I expand the analysis of democratic quality. Not only do we see how conditions facilitating representation can be left undeveloped by democratization, but, critically, how democratization can reduce effective opportunities for political representation. As I shall show, small industry's representative decline is just not a result of the limited reach of Mexico's new democracy, but, rather, is caused by conflicts unleashed by democratization itself.

An important conclusion drawn from this study is that democratization ultimately must be conceived of as a positive project, one that not only relaxes controls and eliminates constraints derived from authoritarianism, but actively provides members of society with the tools to redress their grievances in the public domain. To be sure, designing institutions to provide a new role for associations, to buttress the operational capacity of CSOs, and to strengthen political parties are healthy measures that may make valuable contributions to improving democratic quality, but these measures may leave the challenges of representation unresolved. To improve representation, it is essential to strengthen and consolidate networks of intermediaries and even construct new networks. Refurbishing and constructing networks of intermediaries requires close attention to the basic political characteristics that present distinct representative challenges to different actors. Or, to put it another way, because democratic quality requires social engagement, scholars of democracy need to pay close attention to different actors' capacities for political participation and civic engagement. In the following section I identify the core attributes that contribute to the weakness in one such actor, small industry.

The Challenges of Small Industry Representation

In considering the challenges of small industry representation, it is important to begin by noting the economic and political characteristics that distinguish small firms. I begin this section by highlighting a set of basic size-based economic differences between firms. I then examine the core attributes that define small industry as a political actor, focusing on heightened obstacles to collective action and limited electoral resources. With the distinguishing characteristics presented, in the following section I will then turn to the implications for representation in the context of changing political and economic environments.

Size and the Importance of Representation

Several economic and political characteristics distinguish small firms. Relative to larger businesses, small firms generally have minimal access to credit and technology, they ordinarily operate on less product and market information, their owners and managers often lack critical administrative and professional skills, and they frequently lack the resources to train (and retrain) their employees. The reduced scale of operations for small firms contributes to liquidity problems, as factories need to run at closer to full capacity to meet customer demand, and small firms also often find themselves in disadvantageous positions in bargaining with suppliers and purchasers.

These differences in resources and capacities generate contrasting interests for small and large firms on a variety of public policy issues. Small and large firms typically have clashing orientations toward direct foreign investment, for example, as weaker firms with limited access to credit and technology lack the ability to associate with multinationals via joint ventures and integration into transnational production chains. Differential access to credit and technology also conditions firms' capacity to enter into foreign markets and their capacity to adjust to increased import competition in the domestic market. And because smaller firms depend to a greater degree on domestic sales, small and large firms typically have conflicting positions on macroeconomic policies that affect domestic purchasing power.

Size, thus, is important; and it is particularly important in developing economies, where capital is scarce, credit markets are generally shallow, technological innovation externally driven, and degrees of industrial integration typically low. For example, because integration between big and small firms is significantly higher in the United States than in Mexico, smaller firms in the United States stood to benefit more from the export opportunities created by the North American Free Trade Agreement (NAFTA) (Christensen 1993).[16]

Most analyses of intracapitalist conflict focus on sectoral cleavages such as industry versus commerce or tradable versus nontradable.[17] Firm size constitutes an important line of cleavage too, for size tends to be closely correlated to access to credit and technology. Access and credit, in turn, are key factors in explaining firms' capacity to adjust to international competition. Adjustment capacity, Kingstone (1999) has shown, is a function of many economic and political variables. Resources, it is argued here, is one key variable. In short, the range of feasible adjustment options—not simply increasing competitiveness by improving quality, but also moving into new products, finding new markets, seeking joint ventures—is by size.[18]

When the important size-based differences in business interests are highlighted, the role of encompassing "peak" associations is assessed differently from how it is viewed in the contemporary literature. To the extent that peak associations are encompassing—that they span various sectors of the economy—they are considered potentially useful instruments

16. Subsequently, the lack of small business opposition to NAFTA in the United States is not as puzzling as is the quiescence of small firms in Mexico.

17. See Kingstone 1999, introduction and chapter 1, for a review of various explanations to business's political preferences. See also Haggard, Maxfield, and Schneider 1997.

18. For this reason, small manufacturing firms might be thought of as having comparatively high asset specificity, despite their purported "flexibility." See Frieden 1991 for a model that derives business preferences from degrees of asset specificity.

for overcoming rent-seeking on the part of narrowly defined sectoral interests (Olson 1982). Because they reconcile intracapitalist conflict and present a supposedly general interest of business, peak associations, it is argued, improve government-business collaboration (Schneider 1997, forthcoming 2004; Moore 2001; Durand and Silva 1998). Yet while peak associations may be encompassing in a horizontal sense, allowing them to reconcile intersectoral diversity, they are rarely encompassing in a vertical sense. Peak associations may represent a generalized, intersectoral interest of business—but of big business. They are likely to subordinate the distinct interests and perspectives of smaller firms.

The distinct and often contradictory interests of small and large firms makes it important that a specific representative exist to advocate on behalf of small firms. Without such a representative, where small firms are integrated into business organizations created and controlled by larger firms, for example, their distinct interests are likely to be neglected and subordinated. To be sure, most business organizations maintain that they act in the interest of small firms. Yet representation has to entail more than noting the potential positive externalities of a preferred policy—that what is good for big firms may also be good for small firms. The crux of the issue is who will defend the interests of small firms when their interests conflict with big business. Representation and interest intermediation, we must not forget, is about reconciling conflicting interests.[19]

A Third "Logic of Collective Action"

Departing from Olson's (1965) famous statement on collective action, much of the literature on business collective action has sought to distinguish capitalists' modality of organization from that of workers.[20] Yet many of the attributes that are claimed to broadly distinguish "business" do not apply to small firms. It is necessary to distinguish the organization of small business from the organization of both big business and labor. We can refer, in the broadest sense, to a third logic of collective action.

In comparing the logics of collective action for different actors, it is useful to make assessments along two axes—the relative importance of

19. Recall the title of Schmitter's (1971) classic analysis of interest intermediation, *Interest Conflict and Political Change in Brazil*.
20. Offe and Wiesenthal 1980; Bowman 1989; Streeck 1990; van Waarden 1991; Traxler 1993; Roy and Parker-Gwin 1999; Haydu 1999.

formal organization for a group to defend its interests, and the relative capacity of a group to organize. Small firms are like workers, in that their individual weakness means that they rely on collective representation through formal organizations more than large firms do. At the same time, and despite this heightened importance of organization, collective action is relatively more difficult for small firms.

Because small industrialists (and workers) ordinarily lack the resources to defend their interests individually and informally through the market, they rely on formal organizations to a greater degree for representation. The owners of large firms can often do without formal organizations, because they are more likely to gain individualized access to policy makers, and their market power often places them in positions to collude informally by establishing cartels. Furthermore, since large firms' individual investment decisions reverberate throughout local, regional, and sometimes even national economies, government authorities are more likely to watch out for their interests.[21]

To indicate large firms' reduced dependence on formal organization is not to suggest that they do not act collectively. Societies throughout the world are full of business organizations. Yet establishing associations is but one mechanism by means of which actors can defend their interests. Collective action should be thought of as a second-best solution: most actors would prefer individual strategies, so to avoid coordination problems. The key point is that the feasibility of an individual strategy is a function of resource availability (Traxler 1993).

Because of basic asymmetries in economic and political resources, small firms and workers are less able than large firms to pursue individual strategies. With regard to small industry, just as size limits the available range of firm-level adjustment strategies, so too does size limit the range of political strategies. Individual strategies are generally less available for the owners of small firms, who tend not to have privileged access to state officials and whose individual investment decisions have less of an effect on the economy as a whole.[22] The individual weakness of

21. For example, Offe and Wiesenthal argue that capitalists' important role in the economy "is exploited and fine-tuned by the operation of business associations, but it is by no means *constituted* or created by them. Their success is not accomplished by or because of the organization itself; rather it derives from a power relationship that is logically and historically prior to the fact of any collective action of businessmen" (1980, 86; emphasis in original).

22. And because cartels are formed by a reduced numbers of firms controlling large shares of the market, this strategy is obviously not available to small firms either.

the small firm, subsequently, increases the importance of collective representation through formal business organizations.[23]

The increased importance of organization for small firms is compounded by a more cumbersome set of impediments to collective action, and on this axis small firms are distinguishable not just from large firms but also from workers. Capitalists, generally, overcome barriers to collective action in two reinforcing ways, each of which tends to leave the ensuing associations in the hands of big firms. First, larger firms bear the costs of organization-building. Second, capitalists overcome impediments to organization by fragmenting according to productive activity, or "sector" (Streeck 1990; Traxler 1993). While encompassing, economy-wide organizations do exist in most countries, the more common form of business organization is the sector-specific trade association. Fragmentation facilitates collective action by creating smaller collectivities with more homogenous interests, effectively parceling business into a multitude of "privileged groups" (Olson 1965, 143). For example, fragmentation helps chemical producers organize, not only by creating a smaller collectivity, but also by eliminating the interests of other producers with whom they might enter into conflict on issues of public policy. And, of course, fragmentation into sectors also preserves the key condition of asymmetrical resource distribution, which allows large firms to bear the costs of organization-building within these sectors.

The strategy of forming organizations via sectoral fragmentation has limited utility for overcoming the challenges of small firm representation. Fragmentation can help capitalists overcome the obstacles to collective action that are derived from horizontal, intersectoral conflicts, but it leaves vertical, intrasectoral conflicts to be reconciled internally. Although some small firms will join and participate in associations that are created via sectoral fragmentation, these organizations tend to represent the interests of the larger firms that supply the resources for their creation and continued existence. Furthermore, while fragmentation helps capitalists organize by producing smaller, more homogenous groups that continue to benefit from

23. Haydu (1999) makes a similar point in suggesting that there is greater variability in capitalist collective action than proposed by Offe and Wiesenthal (1980). In Offe and Wiesenthal's framework, the power of individual capitalist firms vitiates the importance of formal organization. Haydu, however, argues that such reasoning makes sense for modern corporations but not with regard to proprietary capitalists of nineteenth century. Thus, for Haydu the crucial variable that affects the importance of organization is the historical period, which ultimately becomes a proxy for firm size. See also Salamon and Siegfried 1977.

an asymmetrical distribution of resources, it is a considerably less effective strategy for small industrialists: fragmentation by size into a collectivity of small firms has the perverse effect of removing the larger enterprises that are potential organization-builders. With small firms left to their own devices, then, organization is particularly difficult, as their number and spatial dispersion complicate coordination and increase the likelihood of free-riding.

Indeed, small firms face more intense obstacles to collective action, not just relative to big business but also relative to workers. Unlike a collectivity of factory workers that are concentrated on the shop floor, for example, individual small firms are more isolated from one another, which increases the difficulties of monitoring participation and sanctioning free riders (D. M. Shafer 1994, 40; see also Haydu 1999, 508). The challenges to small firm collective action are also heightened by the perverse effects of anticipated upward mobility. Workers in larger unions with ample resources retain an interest in increasing worker organization and broadening the labor movement. Among the broad category of "small firms," medium-size firms (e.g., in this study, firms with 101–250 employees) may also have sufficient resources to be potential organization-builders. Yet such firms may be less likely to play the part. This difference can be attributed to the fact that business firms are organizations themselves that can grow in size. Aspirations of upward mobility—of the small firm becoming a big firm—mean the owners of such firms may perceive fewer costs in joining existing organizations that are dominated by larger firms, and less to be gained by promoting organizational cohesion within the small firm sector. Potential organization-builders have less incentive to invest resources in establishing separate organizations to represent the distinct interests of small firms. In effect, the promise (or hope) of developing from being a small firm to becoming a big firm can act as a fetter on collective action.

Electoral Resources

The complex challenges of small industry representation are also evident in the realm of partisan politics. Small industry suffers from an inherently problematic relationship with political parties that makes parties generally unreliable representative agents. Small firms lack the critical electoral resources to make themselves of great value to political parties. Moreover, because small industry's interests often conflict with the actors that can best deliver such critical electoral resources, small firms are likely to see their interests subordinated within electoral coalitions.

Social groups typically gain influence within political parties through the ability to deliver critical electoral resources in the form of finances and votes. In general, business's most important electoral resource is the ability to finance campaigns, while labor's most important electoral resource is the capacity to deliver significant numbers of votes. Because small firms lack these critical resources, they will rarely be in a position to be the core constituents of a political party.[24]

Whereas the financial-resource constraint is obvious, the issue of votes requires some elucidation, since small establishments are so numerous. For example, in Mexico small firms account for 99 percent of all manufacturing establishments (see Figure 1). Yet while small industries dominate the manufacturing sector numerically, we should not expect them to be dominant in an electoral sense. To take numerical dominance within the industrial sector as a predictor of electoral dominance entails questionable assumptions about consistency in voting preferences and relative rates of voter turnout when small firms and other sectors of electorate are compared. Indeed, extrapolating a number of votes from census figures on the number of small establishments is quite complex, given that a family might own more than one business or a single business might have more than one owner (Bates 1997, 81–82). In short, there is little reason to expect small firms to be able to deliver enough votes to serve as a political party's core constituency.[25]

That an actor is not a core constituency obviously does not preclude parties' attempting to cultivate its support. Certain constituencies may be courted not for their own resources, but for the signal that their support sends to others. In the case of small industry, political support helps parties on the Right make neoliberalism appear more competitive and less prone to concentrating resources and power; and support for parties on the Left allows them to emphasize key issues of inequality without appearing antigrowth.[26]

Even while parties across the ideological spectrum appeal to small business to broaden their electoral coalitions, however, a strategy to represent small

24. See Gibson 1996, chapter 1, for further discussion of the relationship between parties and their "core constituencies."

25. It is important to distinguish here between small and medium-size industrial firms and tiny micro firms in the commercial sector. The latter may indeed be able to exert more electoral influence, particularly at the local level. Cross (1998), for example, provides evidence of this in the case of street vendors in Mexico City.

26. As Evans wrote about small manufacturing firms in Brazil, "[B]ecause they are both national and private they represent the ideologically ideal instruments of local accumulation" (1979, 283). See Weiss 1988 for a discussion of political-party strategies toward small firms.

firms may conflict with broader party goals, because small firms' interests tend to conflict with the dominant interests of parties' core constituents. As a result of these conflicts and small industry's comparative lack of electoral resources, small firms' interests tend to be subordinated within electoral coalitions. When interests clash and strategic trade-offs must be made, small firms remain subordinated to the dominant actors in a given party coalition. Ultimately, conflicts between constituencies over critical issues of public policy compel candidates, legislators, and party strategists to decide which actor they are going to represent. Because small firms can deliver few electoral resources relative to big business and workers, we should expect them to be subordinated.

Corporatism, Democratization, and Small Industry Representation

Comparatively heightened obstacles to collective action and reduced electoral resources, the core characteristics that define small firms as a political actor, have important implications for political representation. The point of the analysis in the previous section is not that actors facing difficult collective action problems cannot organize or that actors with minimal electoral resources cannot exert electoral influence, but that doing so is more difficult. The sectoral-based approach to political economy, deriving implications for political activity from actors' core political and economic characteristics (e.g., D. M. Shafer 1994; Frieden 1991), provides an analytic point of departure. Actors' core attributes signal the expected difficulties to be faced and obstacles to be overcome in securing representation. But these attributes do not tell us whether the actors will succeed. The key is to take into account how these capacities are affected by changing economic and political conditions.

State as Opportunity

Although small industrialists' core characteristics predispose them toward disorganization and weakness, it would be a mistake to conclude that they will necessarily remain politically unimportant. There are multiple solutions to the collective action problem (Lichbach 1995), and many groups that face difficult obstacles to collective action become organized with the direct or indirect assistance of the state. Indeed, the provision of selective incentives that facilitate collective action is a fundamental way in which states shape patterns of organization and mobilization.[27] Likewise, parties may cultivate small business support for a variety of ideological and strategic reasons (Weiss 1988; Patterson 1994).

One set of institutions of particular importance to this study are "corporatist" frameworks that structure patterns of interest association. Schmitter (1974, 86) defines corporatism as a "system of interest and/or attitude representation . . . for linking the associationally organized interests of civil society with the decisional structures of the state." Key elements of corporatism include regulations that make membership compulsory to certain organizations and policy-making regimes that give special status to "official," state-licensed associations.[28]

An important implication of distinguishing between big and small firms' collective action challenges is that small industrialists may have a different orientation toward corporatist regulations that affect interest organization. Because *big* firms generally rely less on state concessions to organize, and because they can often escape state-imposed constraints on organization, it is generally argued that the state's capacity to structure patterns of capitalist interest association is weak (Moore and Hamalai 1993; O'Donnell 1977; Offe and Wiesenthal 1980). Not surprisingly, attempts to impose corporatist restraints on big business tend to be relatively ineffective. For small industry, in contrast, the comparatively greater importance of formal organization combined with a comparatively lesser ability to overcome the impediments to collective action suggest that patterns of association are likely to be more sensitive to state institutions.

A staple of the literature on corporatism is that such regulatory frameworks can distort representation. Concessions such as licensing and compulsory membership can serve as invaluable ingredients for overcoming barriers to collective action. However, because concessions extended under one set of political conditions can be withdrawn under other conditions, dependence on organizational concessions can generate vulnerability (D. Collier and R. B. Collier 1977; R. B. Collier and D. Collier 1979). Vulnerability to the removal of such concessions, in turn, can make an organization's leadership less accountable to the membership and more oriented toward satisfying the state. Indeed, reorienting the accountability of an organization's

27. The incentives may be embedded in laws and constitutions themselves, and they may be provided by means of the direct actions of politicians and state officials. See Bates 1990; and Schneider forthcoming 2004.

28. D. Collier (1995) provides an insightful discussion of how the concept of corporatism has been used in the study of Latin American politics.

leadership from the membership to the state is frequently one of the objectives in extending concessions.

While corporatism certainly entails constraints on certain types of political activities, it is important to understand how corporatist regulations can also provide opportunities. To be sure, where regulations on association are imposed from above, a process that Schmitter (1974) labeled "state corporatism," groups risk losing their autonomy to the state.[29] But one has to be careful, analytically, not to prioritize autonomy over organization. The risk of losing organizational autonomy is predicated on the prior existence of organizational cohesion. If a social group that depends on organization for representation is fragmented and unorganized, reduced autonomy is hardly the biggest problem it faces. To the contrary, if a sacrifice of autonomy is the price to be paid for overcoming obstacles to collective action, many weak groups may be willing—if not eager—to pay this price. Weak actors may take advantage of the opportunities presented by corporatist institutions to build alliances with the state.[30]

Rather than regarding the ensuing relationship as entirely state-inspired and state-dominated, we should conceive of corporatism—even state corporatism—as establishing a bargaining framework that includes trade-offs. Social groups acting within a corporatist framework balance the benefits gained from state concessions, for example, increased organizational cohesion, with the costs entailed by dependence on the state, for example, decreased organizational autonomy. We cannot know a priori how actors will weigh these trade-offs, but it is essential to recognize that the political relationships that develop within such frameworks may not simply be imposed by the state but may be part of a strategy of the weak actors that prioritize organizational cohesion over autonomy.

The complex trade-offs between organizational cohesion and organizational autonomy are likely to produce tensions within associations that attempt to represent small firms. Representative organizations must respond to the demands of the membership, of course, and they also need to devise strategies to preserve resources and the capacity to participate in policy making. The tensions between these two tasks, always present for organizations (see, e.g., Schmitter and Streeck 1981), are intensified for organizations representing small firms. This distinction derives from the previous discussion.

29. Indeed, that was often the objective of state officials. Controls were typically imposed on already mobilized and organized groups (see Malloy 1977; and O'Donnell 1973).

30. Foster (2001) makes a similar argument with regard to associations under authoritarian rule in China.

The heightened importance of formal organization means that leaders of an association representing small firms must be acutely concerned about preserving the capacity to represent—to retain the association's seat at the table. Concern with preserving the representative status and capacity of the organization may motivate partial suppression of members' immediate interests on a given issue of public policy. From the organization's perspective, it may seem imprudent to exhaust resources in defeat today, particularly if doing so threatens to jeopardize the capacity to project members' interests tomorrow, against a different (and potentially weaker) array of opposing forces.

The benefits obtained by this sort of representative strategy, however, can become outweighed by the costs. Most important, as the benefits accruing to an association's membership decline, where the membership (or important parts of it) perceive that the organization's input is not generating adequate benefits or that the benefits extracted appear narrowly distributed, a representative strategy that subordinates members' interests to organizational preservation is likely to generate backlash. Again, these standard dilemmas, generic to business organizations, are accentuated in the case of small industry because of the sector's debilitating core attributes.

Complexities of Democratization

Democratization may amplify the divisions over representative strategy discussed above by making the opportunity costs of prioritizing organizational preservation appear greater. Democratization presents social actors with opportunities for new forms of social protest, new avenues of interest articulation, and potentially new alliance partners. Political-party competition, the existence of more active legislatures, the appearance (or reappearance) of civil society, and the emergence of new arenas of contestation can make the previous set of trade-offs seem stale. The availability of new alliance partners, for example, can make it appear that organizational cohesion may be obtainable without autonomy being sacrificed to the state. For those actors embittered by sacrificed autonomy, then, democratization can make alternative strategies appear more feasible and desirable. These different evaluations of opportunity costs, in turn, can aggravate tensions between rival groups within a given organization.

Democratization may also introduce episodes of institutional contestation and transformation, which in turn may exacerbate the difficulties of representation for small business. In general, because powerful actors can benefit more from ad hoc and less routinized forms of representation, they may have less interest in increasing broader societal access to the state. To the extent that democratization threatens to reduce big business's access relative to other social groups, we may witness attempts to take advantage of the opportunities presented by democratization to construct new and more exclusionary mechanisms for interest articulation.[31]

But big firms are not the only actors that may be threatened by democratization. Episodes of institutional contestation and transformation can have perverse effects on small firm representation. Take the issue of corporatism, for example. Although democratization does not require the elimination of corporatism, it subjects such regulations to contestation. We might expect actors constrained by corporatist regulations to take advantage of democratization. After all, democratization opens new possibilities for interest articulation, free of the constraints inherent in operating under corporatist regulations. Yet for actors that have benefited from a given policy-making regime—even "weak" actors—democratization may be regarded as as not so much an opportunity as a threat. Sunk costs and the "practical temptations" of operating under one set of political arrangements may make new and more pluralistic arrangements appear less attractive (Schmitter 1992, 437; Power and Doctor forthcoming 2004). Thus, to the extent that democratization contributes to contestation over the institutions that undergird familiar patterns of state-societal interaction, some actors who secured beneficial positions under authoritarian governments may resist and even oppose democratization.[32] In fact, some actors may exhaust limited resources attempting to preserve existing institutional arrangements.

Although securing representation in authoritarian and corporatist settings presents small firms with the challenge of dealing with dependence on the state, the removal of concessions that are delivered through corporatist frameworks presents the challenge of how to remain organized and how to retain access to the state. First-order difficulties of collective action and organizational cohesion, the same concerns that can make corporatism appear to be an opportunity, can be revealed and returned to prominence under conditions of voluntary membership. In other words, not all groups

31. In fact, this same logic is precisely what underlies skepticism regarding the effects that financial integration and the increased prominence of mobile asset holders might have on strengthening democratic institutions (Mahon 1996, chapter 5). See Armijo 1999 for an overview of various hypotheses regarding mobile asset holders and democracy.

32. More generally, see Middlebrook 1995; Middlebrook uses this insight to call into question Rueschemeyer, Stephens, and Stephens's (1992) expectation of organized labor as protagonist of democratization.

constrained by corporatism are likely to be strengthened by democracy. Potential new opportunities emerge, as impediments to organization are reduced, but democratization can replace organizational dependence and diminished autonomy—the pathologies of corporatism—with organizational instability, decay, and political irrelevance.[33]

It is also worth considering how small firms' core characteristics affect their ability to take advantage of other opportunities of democratization, such as the presence of social movements and CSOs. Democratization and neoliberalism have led to the emergence of a broad array of CSOs throughout the developing world. At the core of many of these movements is a challenge not only to economic policy, but also to a sense of growing political exclusion. A goal that is implicit in many CSOs is to "deepen democracy," whereby there is not merely a criticism of neoliberalism and economic policy, but also the articulation of broader and more fundamental concerns about the ability of citizens to participate meaningfully in politics and have their voices heard (Roberts 1998; Friedman and Hochstetler 2002; Chalmers et al. 1997).

In assessing CSOs as mechanisms of representation, it is worth underscoring some of the underlying tensions that accompany small industry's participation. Small firms are typically welcomed into broader CSOs because their presence lends legitimacy to sharp criticisms of neoliberalism that are neither anticapitalist nor antigrowth. Coalitions can assail the power of big business and the growing concentration of income, all the while supposedly presenting an alternative actor for employment generation—small industry. Small firms make CSOs more comfortable for potential middle-class supporters, whose resources may be critical for sustaining collective action, and CSOs can bring to small firms new allies and increased political visibility.

Yet small industry's participation in CSOs is not without its discomforts. Some of the most basic tensions emerge with regard to labor and regulatory issues. Independent unions pressing for collective bargaining rights are prominent in movement coalitions. More generally, the movements call for strong and consistent state regulations to protect weak members of society and to safeguard public space. Owners of small firms, however, typically do not subscribe to this regulatory vision. To the contrary, they complain incessantly of being subject to "excessive" regulatory burdens. Although the actors within the movements can find common ground by expressing a desire to direct the regulatory burdens at *big* business, where so many workers are

33. See Kurtz 2002 for discussion of the problems that atomization poses for democracy.

employed in small firms, for business regulations to affect people's lives they certainly have to be more universalized.[34]

To this point, the analysis of how democratization can generate complexities for small industry representation has emphasized interest associations and collective action. Yet in considering the relationship between democratization and representation we also need to take into account the other key sociopolitical feature of small firms—comparatively minimal electoral resources. Democratization features parties bidding for support of the electorate, and parties across the political spectrum typically sing the praises of small business. But, as indicated, small firms have an inherently problematic relationship with parties. Because small industry lacks the resources to be a party's core constituency, and because small firms' interests often enter into conflict with those of other actors that have more valuable electoral resources, political parties are likely to be unreliable mechanisms of representation.

We can better understand this problematic relationship by considering the dilemmas faced by parties looking to cultivate business support. To be sure, business enterprises of all sizes share a basic interest in achieving stable property rights, labor control, low inflation, and predictable regulatory environments; and business-based parties may promote these broad interests. Yet, as discussed above, on many policy issues small firms' interests conflict with those of big business. This is particularly so with regard to policies that affect access to credit and degrees of purchasing power in the domestic market, and state responses to challenges posed by international competition. Ultimately, on issues that generate conflict between big and small firms, parties may find it difficult to represent one segment of business without alienating the other. Just as encompassing business organizations that are controlled by large firms are likely to subordinate the interests of small industry, political parties attempting to reconcile the same conflicting mix of interests are likely to have the same tendencies. Moreover, the sorts of programs that small firms might require to remain competitive (e.g., subsidized credit, special tax treatment, and mandated government purchases) tend not to be public goods that the state has incentives to provide, but rather targeted concessions that must be demanded by the recipients (Patterson 1994). Being "pro-business" does not mean that the party will look after this sector.

---

34. These tensions and contradictions, of course, explain why many cross-class coalitions tend to be tenuous. See, for example, O'Donnell's (1978) analysis of "defensive alliances" and Smith's (1991) examination of "transitory pacts of convenience" in post–World War II Argentina.

Or consider the case of a labor-based party. On the one hand, we might expect such parties to emphasize the common concerns of workers and small firms and thus attempt to bring these actors together into an alliance. For example, small firms' tendency to concentrate on the domestic market gives them a stake in maintaining adequate levels of domestic purchasing power, and a shared concern with domestic purchasing power can facilitate cross-class alliances between small, domestic-oriented businesses and workers. Yet small firms tend to have higher relative labor costs, and they tend to be concentrated in sectors of the economy with low barriers to entry. As a result of these situational factors, which sensitize small firms to costs and make them less able to pass along higher costs to their customers, their interests typically conflict with those of workers over such issues as unionization, workplace regulation, and payroll taxes. Thus, here too, conflict over critical issues of public policy compel candidates and party strategists to decide which actor they are going to represent. Because workers can deliver more electoral resources, all other things being equal we should expect small firms to be subordinated.

To summarize, democratization can have the unexpected effect of decreasing representation. Democratization threatens to remove concessions that facilitate small firm organization, but small firms face great difficulties in compensating for the loss of organizational cohesion and subsequently representation in the associational realm. Their core attributes make it difficult to get the most out of the new opportunities for political participation that emerge. This is not to suggest that small firms cannot gain representation, only that securing representation in a democratic environment entails a set of challenges that are significantly more complex than we might imagine. Understanding these challenges—and how they may be overcome—is essential for those interested in understanding and promoting democratic quality.

Overview of Book

In the following chapters I analyze how small industry's core sociopolitical attributes affect the process of representation in changing economic and political environments. Chapter 2, which provides a baseline for the subsequent chapters, contains an examination of the politics of small industry representation in Mexico in the decades following World War II. Particular emphasis is placed on analyzing how corporatist institutions in an executive-dominated authoritarian political system provided the weak segment of local industry with constraints on political activism but also at the same time opportunities to secure representation. Corporatism helped small manufacturing firms overcome obstacles to collective action and unite in an organization called the National Chamber of Manufacturing Industry (CANACINTRA). This organization exploited opportunities made available by the nature of the Mexican political regime and economic policy to seek the state as an ally. The chapter shows how CANACINTRA exchanged autonomy for organizational stability and then how it used organizational stability to gain for small industrialists a valuable role in the postwar Mexican political economy.

In Chapter 3, I examine representation in the context of political and economic liberalization in the mid-1980s. The analysis in this chapter highlights the ways that democratization can raise the opportunity costs of a statecentric strategy. The 1982 debt crisis was followed by movement toward the neoliberal economic model. In the new and more difficult economic environment, democratization—which made available potentially new allies and new possibilities for social protest—prompted a dissenting segment of small industrialists to question the merits of CANACINTRA's alliance with the state. I investigate the roots of this challenge and, importantly, how the state intervened to protect CANACINTRA and thwart the dissidents' attempt to establish new and more autonomous mechanisms of representation. By the late 1980s, CANACINTRA's quasi-monopoly was retained, though the chamber's representative capacity had been diminished.

The transformation of corporatism is addressed in Chapter 4, as are the effects of this transformation on small industry representation. A contrast is made between distinct segments of business's responses to democratization and neoliberalism in the late 1980s and early 1990s. The uncertainty produced by the changing political environment, along with the new opportunities presented by the negotiations for the North American Free Trade Agreement (NAFTA), prompted organizations that were dominated by Mexico's largest firms to embark on a project to restructure state-business interaction. They would develop new and exclusive mechanisms for ongoing consultation with key policy makers. At the same time, democratization provided fertile ground for the dissidents from CANACINTRA to build a broader movement against "business corporatism." Thus, the period witnessed the institutions that regulated business associations coming under siege from above and below. The dual challenges sharply reduced small industry representation: small firms were marginalized from the most important economic policy negotiations; nor did small firms have the organizational capacity to mobilize or participate in opposition to

NAFTA. Democratization and neoliberalism led to an unprecedented decline in small industry's ability to secure representation.

At the heart of Chapters 2, 3, and 4 is a complex relationship between democratization, corporatism, and small business representation. As we shall see, corporatist arrangements provided an opportunity for small firms to enhance their representation in the post–World War II authoritarian regime. Yet the late 1980s and early 1990s witnessed a fundamental transformation of the long-standing corporatist institutions that small firms had been able to exploit, and representation subsequently declined.

What explains the transformation of corporatism? One hypothesis is that corporatism was bound to change as Mexico experienced economic crisis in the 1980s and subsequently adopted a neoliberal economic model. To be sure, economic crisis and liberalization change the role of organized business in society. Liberalization removes many of the incentives for collective action and may also reduce policy makers' interests in helping firms organize. Thus, it is reasonable to expect that a change of economic model would naturally lead to the erosion of corporatism. But it is also clear that associations continue to play an important role in economic governance, even in liberal and open economies (Katzenstein 1984; Streeck and Schmitter 1985; Soskice 1999; Doner and Schneider 2000). The effects of the economic model on corporatism are indeterminate.

To understand the transformation of corporatism, we need to look beyond the economic model and consider the process of democratization itself. As we shall see, democratization is central to understanding both the origins and trajectories of the various movements that emerged to transform corporatism in Mexico. Without democratization and the subsequent concern on the part of Mexico's leading firms that their influence on economic policy making might be diluted, the project to transform corporatism from above would have lacked motivation and rationale. Likewise, without democratization, the sustained attack on corporatism from below—launched by the weakest segment of Mexican business in the late 1980s—almost certainly would have fizzled and come to nothing. But the emergence of opposition political parties with incentives to pay attention to and promote this group's campaign to abolish compulsory membership, and the emergence of an increasingly active and independent judiciary with the capacity to rule on the issue—both functions of democratization—allowed this anticorporatist movement to grow and flourish in the 1990s.

In Chapter 5, I examine the difficulties faced by small firms in attempting to take advantage of the opportunities presented by democratization. I analyze small industry representation via interest associations, CSOs, and the opposition-controlled national legislature in the late 1990s, a period that saw the final removal of the corporatist constraints on association and the introduction of unprecedented high levels of electoral competition. The analysis suggests that small firms' distinct political and economic characteristics make them ill equipped to exploit the opportunities presented by democracy. Notwithstanding the removal of constraints on association and the emergence of a competitive electoral arena, small industry's capacity to participate in politics continued to diminish. Rather than arresting representative decline, democracy orphaned small industry.

The broad lessons of the Mexican case for studying democracy and economic development are extracted in Chapter 6. Here, I build on the Mexico case by considering the relationship between democratization and representation in Argentina and Brazil. Consequently, we see the role that the state plays in helping weak actors increase their ability to participate constructively and meaningfully in politics, even in democracies. The book concludes with a discussion of the importance of increasing the representation of small industry in developing countries in order to enhance these countries' abilities to respond to the challenges of economic development in the contemporary global economy.

Research Design and Data Collection

The analysis is based on a longitudinal comparison that breaks the "case" of Mexico into four separate cases. That is, each of the following four chapters corresponds to distinct time periods, 1940s–1970s (Chapter 2), early to mid-1980s (Chapter 3), late 1980s to early 1990s (Chapter 4), and late 1990s (Chapter 5). Each chapter revolves around an examination of how political and economic contexts shape the opportunities for and quality of small industry representation. A longitudinal approach is essential for demonstrating how democratization can actually reduce effective opportunities for political representation. As discussed above, this is an important contribution to the literature on democratic quality, which has largely been about the unfulfilled expectations of third-wave democracies. Analyzing the causes of declining representation, of course, requires comparative analysis of the same actor over time.

I assess the outcome of small industry representation according to an evaluation of actors' access to state officials and degree of participation in economic policy making. Some of this is in the public record, but in many instances participation can only be ascertained through archival work and extensive interviewing. Of course, individuals' memories fail and they have any number of reasons to distort their accounts of relevant events, to magnify or diminish their participation in a given policy-making forum. Consequently, where participants' own accounts were used as a source of information, every effort was made to consult as many actors as possible that were involved in a given policy-making episode—to consult actors on all sides of the table.

The findings are based on extensive archival research and interviews. The National Archives in Mexico City (AGN) contains rich records on communication between Mexican business organizations and policy makers in the executive branch of government throughout the post–World War II period. The archives of CANACINTRA, the most important business organization for small industry in most of the postwar period, include the minutes of the bimonthly meetings of the chamber's board of directors and of the annual meeting of the chamber's general assembly. In addition to the AGN and CANACINTRA, another source for the findings are also based on the archives of the National Association of Manufacturing Industrialists (ANIT), a group that splintered from CANACINTRA in the mid-1980s, and the personal archives of individuals active in the subsequent dispute between CANACINTRA and ANIT. This material provides new evidence of and insights into the difficult challenges of interest aggregation and representation for small industry, and it allows for the presentation, in this book, of new findings on the important roles of these organizations in postwar Mexican politics.

In Mexico, I conducted more than one hundred open-ended interviews at the following five levels:

(1) *association level,* with leaders and members of a wide range of organizations representing various segments of Mexican business
(2) *civil society level,* with leaders and participants in a variety of CSOs that emerged in the 1980s and 1990s
(3) *party level,* with leaders of Mexico's three principal political parties, including both officials in the national party headquarters and legislators in the Chamber of Deputies and the Senate
(4) *state level,* with officials responsible for small business in the Secretariats of Trade (now named Economy) and Finance, and the National Development Bank
(5) *firm level,* with the owners and managers of micro, small, and medium-size manufacturing firms in a range of sectors

The interviews in Mexico were conducted in 1993, 1994, 1997, 1999, and 2001. I also conducted interviews in Buenos Aires (in 2001 and 2003) and in São Paulo (in 2003). The Appendix provides a list of interviews conducted in all three countries. Most interviews were confidential. Unless quoting or providing information that could only come from a single interview, I do not cite individual interviews in the text.

TWO

Representation via Accommodation
Small Industry and Postwar Developmentalism

The politics of representation in an authoritarian regime will be examined in this chapter, with a focus on small industry in post–World War II Mexico. Small firms' core characteristics make securing representation an uphill struggle in any political system, but in postwar Mexico, the nature of the regime provided fertile territory for small industrialists to secure reliable representation. While authoritarianism and corporatist regulations on interest association were constraining, these conditions also presented small firms with a window of opportunity in which to develop and nurture an alliance with the state.

Particular attention is dedicated here to the role of the National Chamber of Manufacturing Industry (CANACINTRA), which emerged in the 1940s and 1950s as the principal representative of small industry. The nature of postwar economic policy, the particularities of Mexico's authoritarian regime, and a set of corporatist regulations directed toward the business sector had significant effects on the development and political trajectory of this organization. CANACINTRA exchanged autonomy for organizational stability, and organizational stability allowed the chamber to gain for small industrialists a valuable role in the postwar Mexican political economy. The analysis in this chapter provides a baseline for the events of the 1980s and 1990s, when democratization and neoliberalism would introduce a decidedly more difficult terrain for the representation of small industry.

We begin with a broad sketch of postwar economic policy, policy making, and politics. The brief overview points to the important role that business associations played in this period. In the second section we look at how corporatist institutions affected patterns of business organization. While large firms became integrated into a loose network of sector-specific industrial chambers and associations, small industrialists in a wide range of sectors became represented by CANACINTRA. In this section I illustrate the asymmetrical effects of corporatism within the business sector, presenting a point that comes out repeatedly throughout this book. While large firms are better able to organize independently of state-imposed regulations on interest associations, such regulations exert significant influence on patterns of association among small industrialists.

The third section concerns CANACINTRA's response to the challenge of representing the weak segment of local capital in the context of Mexico's post–World War II development model. Here we see corporatism and authoritarianism as both constraints and opportunities. Material and organizational weakness prompted CANACINTRA to seek the state as alliance partner. CANACINTRA adopted a representative strategy that earned small manufacturers regularized access to state officials and policy-making forums. This strategy, labeled "accommodation," consisted, in broad strokes, of adopting a cautious and conciliatory approach toward state officials, avoiding outspoken criticism of postwar economic policy, and bypassing alliances outside the state. By offering support of the government—even a government implementing economic policies that fostered industrial concentration and that clearly bestowed disproportionate benefits on large, multisectoral conglomerates—CANACINTRA exchanged political autonomy for organizational stability.

The fruits of accommodation are the subject of the fourth section. Organizational stability allowed CANACINTRA to participate in national political economy and deliver valuable concessions to small industrialists. To be sure, small manufacturers were not the dominant actor in state-business relations; they did not drive policy. Yet a combination of political and economic factors made accommodation a productive strategy for enhancing small firm representation. CANACINTRA was able to exploit ties to the state—ties cultivated via accommodation—to extract benefits for small firms in the areas of trade, foreign investment, and industrial finance.

Developmentalism, Presidentialism, and Business Politics

In a process initiated during the presidencies of Manuel Avila Camacho (1940–46) and Miguel Alemán Valdés (1946–52), and continuing for most of the following three decades, policy makers in Mexico took increasingly active roles in directing industrial development. In addition to exercising state ownership, to break bottlenecks and lower the cost of critical inputs, policy makers used a wide range of credit, fiscal, and trade instruments to channel investment into targeted and more sophisticated industrial branches. This sort of intervention has been given many labels, including "statism," "mercantilism," "import-substituting industrialization," and "developmentalism." In this book the last term is used. Developmentalism, in Mexico and throughout Latin America, was a "catching-up" strategy for what Hirschman (1968) referred to as "late-late industrialization."[1]

An important aspect of developmentalism, throughout the developing world, was its tendency toward "giantism."[2] Because the sectors with the most developmental potential tended to have greater capital and technological requirements, industrial promotion aimed to facilitate the concentration of capital and the creation of large firms that could lead Latin American countries' insertion into the postwar international economy (Gereffi 1990; Evans 1979). Developmentalist policy instruments subsequently bestowed disproportionate benefits on a reduced number of large industrial firms, both national and transnational.

The giantist biases of Mexican economic policy can be illustrated through a brief examination of investment and credit policies.[3] The postwar decades witnessed significant increases in foreign investment in the manufacturing sector. As the activities targeted by the developmentalist policies had significantly higher technological and capital requirements, investment in manufacturing became increasingly attractive for international firms.[4] Whereas previous direct foreign investment (DFI) tended to be directed toward raw-material extraction and infrastructure, postwar DFI went increasingly toward the manufacturing sector. As illustrated in Figure 2, U.S. manufacturing investment in Mexico rose from less than 3

1. Hirschman, of course, is drawing on Gerschenkron's (1962) discussion of the challenges of late industrialization. For more discussion and illustration of developmentalist strategies, see Prebisch 1950; Hirschman 1958; Amsden and Hikino 1994; Evans 1995; and Amsden 2001.

2. Use of the term *giantism* is borrowed from Weiss (1988).

3. Excellent sources for post–World War II industrial policy in Mexico, works in which the giantist biases are emphasized and industrial concentration is discussed, include Brandenburg 1962; Horvath 1991, chapter 2; Izquierdo 1964; Jacobs and Máttar 1985; King 1970; Reynolds 1970; Sheahan 1987; SPP 1980; Story 1986, 33–38; R. Villareal 1977; and World Bank 1979.

4. The role of U.S. diplomatic pressure to encourage developing-world allies to provide American producers with privileged market-access is important too (Maxfield and Nolt 1990; O'Brien 1999). Thus, the changing volume and composition of capital flows in this period were driven, as always, by a combination of "pull" and "push" factors.

percent of total U.S. investment in 1940 to 75 percent by the 1970s. Not only did the level of foreign investment increase, but foreign firms came to account for increasingly larger shares of total industrial production as well. Indeed, from 1950 to 1972, U.S. manufacturing investment grew by an annual rate of 11.2 percent, a greater rate of growth than that of the Mexican manufacturing sector as a whole (Newfarmer and Mueller 1975, 50).[5] Successive governments responded to the growth of foreign firms by attempting to restrict foreign ownership to a level of less than 50 percent of firms in most sectors.[6] It is important to point out that this "Mexicanization" strategy was designed not so much to exclude foreign capital from the Mexican market as to induce foreign investors to enter into joint ventures with large, local conglomerates (private and public). Not unexpectedly, Mexicanization furthered giantism.[7]

Fiscal incentives provided to industrial enterprises also demonstrated a giantist bias. The 1941 Law of Manufacturing Industries, which was revised in 1946 and then again in 1955, offered tax exemptions to firms in "necessary" industries marked by insufficient supply.[8] Table 2 illustrates the declining number of firms that benefited from tax exemptions, even as the gross amount of tax exemptions increased. More telling than the number of firms benefiting from tax exemptions are figures on the size-distribution of firms benefiting from tax exemptions. Even taking into account peso devaluations in 1948 and 1954, these figures demonstrate a clear tendency away from the practice of targeting smaller firms with tax exemptions.

Another important aspect of developmentalism in Mexico was the fact that the promotional instruments tended to be particularistic. Take, for example, the reliance on import licenses as the principal instrument to regulate imports, a distinguishing characteristic of trade protection in postwar

5. Gereffi and Evans (1981) also provide evidence of the growing role of foreign investors in the Mexican manufacturing sector. Gereffi (1978) and Bennett and Sharpe (1985) document this process in their analyses of the Mexican pharmeuceutical and automotive industries, respectively.

6. The rules on foreign investment were based largely on presidential decrees until the consolidation of the regulatory framework in 1973. See Whiting 1992; and Jenkins 1992.

7. Story (1986, appendixes B and C) illustrates that the benefits of Mexicanization accrued disproportionately to large conglomerates and state enterprises. Nor is Mexico an exception. Indigenization strategies generally tend to concentrate benefits on the largest local firms that can raise sufficient capital to enter into joint ventures with foreign investors (see Biersteker 1987).

8. Industries were classified as "necessary" if the domestic supply was less than 80 percent of demand and where the low level of supply was not attributed to a temporary production setbacks (King 1970, 99). In addition to investment incentives in the form of fiscal exemptions, Mexico had remarkably low corporate tax rates (see Elizondo 1994).

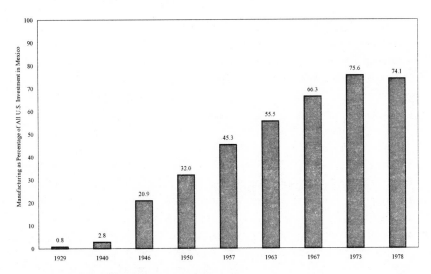

Fig. 2   U.S. investment in Mexican manufacturing
Source: Gereffi and Evans 1981, 36–37, table 1.

Table 2   Distribution of tax exemptions

	1940–50	1951–55	1956–61
Number of Firms Benefiting	570	281	69
(Average per year)	(51.8)	(56.2)	(13.8)
Average Initial Capital of Benefiting Firms (millions of pesos)	1.2	2.04	9.0

Source: Calculations made by author based on data in King 1970, 102–3.

Mexico.[9] Although licensing requirements, covering a small percentage of imports, were originally initiated by decree during World War II, throughout the postwar era more and more goods became subject to the licensing requirement, both to correct balance-of-payments deficits and in response to local producers' demands for protection. Because items included on the list were rarely removed, the government gained expanded authority during this period. Importantly, the process by which licenses were requested

9. The tariff structure was complex as well, but tariffs were not particularly high in comparative perspective. Izquierdo (1964) and Wallace (1980) provide detailed analyses of Mexico's post–World War II trade policy regime, with particular emphasis on the politics of import licenses. See also King 1970, 78–83; and Balassa 1983.

and either granted or denied was highly discretionary and nontransparent. Sectoral committees were established to advise officials in the Secretariat of Industry and Trade (SIC), but the committee's advice was not binding and SIC's decisions were announced without appeal.

In addition to economic policy being giantist and particularistic, the political system was authoritarian and presidentialist. Government was dominated by the Institutional Ruling Party (PRI), and party competition was minimal. Elections were routine in Mexico's civilian-authoritarian regime, but these simply confirmed the PRI's hegemony. From the 1950s until the 1980s, the party would win presidential and legislative elections overwhelmingly, using the resources of the state and control over electoral institutions to retain control of the presidency and dominate virtually all state institutions (Molinar 1991; González Casanova 1970; Reyna and Weinert 1977).

Policy, policy making, and the nature of the Mexican regime had important effects on business politics. The most important issues of public policy affecting firms on a day-to-day basis were not made in the legislature, where parties might have been more important, but in the nontransparent setting of the back rooms of the executive. That key policy decisions were made in a discretionary form by state officials meant that much of the lobbying activities on the part of business were directed toward the state bureaucracy itself.[10] Of course, in Mexico's PRI-dominated and presidentialist regime, not just business but virtually all sectors oriented their strategies of interest articulation through the official party and directly to the executive. Yet whereas workers, peasants, and an amorphous group of "middle sectors" were formally integrated into the PRI, business, either individually or collectively, dealt directly with policy makers and officials in the executive, typically bypassing the ruling party (Maxfield and Anzaldúa Montoya 1987; Purcell 1975; Vernon 1963).

It is worth underscoring the importance of interest organizations in the postwar Mexican political economy. Associations provided a vital service to individual firms, acting as delegates for dealing with the highly interventionist and particularistic state. Returning to the case of import licenses, some of the sectoral advisory committees met with state officials up to three times weekly (Izquierdo 1964, 255). The discretionary, case-by-case nature

10. See Izquierdo 1964, 255–60, and Story 1986, 130–33, for discussions of how particularistic aspects of economic policy, the high degrees of state discretion, and regulatory uncertainty motivated business strategies for affecting policy at the level of implementation. That economic policy encouraged this sort of lobbying behavior is a point underscored and lamented by critics of "rent-seeking" (Krueger 1974; Olson 1982).

of state intervention increased the importance of developing sound working relationships with officials in the state bureaucracy. If policy was made in the executive branch and if policy making consisted of ongoing negotiations, having access to the executive branch and good relations with policy makers in the relevant agencies of the state bureaucracy was essential.

The most important association for representing small industry during this period was CANACINTRA. To be sure, many small firms were not officially members of the chamber; nor, as we shall see, were all the firms that were officially members of the chamber small firms, but throughout the post–World War II period CANACINTRA served as the principal representative of small industrialists in the Mexican political economy. The chamber articulated the interests of the weak segment of local industry, working with the executive and attempting to push for policies in favor of small firms; and it advocated on behalf of small industrialists in a variety of day-to-day issues before the state. In the remainder of this chapter I will examine the process by which small industrialists became organized in CANACINTRA and how the chamber responded to the challenge of representing small industry in the context of developmentalist economics and authoritarian politics.

Corporatism and Business Organization

The cornerstone of the corporatist framework that regulated business organizations in Mexico was the Chambers Law (Ley de Cámaras) of 1936, revised in 1941. The 1936 law required all Mexican firms to join state-sanctioned chambers of commerce and industry, which, in turn, were obligated to join the national Confederation of Chambers of Commerce and Industry (CON-CANACOMIN).[11] This confederation was formed by combining the Confederation of Chambers of Commerce (CONCANACO) and the Confederation of Chambers of Industry (CONCAMIN), founded in 1917 and 1918, respectively. The law defined the chambers and the confederation as "public autonomous institutions," designated them as the private sector's official representative bodies, and provided the state with various mechanisms of control over the formation and functioning of both sorts of official organizations.

11. This requirement did not apply to financial services. Banks, insurance companies, and later stock brokerages each formed their own organizations, which were not regulated by the Chambers Law. In this chapter I analyze the organization of small industry within the corporatist framework. See Schneider 2002 for a discussion of independent business organizations that operated outside the corporatist framework.

The key innovation of the 1941 Chambers Law was to make a statutory distinction between industry and commerce. From this point forward industrialists would join specifically *industrial* chambers, which would be members of the reconstituted CONCAMIN, while retailers and service providers would join chambers of commerce, affiliated to CONCANACO. The revised law was a response to the growth of industry in the 1930s. The manufacturing sector's contribution to total national production had increased from 11.6 percent in 1932 to 24.3 percent by 1940 (Vera Blanco 1960, 272), yet industry remained subordinated to commerce within chambers of commerce and the national confederation. Not surprisingly, leaders of the emerging industrial sector, principally in and around Mexico City, pushed for the reformed Chambers Law, which separated industry from commerce.[12]

CANACINTRA and Small Industry

Mexico had few specifically industrial chambers at the time of the 1941 Chambers Law, because the dominant pattern of business association since the 1800s had been for all businesses, regardless of sector, to join multisectoral chambers of commerce. After 1941 manufacturers would request permission from the state to form the new industrial chambers that were now legal, and CONCAMIN's membership would grow. At the same time, the state collaborated with a group of industrialists in Mexico City to create a new industrial chamber, also part of CONCAMIN, that would include firms from a range of sectors. This chamber was CANACINTRA.

CANACINTRA was not established as an organization for *small* industrialists per se, but rather as a mixed-activity industrial chamber for firms of all sizes in new manufacturing activities that did not have their own chambers. Neither the Chambers Law nor CANACINTRA's statutes mention firm size in establishing membership criteria. However, the pattern of business association that followed the 1941 Chambers Law transformed CANACINTRA into the de facto representative of smaller, domestic-oriented, Mexican industrialists. The organization underwent rapid growth throughout the postwar era, as thousands of industrialists in unorganized sectors became legally obligated to join and pay dues to the chamber. Founded with 93 members in 1941, CANACINTRA had 6,730 members by 1945, 8,970 members by 1950, and 11,535 by 1960. At the same time that it was growing, however,

---

12. R. J. Shafer 1973, 46; Franco 1980, 20; Davis 1994, 109; Lütke-Entrup 2000, 98–110. See also Juárez González 1984, 1991.

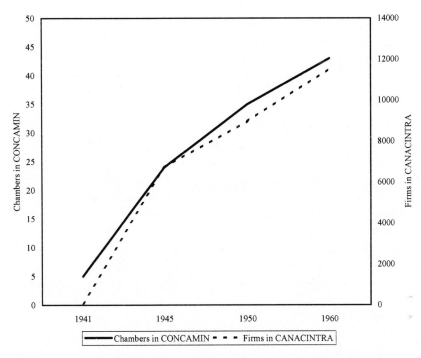

Fig. 3   CANACINTRA and CONCAMIN growth, 1941–1960
Sources: Chambers in CONCAMIN: R. J. Shafer 1973. Firms in CANACINTRA: CANACINTRA 1961;
Garza 1993.

CANACINTRA also lost members to new industrial chambers that were affiliated directly with CONCAMIN. CONCAMIN, whose membership consisted of
five chambers of industry in 1941, including CANACINTRA, had twenty chambers by 1944, thirty-five by 1950, and forty-three by 1960.[13] Figure 3 illustrates the similar growth trajectories of the chamber and confederation in
the 1950s and 1960s.

The pattern of organizational development that followed the 1941 Chambers Law—from CANACINTRA into new chambers—had two important dimensions: region and size. The regional dimension left industrialists from Mexico City in control of CANACINTRA, and the size dimension left the chamber
in the hands of small industry.

13. Note that as a confederation, CONCAMIN has a membership that consists of chambers, while the
industrial chambers' membership consists of individual firms. Industrialists who joined these new chambers were no longer members of CANACINTRA.

By 1944, manufacturers from Monterrey and Guadalajara, the second- and third-largest cities in the country, would not be members of CANACIN-TRA. In both instances, the requirement to join national organizations located in Mexico City was anathema to industrialists with long histories of local, autonomous organization. Encouraged by the green light given to mixed-activity manufacturing chambers, such as CANACINTRA, but not wishing to join the Mexico City–based organization, industrialists from Monterrey and Guadalajara created their own regional manufacturing chambers. In Monterrey, the area's leading industrialists created the Chamber of Manufacturing Industries of Nuevo León (CAINTRA).[14] Similarly, industrialists in Guadalajara, in the western state of Jalisco, created the Regional Chamber of Manufacturing Industries of Jalisco (CAREINTRA). Because Guadalajara lacked the internal hierarchy and integration that distinguished the Monterrey business community, in which a handful of powerful families and gigantic firms dominated the region, the quest for autonomy from Mexico City led not just to one regional, mixed-activity chamber, CAREINTRA, but eventually to more than a dozen different industrial chambers representing manufacturers from the region (Alba Vega 1990, 26–31; Concheiro, Gutiérrez, and Fragosa 197,: 279; Alba and Kruijt 1988). Importantly, the creation of regional chambers in Mexico's second- and third-largest and most industrialized areas meant that CANACINTRA, its name notwithstanding, would not be a *national* organization; manufacturers from the center of the country would be unrivaled in their dominance of CANACINTRA.

The second dimension of organizational development transformed CANAC-INTRA into an organization whose active membership consisted principally of small and medium-size firms. The establishment of new, sector-specific chambers separate from CANACINTRA was most pronounced in those sectors dominated by larger firms. Postwar developmentalist policies engendered significant structural change and differentiation within the industrial sector, as thousands of firms emerged in new sectors, and sectors that scarcely existed at the time of the 1941 Chambers Law began to make increasingly important contributors to industrial output and employment (King 1970; Vera

14. Monterrey, the primary city in the state of Nuevo León, had experienced significant industrial development since the late 1800s, and industrialists from this city sought to remain members of the multisectoral Monterrey Chamber of Commerce. The establishment of CAINTRA followed the Mexican Supreme Court's rejection of the Monterrey industrialists' request for an injunction against the new industrial-commercial division. See Mendirichaga 1989, 18–24; R. J. Shafer 1973, 54–55; and Concheiro, Gutiérrez, and Fragosa 1979, 279. For discussions of Monterrey business elites in this period, see Saragoza 1988; and Fuentes 1976.

Blanco 1960). Prominent industrialists in growing sectors housed within CANACINTRA came to desire their own organizations that would respond to their particular interests and provide distinct services (Brandenburg 1958).

The desire of large Mexican firms, and local subsidiaries of foreign firms, to create separate organizations was complemented by a greater capacity to do so. As discussed in Chapter 1, larger firms have a relatively easier time overcoming the barriers to collective action that typically impede the formation of organizations. Indeed, the creation of sector-specific organizations is precisely the sort of sectoral fragmentation that is emphasized by analysts of business association, in which the obstacles to collective action derived from intrabusiness conflict and free-riding are resolved via the creation of smaller collectivities with more homogenous interests (Streeck 1990; Traxler 1993). These large firms were also better equipped to satisfy the legal requirements involved in establishing new chambers, and they were more likely to have adequate contacts and resources to sway the appropriate state officials responsible for authorizing the creation of new chambers. To the extent that the likely solvency of the new chamber was an important criterion in state rulings, for example, faster-growing sectors were more likely to receive state approval.[15]

The interaction between these factors generated a self-reinforcing dynamic that shaped the patterns of Mexican business-interest organization: larger firms' exodus from CANACINTRA transformed the business organization into the representative of smaller firms, and CANACINTRA's vocation as the representative of small industrial firms heightened larger firms' desire to leave the chamber. In fact, both CONCAMIN and CANACINTRA implemented internal changes that reflected and encouraged this bifurcation. Within CONCAMIN, a change in the confederation's statutes reallocated voting weights according to the share of each chamber's financial contribution, rather than the size of the chamber in terms of members. This reduced CANACINTRA's influence within the confederation, giving more power to newer chambers that were controlled by the nation's largest firms. Likewise, CANACINTRA moved in the opposite direction, replacing a system whereby votes were weighted according to size of contribution (thus firm-size) with a system of one vote per firm.[16]

---

15. Although the solvency criterion was not explicit in the law itself, archival research reveals that demonstration of solvency featured prominently in petitions for state authorization of new industrial chambers. The founders of new chambers routinely emphasized the size of the firms involved and assured the state that the organization would have sound finances.

16. The CONCAMIN change is discussed in Zabludovsky 1984, 74. The CANACINTRA change is noted in the minutes of the board of directors, 11 October 1950.

CANACINTRA's Dependence

The creation of new chambers in CONCAMIN increased both the material and organizational dependence of CANACINTRA on the state. As indicated, the sectors leaving CANACINTRA tended to be those with the fastest growth, in the most dynamic areas of the economy. By the early 1950s, new chambers existed in sectors such as paper and pulp, pharmaceuticals, rubber, and steel and iron—each of these dominated by a handful of large firms. Yet while rubber manufacturers formed their own chambers and joined CONCAMIN, for example, the assortment of smaller firms dedicated to tire rebuilding remained in CANACINTRA. Likewise, while large steel firms created a chamber that joined CONCAMIN, smaller foundries and ironworks remained in CANACINTRA. And whereas pharmaceutical firms joined CONCAMIN, basic chemical producers remained in CANACINTRA.[17] In short, in broad sectors of great importance, the major firms that policy makers depended on to spearhead industrialization and Mexico's integration into the international economy were not those in CANACINTRA, which had come to represent a collectivity of firms from relatively weaker segments of Mexican capital.

This bifurcated pattern of business organization fundamentally changed CANACINTRA's relationships with both CONCAMIN and the state. In the years immediately following the creation of CANACINTRA and the reestablishment of CONCAMIN, the chamber and confederation were tightly linked. CANACINTRA was a member of CONCAMIN, and working together they gave the emerging manufacturing sector a single voice on most issues of public policy. The two organizations shared office space, for example, and, in fact, the first president of CANACINTRA, José Cruz y Celis (1941–43), was also the president of CONCAMIN at the time.[18] Yet by the 1950s, CANACINTRA and CONCAMIN came to represent distinct branches of Mexican industry: the former representing smaller, domestic-oriented firms, the weak segment of local capital, and the latter representing larger and more internationalized firms.

The pattern of association also produced an asymmetry in terms of CANACINTRA's relationship with the state, in that its members depended on the

---

17. See Stockbridge 1954, 26–27 for a comparison of the emerging distinction in sectors included in CANACINTRA versus CONCAMIN. R. J. Shafer (1973, appendixes 4 and 5) lists the sections in CANACINTRA and the chambers in CONCAMIN.

18. CANACINTRA, on behalf of CONCAMIN, was the principal representative of industry at the 1945 Chapultepec Conference, in which the United States and Mexico discussed binational trade relations after World War II (Stockbridge 1954; Mosk 1950; Roxborough 1992b, 200). And in 1946, a much publicized industry-worker pact was signed by CANACINTRA, again in an official capacity on behalf of the entire manufacturing sector.

state for trade protection, subsidies, and government purchases much more than the state depended on these smaller firms' contributions to economic activity. Of course, manufacturing firms of all sizes, Mexican and transnational, benefited from and depended on state concessions during this period. Yet larger firms, on account of the size of their assets and their contributions to economic activity and employment, had a degree of leverage that smaller firms lacked. The typical dependence of the state on capital was diminished in the case of the weaker firms represented by CANACINTRA.[19] These differences grew more important as the Mexican economy became increasingly internationalized in the decades following World War II, and the gap widened between large financial-industrial conglomerates and small, independent manufacturing firms.[20]

A critical effect of this material weakness was an erosion of CANACINTRA's position in state-business consultation. With its membership consisting of weaker firms upon which the state was less dependent, the chamber could not expect to be consulted by policy makers as a matter of course. Instead, the government increasingly relied on CONCAMIN and the new sector-specific organizations as interlocutors. Indeed, beginning in the late 1940s and continuing throughout the postwar era, business organizations representing large firms assumed more prominent positions on state policy-making boards. The close relationship that CANACINTRA and CONCAMIN enjoyed in the immediate aftermath of the Chambers Law was replaced by rivalry. Although CANACINTRA had once represented the manufacturing sector, on behalf of CONCAMIN, on a number of important issues, by the 1950s CONCAMIN came to dominate and worked to exclude CANACINTRA.

CANACINTRA developed what its leaders self-consciously labeled an institutional "foreign policy" to retain access to state officials and keep itself on the radar screen.[21] In addition to standard activities of business associations (e.g., undertaking economic analyses and disseminating information to members), the chamber initiated a constant effort to cultivate links to key state officials, requesting meetings with policy makers to discuss economic policies that affected small firms. CANACINTRA also attempted to

19. For statements of the state's dependence on capital, see Lindblom 1977, 1982; Offe and Wiesenthal 1980; and Przeworski and Wallerstein 1982. The material dependence of CANACINTRA's members during this period has been highlighted by Mosk (1950), Vernon (1963), and Elizondo (1992). See also Concheiro, Gutiérrez, and Fragosa 1979.

20. See Jacobs and Máttar 1985 for an analysis of the changing position of small firms in the Mexican manufacturing sector. See also King 1970; Horvath 1991; and Concheiro, Gutiérrez, and Fragosa 1979. For discussions of distinct entrepreneurial backgrounds, see Vernon 1963, 156–57; and Derossi 1971.

21. This is literally referred to as a "política exterior" in CANACINTRA's internal documents.

increase its importance to the state as a provider of economic analysis. To that end, officials would regularly send copies of the monographs and studies produced by the chamber to the president. The effort to make CANAC-INTRA a valuable interlocutor included organizing large public events, such as National Congresses on Manufacturing, the records of which were published and disseminated throughout the government (CANACINTRA 1953).[22]

CANACINTRA also became increasingly dependent on the state for organizational support, in that the process of fragmentation made it more difficult to sustain collective action and retain organizational coherence. As discussed in Chapter 1, business collective action typically benefits from asymmetrical distribution of resources within the collectivity, which increases the likelihood that there will be larger firms that are able to bear the burdens of organization-building (van Waarden 1991; Olson 1965). In the case of CANACINTRA, however, at the same time as its membership was growing, the chamber was losing the large firms that might have simplified and facilitated organization. Many of the remaining members tended to be smaller and less stable, increasing the chamber's dependence on compulsory membership for organizational cohesion.

Furthermore, the creation of new chambers eroded CANACINTRA's membership base and resources. Even though the creation of new chambers was led by large firms, it occurred within a legal framework that required sectoral chambers to be comprehensive. Because the Chambers Law made membership in the new chamber compulsory for *all* firms in the sector—not only the handful of big firms that petitioned for the new chamber—the establishment of a new chamber therefore meant that hundreds of dues-paying members of all sizes would leave CANACINTRA.[23]

The Chambers Law made state authorization a prerequisite for the creation of new chambers, and the vagueness of the law left state officials with a substantial degree of discretion. According to the Chambers Law, the Secretariat of the Economy was to determine when a new chamber could be

---

22. CANACINTRA held its first such national congress in April 1947 and the second in August 1953. It is worth noting, as an indication of the cleavage that had developed within the industrial sector, that on the eve of the second congress, twenty-three industrial chambers from CONCAMIN jointly wrote President Ruíz Cortines, who was scheduled to deliver the inaugural address, encouraging him not to attend. These chambers maintained that the event staged by CANACINTRA was unrepresentative of the positions on economic policy of Mexico's largest manufacturing firms (Archivo General de la Nación/Fondo Adolfo Ruíz Cortines [AGN/FARC] 111/909).

23. Officially, the smallest firms were exempted, but this clause became increasingly irrelevant over the years, since the minimum level of capital established in 1936 as a threshold was not adjusted for inflation.

created and which firms should join which chambers.[24] But the law did not clearly specify the requisites for establishing separate industrial chambers; nor, critically, did it define the criteria by which the state determined whether groups of manufacturers should form their own chamber or remain members of CANACINTRA. Article 9 simply stipulated that in order for state authorization to be given, the request needed to be made by a group of at least twenty industrialists in the same sector and an industrial chamber could not already exist in that sector.[25]

Throughout the 1950s, CANACINTRA implored state officials to revise the Chambers Law in a way that would raise the barriers to secession and strengthen the chamber. CANACINTRA officials focused on the articles delineating sectoral boundaries and establishing the conditions for chamber registration, arguing that the minimum requirement of twenty firms for the creation of new chambers was too easy and requesting that the impediments to establishing separate chambers be heightened. And the chamber emphasized the importance of retaining compulsory membership, arguing that otherwise small firms would be unorganized and subsequently underrepresented.[26]

CANACINTRA also attempted to block the creation of new industrial chambers. The protracted and uncertain process by which these chambers received authorization opened up opportunities for CANACINTRA to lobby state officials, and the chamber leadership spared little in its campaign to persuade state officials to deny authorization of new chambers. As industrialists from sectors within CANACINTRA petitioned the state to authorize new chambers, CANACINTRA almost invariably objected, using a variety of means to convince government officials to block authorization. CANACINTRA published open letters in the press denouncing proposed organizations, it presented challenging legal documents, and it took advantage of opportunities that were presented by meetings with the president and key cabinet officials to discuss the problem of chamber creation. In short, the chamber exploited all available means and dedicated substantial amounts of time and resources

24. Jurisdiction was transferred in the 1960s to the Secretariat of Industry and Trade (SIC), and in the 1980s to the Secretariat of Trade and Industrial Development (SECOFI).

25. The ambiguity here derives from the inherent uncertainties in establishing the boundaries between sectors. CANACINTRA frequently argued that the firms petitioning for new sector-specific chambers were actually from different sectors.

26. CANACINTRA's warnings in this period foreshadowed the arguments made in the 1990s, when democratization would strengthen a campaign led by a dissenting group of small industrialists to reform the Chambers Law and eliminate compulsory membership. The ensuing conflict and CANACINTRA's response are analyzed in Chapter 4.

in the mission to limit the creation of new chambers and thereby preserve CANACINTRA as a coherent and unified organization.[27]

Thus, in the decades following the 1941 Chambers Law, CANACINTRA came to depend on the state in a variety of important ways. Representing the weak segment of local capital, the chamber had to fight for access to policy makers that it could not expect as a matter of course. The chamber also depended on compulsory membership, for that is what guaranteed the organization an expanding base of dues-paying members, members who otherwise might face daunting obstacles to collective action and suffer from free-riding. And CANACINTRA depended on favorable application of the Chambers Law, particularly with regard to rulings on the creation of new chambers, for that is what saved the chamber from undergoing a massive hemorrhaging of members and resources.

Alliance Formation from Below

Dependence on the state encouraged CANACINTRA to develop a strategy of organizational preservation. From a very early period in the chamber's history, CANACINTRA's labors were twofold—representing the interests of its members, and preserving the chamber's status vis-à-vis the state. The relationship between these two tasks is important: the former is dependent on the latter. That is, CANACINTRA's capacity to represent its members was predicated first on organizational stability and cohesion.

CANACINTRA's strategy for representing small industry must be considered in light of the challenges of reconciling these dual tasks and the chamber's precarious organizational condition. Because separate chambers could not be created without government authorization, and because the Chambers Law was vague with regard to the criteria for creation of new chambers, the continued existence and viability of CANACINTRA came to depend largely on the state's discretion.

CANACINTRA responded to these challenges by cultivating an alliance with the state, articulating enthusiastic and public support of the ruling PRI on a wide range of economic and political issues. Critically, the chamber bypassed alliance alternatives outside the state, refusing to support

---

27. Not all of CANACINTRA's initiatives to curtail the establishment of new chambers were directed toward the state. Internally, as the leadership came to regard sectoral sections within the chamber as stepping stones toward creation of separate organizations, CANACINTRA began working to make it more difficult to form sections and to limit the sections' autonomy (CANACINTRA General Assembly, 28 January 1954).

opposition movements that articulated economic policy interests closer in line with the chamber's own theses. At the heart of this alliance-building project was a strategy of organizational preservation, labeled "accommodation," in which CANACINTRA sacrificed political autonomy in exchange for organizational cohesion and stability.

Accommodation

CANACINTRA supported the state on a wide range of economic and political issues. The chamber supported policies that generally benefited its members, such as trade protection and the provision of consumption subsidies that bolstered local demand. The chamber also supported the growing state role in the energy sector, as provider of low-cost inputs. For example, CANACINTRA defended continued state ownership in the oil sector and actively celebrated the nationalization of the electricity sector.[28]

At the same time, the chamber generally refrained from offering strong criticism of economic policies that were less favorable to small firms. It is important to recall the giantist biases of postwar economic policy discussed earlier in this chapter. Beginning with the Alemán administration and continually throughout the postwar period, successive governments welcomed foreign investment in the manufacturing sector and implemented tax and credit policies that facilitated the emergence of large multisectoral conglomerates, often taking resources away from programs dedicated to smaller firms. And postwar governments also restrained public spending and curtailed the process of land distribution, thus restricting expansion of the domestic market.[29] To be sure, the members of CANACINTRA had myriad grievances about the nature of economic policy. Records of the chamber's meetings during this period at which leaders interacted with members, for example, CANACINTRA's annual general assemblies and bimonthly meetings of the board of directors, are filled with a litany of complaints and demands. Small industrialists complained to their associational representatives about, among other things, the difficulties they faced in obtaining credit and what they regarded as unfair competition in the form of large, powerful multinational firms entering Mexican markets.

28. Wionczek (1964) provides an analysis of the ongoing conflict between the state and the foreign-owned firms controlling the distribution of electricity, with the role of CANACINTRA in this conflict and the chamber's reactions to the nationalization discussed on pages 85–90. See also Alcazar 1970, 53 and Puga 1984, 199.

29. For overviews of the changes in economic strategy from the 1940s through the 1960s, see Hansen 1971 and R. Villareal 1977.

More important than the merits—or demerits—of prevailing economic policies, the recurrent issue debated within the chamber was *how* to address the state—how to articulate policy grievances in light of the constraining economic and political circumstances. CANACINTRA officials expected that accommodation could be rewarded, in terms of organizational concessions, access to policy makers, and the ability to deliver benefits to members. At the same time, they also were keenly aware of the fact that the chamber's precarious organizational condition meant that public and outspoken criticism of the state could be costly. Repeatedly throughout this period, the chamber leadership would discuss what to do with internal studies indicating that one or another aspect of economic policy was damaging to small firms, consistently deciding to refrain from public criticism and instead seek private sessions with relevant officials.

The chamber did not remain silent on policy issues, but rather went out of its way to express opposition through nonconfrontational means. Indeed, part of CANACINTRA's "foreign policy" was a media strategy to proclaim generally supportive positions in the press, the chamber opting to voice criticisms in less visible settings. Thus, those declarations that were public tended to be relatively uncritical of the state, and those that were critical of the state tended to be made not publicly but rather behind closed doors. CANACINTRA's leaders generally refrained from strong public criticisms of policy, and even the criticisms that were made tended to be directed toward errors of omission rather than commission. That is, the chamber would artfully integrate policy advocacy into celebrations of the state's otherwise "revolutionary" achievements.[30]

An important example of this is evident in the realm of foreign investment. The increased presence of foreign capital in the manufacturing sector in the decades after World War II was quite threatening for the smaller local firms represented by the chamber. Mexicanization fell far short of the sorts of regulations that CANACINTRA advocated, and CANACINTRA's intense criticisms of the growing presence of multinational corporations (MNCs) is well documented.[31] Somehow CANACINTRA needed to reconcile

30. For examples, see CANACINTRA 1952, 1961a, 1961b; and Lavín 1960. CANACINTRA also went out of its way to support the state on an array of issues that took on special significance in Mexico's postrevolutionary environment. For example, CANACINTRA actively defended government proclamations in support of the Cuban Revolution, though doing so isolated the chamber within the business community.

31. CANACINTRA (1953) and Amaro (1958) offer the most concise statements of the chamber's theses on foreign investment. Also noteworthy is Domingo Lavín's (1954) 428-page polemic, in which the ex-president of CANACINTRA attributes cycles of decapitalization to waves of foreign investment into Mexico. Alcazar (1970, 57–61) contrasts CANACINTRA's position with that of the other major business organizations, especially CONCAMIN, CONCANACO, and the Mexican Employers' Confederation (COPARMEX).

its strong opposition to increased foreign investment and its concern with remaining in the good graces of state officials with the reality of the situation, which was that the government's position vis-à-vis foreign investors was quite welcoming. How was CANACINTRA to criticize foreign investors while also remaining supportive of a government that was so welcoming of DFI? The strategy was to assail the foreign investors themselves, and their allies within the Mexican business community, but not the policies that facilitated so much investment. To the contrary, any steps taken by the government to regulate foreign capital, minimal as they were, were strongly applauded by CANACINTRA.

A critical dimension of accommodation, and related to the chamber's generally supportive public positions on economic policy, was CANACINTRA's tactic of disassociating small industry from opposition political movements that challenged the governing PRI's economic policy. To be sure, the significance of active partisan opposition in this period was minimal: Mexican politics were dominated by the PRI, and electoral institutions—also controlled by the PRI—were designed to reproduce this dominance (Molinar 1991; Gonzalez Casanova 1970). Opposition parties faced enormous obstacles to gaining official registration, and electoral competition was extraordinarily uneven. Nevertheless, small electoral movements emerged, particularly in the late 1940s and early 1950s as the PRI moved further away from the redistributive sorts of policies that had been implemented during the reformist presidency of Lázaro Cárdenas (1934–40).[32]

Although many of the opposition movements articulated positions on economic policy that one would expect to have resonated with CANACINTRA, a key aspect of the accommodationist strategy was to bypass such alliance alternatives. An important and prominent instance of this occurred during the 1952 presidential elections, when a number of ex-*priísta* forces united in opposition to the candidacy of Adolfo Ruíz Cortines. This movement was based on the candidacy of General Miguel Henríquez Guzmán, who had been expelled by the PRI in 1951 for announcing his own candidacy and assailing the giantist orientation of the Mexican regime (Morris 1995, 176–77). Henríquez united a wide range of dissenting groups and political movements in the Federation of Popular Parties (FPP). At the same time, another important movement of dissent in this period came from the Constitutionalist Party, which supported the candidacy of Gen. Francisco Múgica. Múgica had

---

32. See Cornelius 1973; Hamilton 1982; Collier and Collier 1991, 232–50; and Knight 1994 for analysis of reformism under Cárdenas.

been the heir apparent to President Lázaro Cárdenas, but Cárdenas, in response to the growing backlash against his reformist government, selected the more conservative Avila Camacho as his successor for the 1940 election.

In programmatic terms, very little distinguished the economic policy positions of CANACINTRA, on the one hand, and the *henriquistas* and Constitutionalists, on the other: the criticisms voiced *internally* at CANACINTRA meetings read like the campaign materials of the PRI's fledgling opponents. In fact, an ex-president of CANACINTRA, José Colín (1945–46), who disassociated himself from CANACINTRA and published a series of missives lamenting the "death" of the Mexican Revolution, participated actively in Múgica's campaign (see Colín 1948, 1954, 1966). The trajectory of Colín, who had represented the industrial sector in the famous worker-industry pact (CANACINTRA 1946) but soon thereafter was assailing the Alemán government for restoring "the oligarchy," illustrates the tensions between small industrialists regarding the appropriate and prudent response to the PRI and to potential alliance alternatives outside the state.

While CANACINTRA's former president became a political maverick and challenged the PRI, the chamber's leadership went out of its way to distance itself from both Colín and the political opposition. At one juncture the leadership decided to suppress an internal study on MNC pricing practices, practices that the chamber blamed for increasing the cost of living and bringing about "immiseration." The explicit rationale for this decision, according to minutes of the meeting of the board of directors, was to avoid sounding too much like the PRI's opponents. Instead, the chamber resolved to create a commission that would study the problem of monopolies and present these findings to the government, with a strong emphasis on being cautious, avoiding grand proclamations, and carefully not appearing to look like the political opposition.[33] In the same election, CANACINTRA and other Mexican business organizations received a long questionnaire on economic policy from Ruíz Cortines's campaign. The board of directors considered taking advantage of the opportunity to make its positions known by sending the chamber's response to each of the candidates and publishing it in Mexico City newspapers. This suggestion was overridden, however, as the leadership voiced concerns that disseminating the chamber's positions to all the candidates would somehow give the appearance of political impartiality. The decision was made to respond only to the PRI's candidate.[34]

---

33. CANACINTRA board of directors meeting, 11 July 1951.
34. CANACINTRA board of directors, 28 May 1952.

A similar strategy regarding political positioning is made evident through an examination of CANACINTRA's relationship with organized labor. While the chamber collaborated with "official" state-linked unions in the Confederation of Mexican Workers (CTM), CANACINTRA refused to work with the independent union movement, which was most active in challenging the conservative orientation of postwar economic policy. Indeed, the Mexican labor movement featured a long tradition of more independent unions that sought to operate outside the CTM and looked for allies to oppose the direction of post–World War II economic policy. While workers from smaller and weaker unions were eager to establish alliances with the state during this period, workers from large, national industrial unions with greater market power remained more militant and feverishly sought to protect their autonomy.[35] The sectors in which independent unions were strongest, such as petroleum, railroads, and steel, were sectors where CANACINTRA had few active members at the time. Thus, economic conditions would suggest that these unions might be comparatively unthreatening to the chamber, as the costs would be borne by firms in other sectors of the economy. Yet CANACINTRA was publicly supportive of steps taken by Presidents Alemán and López Mateos to purge independent labor leaders and suppress dissident unions. In standard fashion, the chamber's leadership went out of its way to express its support for such actions in the press.

These observations on CANACINTRA's strategy affirm the importance of archival work for understanding this period. It is important to underscore the extent to which CANACINTRA's declarations in the press on a variety of issues differed from the positions articulated internally within the chamber. By making it possible to contrast these external and internal positions, archival work allows us to reinterpret as political strategy the support of the state, which many analysts have regarded as a reflection of small firms' interests (e.g., Story 1986; Hobbs 1991). CANACINTRA's leaders were not simply acting as the members wanted; representation often entailed suppression of firms' immediate interests for the sake of organizational preservation.

Importantly, the analysis presented here also contradicts assertions that CANACINTRA was essentially a mouthpiece of the government (R. J. Shafer 1973; Purcell and Purcell 1977).[36] To the contrary, the supportive positions were not imposed from above, but, rather, designed to exploit opportunities

---

35. See Middlebrook 1995, chapters 3–4, for an analysis of the conflicts between the more docile CTM and the more independent unions.

36. For example, R. J. Shafer writes that "CANACINTRA obviously always has represented the views of the political masters in Mexico" (1973, 107).

to improve representation for small industry in the authoritarian and developmentalist regime. The postwar political and economic environment created both challenges and opportunities for small firms, and CANACINTRA took advantage of the opportunities to forge an alliance with the state.

Protecting CANACINTRA

In 1960 CANACINTRA was awarded for its labors with the most substantive reforms that the Chambers Law would undergo until the late 1990s.[37] The 1960 reforms made separation from CANACINTRA more difficult by increasing the threshold for allowing industrialists to petition for authorization of new chambers. Whereas Article 9 had required that the petition be made by a minimum of twenty industrialists, the revision stipulated that the petition must include the signatures of 80 percent of the industrialists in the specific sector. To be sure, the 1960 reforms did not eliminate the state's discretionary power (e.g., the state retained the authority to determine which activities fell within which industrial sector, and the criteria for determining how the state rules on petitions remained vague), but they unquestionably provided CANACINTRA with a cushion against secessionist groups. The chamber's leadership had fought doggedly for this change, and the organization's newfound stability was celebrated in ceremonies surrounding the chamber's twentieth anniversary (CANACINTRA 1961a, 1961b). With its future secure, the chamber's leaders began constructing a new ten-story office complex in Mexico City.[38]

By making the creation of new chambers less likely, the 1960 reforms established the conditions for CANACINTRA's membership base to expand exponentially. New chambers could (and would) continue to emerge, but the 80 percent requirement meant that it would be difficult for such chambers to be created in sectors that were populated overwhelmingly by small firms. While CANACINTRA had 11,535 members in 1960, by 1970 its membership

37. Published in *Diario Oficial*, 16 January 1960. Although this was the only significant reform of the Chambers Law until it was replaced in 1997, the law underwent minor revisions on various occasions, as published in *Diario Oficial* on 2 February 1943, 4 February 1963, 24 December 1965, 23 December 1974 (as part of a broader constitutional reform), 30 December 1974, and 7 January 1975.

38. In a well-publicized ceremony attended by President Gustavo Díaz Ordaz (1964–70) and prominent members of his administration, CANACINTRA president Raul Ollervides inaugurated the gigantic "house of industrialists" on 30 June 1965. CANACINTRA 1965 reproduces the speeches delivered at the opening ceremony by Díaz Ordaz and Ollervides, along with articles and editorials from six Mexico City newspapers.

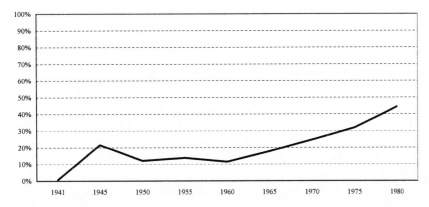

Fig. 4   CANACINTRA: Members as share of all industrial firms, 1941–1980
Source: CANACINTRA 1961a; Garza 1993.

would almost triple, reaching 29,542, and by 1979 the chamber would have 56,000 members. This growth in membership, of course, partially reflects the demographic change that Mexico underwent in the 1960s and 1970s, as the country became increasingly urbanized and industrialized. The important point, however, illustrated in Figure 4, is that after 1960 the chamber's membership grew rapidly not only in absolute terms but also as a share of Mexico's expanding industrial sector. After declining in the fifteen years after 1945, this ratio increased dramatically after 1960.

It is essential to underscore that the 1960 reforms to the Chambers Law further buttressed the size-based cleavage between CANACINTRA and CON-CAMIN. Had the threshold for establishing new chambers and leaving CANAC-INTRA been set high in the original Chambers Law, large firms most likely would have simply commandeered the new chamber immediately, and CANAC-INTRA would never have emerged as a representative of small firms. Yet coming when they did—after an extensive process of industrial differentiation and two decades of organizational development had already produced this bifurcation—these reforms simply inspired Mexico's leading industrial firms to adopt new strategies to continue separating themselves from CANACIN-TRA and affiliating with CONCAMIN.

The dominant strategy by which large firms separated from CANACINTRA was to create sector-specific trade *associations,* which were not official "chambers" and to which membership was voluntary. In fact, this strategy was not altogether new in the 1960s, as large firms had been creating such voluntary associations since the 1940s. Because these associations operated outside the corporatist system, they could engage in a variety of activities that were off limits to official chambers; and sectoral trade associations were also useful steps along the way toward establishing sector-specific chambers.[39] The creation of voluntary associations was a loophole in the corporatist regulations that was disproportionately available to larger firms, underscoring the fact that larger firms were less constrained by state-imposed regulations on interest organization. With the creation of new chambers made more difficult after 1960, leaders of large firms instead opted to formalize sectoral trade associations. CONCAMIN, in turn, eagerly accepted these associations as nonvoting members with access to the confederation's services and a voice in internal affairs.[40] Whereas CONCAMIN had only three associations in 1954, by 1967 fourteen such associations were affiliated with CONCAMIN; by 1983 the number had reached twenty-six, and by 1993 thirty-five.[41]

The proliferation of associations in CONCAMIN certainly reinforced the pattern of bifurcation that had marked organizational development in the industrial sector since the 1940s, because these associations typically had few small firms as members.[42] Sectoral associations, like the sector-specific chambers discussed above, were created by the leading firms in the given sector. Unlike chambers, however, which were subject to the compulsory-membership clause of the Chambers Law, associations attracted only the firms that elected to join. Because associations tended to service the specialized needs of the larger firms that inspired their creation, they had less to offer in the way of services for smaller firms. Furthermore, membership in a voluntary association implies payment of additional membership fees, beyond what firms are legally obligated to pay their official organization. Since membership dues to voluntary associations tend to be higher than those paid to chambers, to compensate for the absence of the compulsory-membership "subsidy," smaller firms are less likely to join.

---

39. As indicated, banks and insurance firms were not obligated to join chambers. Their voluntary associations, such as the ABM (Mexican Bankers' Association) and AMIS (Mexican Association of Insurance Institutions), were the principal representatives of the sectors. With the development of large industrial-financial conglomerates, large manufacturing firms had representation outside corporatism.

40. Because the Chambers Law stipulated that CONCAMIN's members must be chambers, these associations were restricted to voice but not vote within the confederation.

41. The 1967 figure comes from R. J. Shafer 1973, 212–13; the 1983 figure comes from Story 1986, 89; and the 1993 figure comes from CONCAMIN 1993.

42. These observations contrasting associations with chambers are drawn from various interviews with directors of official chambers and voluntary associations, and it was a topic that I consistently covered in firm-level interviews. See also Puga 1992, 35–36; R. J. Shafer 1973, 73–76; Camp 1989; and Arriola 1981.

This slightly revised pattern of organization also stabilized CANACIN-TRA's resources, since members of voluntary associations were legally obligated to continue to pay membership dues to CANACINTRA. But they did little else. After all, the association provided essential services, and with membership in CONCAMIN, the associations obtained quasi-official status. CANACINTRA had little to offer. To the contrary, the chamber's internal, majoritarian, democratic structure discriminated against large firms, which were of course fewer in number. And a progressive dues schedule meant that these larger firms provided a significant share of the chamber's revenues.[43] Small industrialists thus had control over an organization that was financed by the compulsory membership dues, not only of thousands of small firms, but also of larger firms that remained as generally disinterested and inactive members.

Mitigating Giantism

With the chamber stabilized and access to policy makers somewhat secured, CANACINTRA could extract important material benefits for the membership. As indicated, an important characteristic of postwar developmentalist economic policy was its particularistic nature, which, in turn, increased the importance of interest organization in the political economy. This increased importance was particularly relevant in the case of small industrialists, who typically lacked well-developed managerial and legal staffs and rarely had individual government contacts. Small manufacturers counted on CANAC-INTRA to act as intermediary and deal with state officials on their behalf; and CANACINTRA was able to parlay its official status to gain access to important policy-making arenas.

Representing Small Industry

CANACINTRA had a seat on the board of directors of key state enterprises. By including the chamber on commissions and policy-making boards, the state provided CANACINTRA with access to policy makers and, effectively, patronage resources to distribute to members. CANACINTRA was also able to take advantage of its official status to assist its members with the day-to-day difficulties they faced, providing to members the invaluable service known

43. And since many of the large firms conducted business with the state, they would not risk their privileges by refusing to pay their membership dues, even to a chamber that they largely ignored.

as *gestión*—obtaining necessary permits, cutting through bureaucratic red tape, bribing inspectors and regulators, and so on. To label these benefits "selective incentives" to membership would not be entirely accurate, as chamber membership was compulsory under the Chambers Law. With or without these benefits, firms still had to join the chambers, and they had little choice about which chamber to join. Yet CANACINTRA's ability to assist firms in this way was certainly an incentive to active participation in the chamber and a disincentive to dissent.

The importance of CANACINTRA to small firms is further illuminated through examination of the chamber's role as intermediary in three realms of postwar economic policy: trade strategy, foreign investment regulation, and industrial finance. The fact that licenses, and not tariffs, were the key instrument of trade protection, and that license requests were decided on a case-by-case basis, made it especially important for small firms to have a representative with access to the right decision-makers. The chambers' role in requesting import permits was not formally required, as individual firms could petition the state directly, but small firms were less likely to have the resources to successfully make their cases on their own. Many lacked the legal expertise and understanding of the process, and individual requests coming from small firms were typically put at the end of the queue. CANACINTRA, subsequently, encouraged members to channel their requests through the chamber. The chamber could also provide small industrialists with input on the sectoral advising committees that participated in the licensing process.

Similar dynamics were evident in terms of CANACINTRA's role as intermediary in the area of foreign investment. As indicated, an array of presidential decrees governed this issue area, requiring authorization and registration of foreign enterprises. As with trade policy, rulings were again made on a case-by-case basis and featured large degrees of state discretion; and as with trade policy, small firms relied on their intermediary to defend their interests. Small firms that were threatened by the pending entry of a foreign investor depended on CANACINTRA to represent them, and the chamber routinely lobbied regulatory officials in the executive branch to block entry or at least delay the authorization of foreign firms.

Assessing representation in this context raises difficult questions of observation and measurement. Data on the number of petitions for foreign investment denied or delayed are not available. Nor are data that might link denial or delay of entry to CANACINTRA's activities. Thus, it is difficult to demonstrate that CANACINTRA wielded influence on behalf of small firms in this regard. However, archival records, those both of the chamber and of the presidency, make it clear that small firms relied on CANACINTRA to represent them and that the chamber exhausted significant resources advocating on behalf of individual firms that lacked the resources to contact state officials directly. It is evident that CANACINTRA exploited the close relationships that were cultivated and developed through accommodation to advocate on behalf of small industries within the context of the developmentalist economic model.

Perhaps the most important dividend of accommodation came in the realm of industrial finance. A critical challenge facing small firms throughout the world regards access to credit. In postwar Mexico, these difficulties were exacerbated by tight monetary policy and an oligopolistic commercial banking sector, in which six institutions controlled roughly 80 percent of all assets (King 1970, 68). The structure of the local financial sector and the emergence of tight relationships between local banks and large industries meant that large firms benefited from preferential access to finance, while small firms were increasingly squeezed out of commercial credit markets. Not surprisingly, members of CANACINTRA deluged the chamber with complaints and requests, criticizing the Bank of Mexico for settling high interest rates, assailing the private banks for discriminating against them, and beseeching the chamber to do something to improve the availability and terms of credit.

CANACINTRA was able to use its official status to encourage state officials to help improve access to credit. In 1953, with the assistance of the state development bank (NAFIN), CANACINTRA initiated a credit union to provide members with subsidized loans. In the same year, government officials introduced a trust fund to provide loan guarantees for small firms, the Guarantee Fund for the Development of Medium and Small Industry (FOGAIN). Not only was CANACINTRA active in the creation of FOGAIN; it also attained a seat on the Technical Committee, which managed the fund.[44]

CANACINTRA successfully parlayed its seat on the management committee to increase the size of FOGAIN, and, subsequently, the amount of loans supported by the fund. From 1954 to 1960, FOGAIN guaranteed an average of roughly 650 loans per year, increasing to roughly 750 loans per year from 1961 to 1973. In 1974 alone, the number increased to 2,900 and stayed at this level throughout the decade.[45]

44. Along with CANACINTRA's representative, the five-member Technical Committee consisted of representatives from the Secretariat of Finance (Secretaría de Hacienda y Crédito Público [SHCP]), the Bank of Mexico, NAFIN, and CONCAMIN. For additional analyses of FOGAIN, see Jacobs and Máttar 1985; Alvarez Uriarte 1990; Horvath 1991; López Espinosa 1994; and de María y Campos 2002.

45. The calculations are based on data provided by FOGAIN and by Horvath 1991 and de María y Campos 2002.

In assessing the effects of the accommodationist strategy, it is important to distinguish between representation and power. The argument here is not that small industrialists drove postwar policy. As is well documented, the lion's share of fiscal and trade incentives went to Mexico's largest firms (e.g., King 1970); foreign investment continued to flood into the manufacturing sector at a much greater rate than CANACINTRA's members would have desired (e.g., Gereffi and Evans 1981); and small firms remained marginalized from commercial credit markets, notwithstanding the emergence and expansion of FOGAIN (e.g., Horvath 1991). Yet there is little doubt that the concerns of small firms were voiced and heard by relevant policy makers. Small industrialists lacked power, but not representation: they had an advocate. CANACINTRA's labors could deliver benefits, albeit on the margins of economic policy, and thus help mitigate the giantist biases of the postwar development strategy.

Conclusion

In this chapter we have examined the material and institutional roots of CANAC-INTRA's strategy to represent small industry in post–World War II Mexico. A developmentalist economic model, an executive-centered authoritarian regime, and the corporatist framework provided CANACINTRA with opportunities to gain an important role in the postwar Mexican political economy.

Small firms' collective action difficulties encouraged CANACINTRA to prioritize organizational preservation, even if stabilizing the organization entailed partial suppression of members' interests. Thus, CANACINTRA effectively exchanged political autonomy for organizational stability. The chamber's subsequent strategy of accommodation—refraining from public and confrontational criticisms of the state and withholding support from groups challenging the ruling PRI—earned small manufacturers access to the policy-making apparatus, more access than might be expected, given these firms' subordinate economic position.

With the organization protected, the chamber was able to deliver critical material concessions to members. CANACINTRA helped small firms navigate the complicated terrain of Mexico's import licensing regime. The chamber sought protection for small industrialists from the practices of MNCs, which played an increasingly prominent role in manufacturing after World War II. And CANACINTRA worked closely with the state to develop and secure continued expansion of an industrial financing program for small firms.

The discussion of representation in this chapter underscores a critical point in this book, that small firms' individual weakness increases the importance of organization. Because CANACINTRA developed and retained links to the right policy makers within the state bureaucracy, the chamber could provide small industrialists with representation that they might otherwise have lacked. CANACINTRA could provide this service because of the discretionary nature of economic policy itself and because of the organization's success at cultivating and retaining close ties with the state. Material and organizational dependence encouraged the chamber to seek out the state as an alliance partner, and the ensuing strategy of accommodation secured the organizational resources necessary to represent small industry in the postwar period. By stabilizing the organization, accommodation allowed CANACINTRA to deliver concrete material gains to small industrialists in the decades after World War II. Though CANACINTRA, representing the weak segment of capital, clearly did not drive economic policy, accommodation allowed the chamber to mitigate some of the giantist effects of developmentalism.

This chapter provides new insights for understanding postwar Mexican political economy. The literature on this period frequently depicts CANACINTRA as a powerful and influential player (e.g., Hobbs 1991; Story 1982, 1986; Hellman 1988). Yet it is clear that the chamber, representing the weak segment of local industry, was neither powerful nor influential. The pattern of the 1940s, when CANACINTRA (on behalf of CONCAMIN and the emerging industrial sector more generally) exercised significant influence (Mosk 1950; Reyes Heroles 1951; Lombardo Toledano 1951), did not continue throughout the postwar decades. To the contrary, industrial differentiation produced new sources of power and new patterns of government-business interaction. The archival record makes it abundantly clear that CANACINTRA's leaders were well aware of the fact that the chamber lacked significant influence over the broad parameters of economic policy. Indeed, CANACINTRA's representative strategy was conceived and designed self-consciously in the context of small industrialists' and the organization's weakness within the Mexican business community.

Moreover, framing an assessment of accommodation in terms of CANACINTRA's power and influence over the broad direction of economic policy is seriously misleading. CANACINTRA's role in Mexican political economy should be assessed not in terms of its influence over development strategy per se, but in terms of the chamber's capacity to extract benefits that were available within the model and thus mitigate the effects of industrial giantism for its members. CANACINTRA did not arrest the giantist biases of developmentalism, but representation via accommodation did allow CANACINTRA to provide small industrial firms with a more propitious environment than they might have had otherwise.[46]

In conclusion, and foreshadowing the events of the 1980s, it is important to underscore that CANACINTRA's strategy remained a divisive issue among small industrialists. Representation via accommodation entailed trade-offs. Yes, the chamber was able to provide small manufacturers with access to policy makers. But the fact of the matter is that many small industrialists' concerns went unheeded by the leadership, and many of the chamber's concerns went unheeded by the state. It was precisely because CANACINTRA could not prevail on the major policy issues of the day that the strategy of accommodation was controversial.

Ultimately, one's assessment of the accommodationist strategy is based on the counterfactual of how small industry's representation might have been affected by a different strategy vis-à-vis the state. Throughout the postwar period many in the chamber resented CANACINTRA's sacrifice of autonomy and charged that the benefits obtained were too few. These fledgling dissident movements, of which the discussion of ex-president José Colín provides an illustration, called for the strategy of accommodation to be revised. Indeed, throughout the postwar period tensions developed between the chamber's leadership, which saw accommodation as the appropriate response to organizational dependence, and those resenting the chamber's loss of autonomy, which they blamed for the failure to present more critical positions on policy. Yet the leadership defended its actions by pointing to the results. The proof was in the pudding, so to speak: CANACINTRA was afforded access to policy makers, and access allowed the chamber to deliver material benefits to the membership. Thus, the advocates of accommodation prevailed, and they managed to prevent any significant and lasting divisions within the organization.

As we shall see, economic crisis, the emergence of a neoliberal economic model, and democratization would exacerbate this latent conflict in the 1980s. At the same time as crisis and the removal of discretionary state economic interventions would effectively reduce the payoffs to accommodation, democratization, the proliferation of new forms of social protest, and the associated emergence of new alliance alternatives would make the opportunity costs of small industry's alliance with the state appear excessively high. In the following chapters I analyze these changes and the effects that conflicts unleashed by democratization would have on the representation of small industrialists in Mexico.

---

46. Chapter 6, which includes analyses of small industry representation in Argentina and Brazil, places CANACINTRA's representative strategy in cross-national comparative perspective.

THREE

The Challenges of Change
Crisis, Democratization, and the Quest for Representation

Economic crisis and democratization can unleash conflicts that heighten the challenges of small industry representation. Reduction in available material benefits, combined with the emergence of new forms of social protest and potentially new alliance partners, can make the opportunity costs of a representative strategy prioritizing organizational preservation appear too high. The result of this is that the latent tensions within organizations representing small firms can be brought to life and intensified. In this chapter I examine these dynamics as they existed in the 1980s, when economic crisis and democratization unleashed a series of conflicts that would have significant effects on the representation of small industry.

In 1982, the Mexican economy was on the brink of collapse. A decline in export revenues, a dramatic increase in servicing obligations on floating-rate external debt, precipitous loss of foreign reserves as a result of private capital outflows, and the inability to contract new financing left Mexico unable to meet payments on its external debt. The following years would be marked by deep and protracted economic crisis. With monetary and fiscal austerity producing a contraction of the domestic market, economic growth during the presidency of Miguel de la Madrid (1982–88) would be lower than that of any presidency during the postwar period.

The mid-1980s also witnessed the dismantling of Mexico's developmentalist trade and industrialization strategy, as indebtedness and economic crisis increased the government's vulnerability to pressures to implement deep structural reforms. The pressures were both external, from creditors, creditor governments, and international financial institutions (Aggarwal 1996, chapter 11), and internal, from a sector of more internationally oriented Mexican business that perceived new opportunities in a more open-ended form of integration with the global economy (Thacker 2000). Throughout the 1980s, developmentalist instruments were retired, and Mexico came to adopt a neoliberal economic model that featured the removal of most restrictions on trade and investment, along with extensive privatization and a new commitment to fiscal and monetary orthodoxy.[1]

The dramatic changes in the Mexican economy would be accompanied by equally significant changes in that country's political system. To be sure, the PRI continued to dominate all branches of national government during the de la Madrid presidency, and strong party discipline within the ruling party subsequently made the legislature irrelevant as a policy-making forum. Yet while Mexico clearly was not a democracy in the 1980s, unprecedented opportunities for dissent began to emerge. For example, electoral reform lowered the barriers for party formation and introduced new actors into the electoral arena (Middlebrook 1986). Significantly, the debt crisis and perceptions of economic mismanagement also gave rise to new forms of political protest that spanned the political spectrum. On the Left, urban social movements and dissident factions of the labor movement pressed for regime opening and policy change.[2] On the Right, prominent business leaders in the north of Mexico launched vociferous protests against the PRI, many lending support at the local level to candidates from the opposition PAN.[3] Thus, de la Madrid's election in 1982 would be the last of the virtually uncontested presidential elections that had been a hallmark of the Mexican regime since the 1950s. The ensuing years would witness a process of fledgling democratization, featuring increased social mobilization and the progressive decay of PRI hegemony.

The following analysis of how the changing economic and political environment of the mid-1980s affected small industry representation consists of three sections. The first section contains an examination of a conflict within CANACINTRA over the strategy of accommodation. Economic crisis, the threats of neoliberalism, and the new opportunities presented by democratization gave new life to the latent tensions that had existed within CANACINTRA for decades. At the same time as a worsening economic environment

1. See Lustig 1998; Ros 1993; Ten Kate 1992; and Aspe 1993.
2. See Cook 1996; Foweraker and Craig 1990; Haber 1994; and Middlebrook 1995, chapter 7.
3. See Elizondo 1992; García Figuroa 1992; Hernández Rodríguez 1986, 1990; Mizrahi 1994; Montesinos Carrera 1992; Story 1987; and Valdés Ugalde 1994, 1996, 1997.

indicated to many members of the chamber that the strategy of accommodation was producing limited returns, democratization made alternative strategies appear more fruitful. The subsequent conflict would have important consequences for small industrialists' representation in Mexico. Failing to gain control of the chamber, a dissenting group of industrialists created a rival association, challenging CANACINTRA as a representative of small industry. In the second section I examine how the state intervened into this interorganizational dispute to help CANACINTRA ward off the challenge of the National Association of Manufacturing Associations (ANIT). State intervention not only protected CANACINTRA, but also thwarted the dissidents' efforts to provide alternative small industry representation. The effects of corporatism and lack of access to the state on the complex process of small firm collective action are discussed in the third section.

Questioning Accommodation:
Economic Change and Small Industry in the Early 1980s

The new commitment to trade liberalization and industrial rationalization, with an eye toward export orientation, was made explicit in the 1983–88 National Development Plan (PND), released in May 1983. Mexico had originally responded to the 1982 crisis not by liberalizing trade but by heightening import controls, a standard reaction to balance-of-payments crises, by expanding license requirements to cover all imports. But these were only temporary measures. In mid-1983, with the foreign-exchange crisis seemingly under control, de la Madrid began to liberalize the trade regime. By 1985, licensing requirements would be dramatically reduced and the following year Mexico would enter the General Agreement on Tariffs and Trade (GATT). By the end of the de la Madrid presidency, licensing requirements had been almost entirely abolished, and the maximum tariff was reduced to a comparatively low 20 percent.

Economic crisis and the specter of liberalization presented CANACINTRA with a difficult set of challenges. After decades of protection, Mexican industry, in general, was less competitive than what would be required to compete globally; and for smaller firms, with less access to capital, fewer ties to foreign firms, and even less experience in export markets, adjustment would be particularly difficult.[4] Thus CANACINTRA would demand that trade liberalization be gradual, as it had throughout the 1970s.

---

4. Rubio (1988), in contrast, depicts small firms as generally more flexible and thus well equipped to adjust to changing economic conditions.

But the constellation of factors pushing for liberalization left CANAC-INTRA with a particularly weak hand in this period. In addition to the stark changes in Mexico's external economic position, the early 1980s were also marked by fundamental changes in the makeup of the state bureaucracy. As secretary of planning and budget during the presidency of José López Portillo (1976–82), de la Madrid had been among those cabinet members who were most supportive of trade liberalization and entry into the GATT in 1980.[5] Upon ascending to the presidency in 1982, he maintained his commitment to open the Mexican economy, surrounding himself with a coterie of like-minded economists. Of the eighteen original cabinet appointees, thirteen came from the so-called financial secretariats—the Secretariat of the Treasury (SHCP), the Secretariat of Programming and Budget (SPP), and the Bank of Mexico (Kaufman 1988, 83; Hernández Rodríguez 1987).

Although small industry, through CANACINTRA, could expect to work closely with officials from the trade secretariat, now renamed the Secretariat of Trade and Industrial Development (SECOFI), all indications were that the role of this ministry would be reduced.[6] The debt crisis sparked ongoing negotiations with the International Monetary Fund and commercial banks, for example, and the officials responsible for these interactions with external actors were principally from the Treasury and the Bank of Mexico.[7]

The early 1980s would also witness the state's seeking the collaboration of private-sector organizations that were more supportive of the new economic orientation. In order to prepare the initial groundwork for trade liberalization, for example, the de la Madrid government commissioned the National Foreign Trade Council (CONACEX), one of the country's most prominent export organizations, to undertake an analysis of Mexico's trade regime. The CONACEX analysis would be used as the baseline for a process of consultation on trade policy that was to begin the following year. In a report titled "To Make Mexico an Export Power," CONACEX called for a thorough reorientation of trade policy, one that would make increasing manufactured

5. For analyses of Mexico's flirtation with the GATT in 1979–80, see Story 1982; Helms 1985; Mares 1985; and Escobar Toledo 1987.

6. SECOFI was created in 1982, fusing the Secretariat of Industry and Commerce (SIC) and the Secretariat of National Patrimony and Industrial Development (SEPAFIN) into a single cabinet agency. In 2000, SECOFI was renamed Secretariat of the Economy (SECON).

7. Not only did CANACINTRA lack close ties to these agencies, but the leaders of these more technocratic agencies made little secret of their disdain for the "protectionist" chamber. For further discussions of the policy-making currents within the state bureaucracy, see Bailey 1988; Centeno and Maxfield 1992; Centeno 1997; and Cleaves 1987.

exports, and not rejuvenating the domestic market, the highest priority and the centerpiece of development policy (Hobbs 1991, 248–49).

CANACINTRA's Response

The depth of the economic crisis and the extensive momentum that was building behind liberalization, within the state and the private sector, called for a reassessment of CANACINTRA's strategy for representing small industry. Chamber officials were aware of the fact that most of de la Madrid's cabinet consisted of officials who had favored GATT entry in 1979–80, and they recognized that the chamber had alienated many of these officials with its opposition to the GATT. In addition, the CONACEX report was widely accepted among Mexico's most prominent business organizations, such as the peak Business Coordinating Council (CCE).[8]

The sunk costs of decades of accommodation encouraged continuity in political strategy. CANACINTRA's leaders had exhausted significant resources— economic and political—in their efforts to develop the organization and cultivate links to the state, and the chamber's leadership expected that these ties could continue to be exploited. Furthermore, the leadership maintained that economic and political weakness continued to make accommodation the most prudent strategy. Although aware of the new style of economic management and the likelihood that the chamber would have less ability to obtain access to appropriate state officials, CANACINTRA's top officials continued to fear the consequences of public dissent. Thus, CANACINTRA attempted to adapt the accommodationist strategy that had been developed over the course of the postwar period to the new environment.

As in the preceding period, the key issue was not *whether* to express opposition but *how* to do so—accommodation did not and would not mean sycophantic support of the state. In the 1980s, while policy makers and much of the Mexican business community began to preach the importance of export orientation, CANACINTRA continued to advocate economic recovery via expansion of internal demand and retained its support for restrictive investment and trade policies. Yet the critical dimensions of the accommodationist strategy remained most salient: CANACINTRA would refrain from strong public criticism, and it would not sustain opposition or attempt to mobilize small industrialists against the introduction of threatening economic policies. CANACINTRA would express opposition in "appropriate" settings and refrain

8. The changing role of the CCE is analyzed in the following chapter.

from activities that could threaten the organization, such as outspoken public declarations or displays of solidarity with other dissenting actors. By preserving the organization's capacity to represent its members, CANACINTRA officials expected that accommodation would allow it to continue to extract benefits for its members and cushion them against the effects of crisis and liberalization.

From the leadership's perspective, the merits of this strategy were quickly demonstrated in the first major challenge of the 1980s, the formation of the National Program for Industrial Development and Foreign Trade (PRONAFICE) in 1983 and 1984. CANACINTRA had attached a high priority to the PRONAFICE negotiations and worked stubbornly to remain involved. Although eight different business organizations participated in the consultations, CANACINTRA, along with CONCAMIN, was by far the most active. CANACINTRA participated in six official forums during the consultation process, while most other organizations participated in only one or two (Hobbs 1991, 269–72).

CANACINTRA officials were quite pleased with the nature and outcome of the PRONAFICE negotiations. When PRONAFICE was announced in 1984, the program did not entail the radical policy changes that CANACINTRA had feared. Rather, it simply grafted selective export incentives onto an already existing industrialization strategy, retaining a significant amount of trade protection. To the extent that PRONAFICE introduced import liberalization, this would occur gradually. PRONAFICE also purported to preserve SECOFI's control over the implementation of trade policy, in that all future changes to the trade regime were to follow ongoing negotiations between the secretariat and Mexican business organizations, with negotiations to occur through a newly created Consultative Commission of Industrial Planning.[9]

The chamber's leadership cited PRONAFICE as a vindication of the accommodationist strategy, as proof that accommodation could still benefit small industrialists in the 1980s, and they celebrated their accomplishments at the annual "National Meeting of Industrialists" in Mexico City in 1984. Faced with policy makers who were intent upon liberalizing trade, it was argued, accommodation allowed CANACINTRA to remain involved in the negotiations.[10] And not only would trade liberalization be gradual; because

---

9. It was precisely the same points that CANACINTRA regarded as accomplishments that many of PRONAFICE's detractors criticized. For example, one group of prominent Mexican academic critics assailed the lack of firm commitment to rapid liberalization and maintained that the program was "meant to liberalize as little as possible from the outset" (Rubio, Rodríguez, and Blum 1989, 170).

10. According to Hobbs (1991, 273), one high-level chamber official claimed that CANACINTRA and SECOFI "worked as a single team."

CANACINTRA had a seat on the consultative commission, the chamber was assured it would be closely consulted on future policy changes. Thus, for the chamber's leadership PRONAFICE was more than a victory of substance; it demonstrated that CANACINTRA could continue to represent its members even under more constraining economic and political conditions. In contrast, a more confrontational response, the leadership argued, would have minimized access to state and limited CANACINTRA's influence on policy making.[11]

The Dissidents' Challenge

While CANACINTRA's leadership remained committed to accommodation, a faction of dissenting industrialists within the chamber advocated a more confrontational strategy in response to the changing economic and political environment. The debt crisis and the new policy orientation of the de la Madrid government exacerbated an emerging division within CANACINTRA; and what began as a intersectoral conflict within the chamber would ultimately develop into a full-scale challenge to CANACINTRA's leadership and to the prevailing strategy for representing the weak segment of Mexican capital.

The dissident movement had its roots in Mexico's emerging capital goods and metalworking industries. These sectors had expanded rapidly in the 1970s, as a result of both increased demand from state enterprises during the oil boom and activist industrial strategies under the governments of Presidents Luis Echeverría (1970–76) and López Portillo. Responding to the increasingly higher shares of Mexico's imports that were in capital goods, both Echeverría and López Portillo had emphasized the development of local capital goods industries as part of a larger strategy to increase industrial integration.[12] For example, fiscal incentives that encouraged the importation of capital goods were replaced by subsidies to import machinery to produce such goods locally.

The combination of increased public-sector demand and fiscal incentives led to the proliferation of new capital goods and metalworking firms in the 1970s. As Figure 5 demonstrates, the growth of such firms significantly outpaced the growth of manufacturing more generally. From 1975 to 1980, for example, while the total number of manufacturing firms increased by

11. Interviews with Carlos Mireles García, president of CANACINTRA, 1984–86, and Juan José Moreno Sada, president of CANACINTRA, 1986–88. Moreno Sada was director of foreign trade for the chamber during Mireles's presidency.

12. González Marín 1996; Villalobos 1989; SPP 1980; Solís 1979; NAFIN-ONUDI 1977.

10.4 percent, the number of firms in these sectors increased by nearly four times as much. Indeed, over the course of the fifteen years recorded in these data, the growth of firms in these sectors was nearly ten times that of manufacturing firms more generally, and by the mid-1980s such firms accounted for more than one-fifth of all manufacturing firms. With regard to size, though the data in Figure 5 are not restricted to small firms per se, the 1986 census reveals that 98 percent of the firms in these subsectors had fewer than 250 employees (INEGI 1989, table 6). In fact, by 1984, according to a government survey (NAFIN-ONUDI 1985), the metalworking and nonelectrical-machinery sectors alone came to account for approximately 19.8 percent of all small firms in Mexico.

Under the regulations of the Chambers Law, most of the thousands of new capital goods and metalworking firms that emerged in this period were affiliated with CANACINTRA.[13] The industrialists of these firms, from what might be regarded essentially as Mexico's final wave of infant industries, became increasingly active in CANACINTRA. Although originally placed into subdivision within the Metalworking Council, they created new sections within the council. In 1981 five of the sections separated from the Metalworking Council and founded a new Capital Goods Council; quickly, another seven sections became affiliated.[14] By the end of 1981 these two councils, Metalworking and Capital Goods, had essentially come to represent this wing of small industry.

The conflict within CANACINTRA has its origins in the chamber's representation of capital goods and metal producers in policy-making forums. For even as the industrialists gained prominence within the chamber, controlling the presidency of the capital goods and metalworking councils and a number of sections within these councils, for example, they remained unsatisfied with CANACINTRA's activities on their behalf. The leaders of this wing of the chamber sought more active defense of their sectors, and they pushed the chamber to adopt more critical positions of government policy. Even if CANACINTRA resisted across-the-board trade liberalization, they maintained, the chamber was not pushing the de la Madrid government to continue developing these sectors.

13. As indicated in Chapter 2, firms in the states of Nuevo León and Jalisco were not obligated to join CANACINTRA. As of 1985, 16.5 percent of the firms in these sectors were located in these two states (INEGI 1989, table 3, p. 93).

14. CANACINTRA's sectoral structure consists of sector-specific sections that are integrated into broader coordinating councils. At its peak, there were approximately 115 sections in ten councils. The Metalworking Council had existed since 1958.

Table 3   Capital goods and metalworking firms in the 1970s and early 1980s

	Number of Firms			Rate of Increase		
Year	All Sectors	Subsector	Period	All Sectors (%)	Subsector (%)
1970	119,963	12,993 (10.8%)	—	—	—
1975	119,212	16,276 (13.7%)	1970–75	−0.6	25.3
1980	131,625	22,963 (17.5%)	1975–80	10.4	41.1
1985	135,075	28,414 (21.0%)	1980–85	2.6	23.7
			1970–85	12.6	118.7

Source: Calculations by author, based on data in SIC 1973, table 8; SPP 1979, table 8; INEGI 1988, table 4; INEGI 1989, table 6.

Note: Because the classification systems used to identify sectors, subsectors, and branches changed over the course of these four industrial censuses, it was necessary to use expanded definitions. These data include the following types of firms: metalworking, machinery (electric and nonelectric), and transportation equipment.

To understand the intensity of these complaints, it is important to consider the difficulties that capital goods and metal producers faced in the early 1980s. Economic crisis and fiscal austerity implied the end of the fiscal incentives that had nurtured these sectors in the past. Furthermore, these sectors were heavily dependent on the state sector as a source of demand. According to a survey of small firms, for example, only newsprint and petroleum products reported a higher share of firms with sales to the public sector, and no sector indicated higher volumes of sales to the government (NAFIN-SPP-INEGI 1988, table 20).[15] Consequently, these sectors immediately felt the effects of the sharp reductions in public spending that followed the negotiations on Mexico's external debt. Although declining domestic demand could, hypothetically, have been offset by the increased protection that all sectors received in 1982–83, in fact production in the capital goods and metalworking sectors, which had increased by an average of 10.4 percent annually from 1971 to 1981, declined by approximately 17.1 percent in 1982 and 23.8 percent in 1983. And even with some recovery, production levels as of 1986 would not reach the precrisis levels (González Marín 1996, 44; Villalobos 1989, 17).

The dissidents' first response to CANACINTRA's alleged failure to represent them adequately was to attempt to create a separate organization. As

15. The same survey indicates that across the entire manufacturing sector, small firms sold 34.7 percent of their production to the state, while the corresponding figure for large firms was 27.5 percent. NAFIN-ONUDI (1985) also emphasizes these sectors' reliance on demand from the public sector.

we have seen, throughout the history of CANACINTRA, groups of industrialists had left CANACINTRA and formed separate, sector-specific chambers that provided them with more specialized representation and services. Typically, leaving CANACINTRA had been a strategy of large firms; now it was that of small firms. In 1984 the same industrialists who had been prominent in expanding representation within CANACINTRA for the capital goods and metal sectors, and who were outspoken in their criticism of the CANACINTRA leadership, began circulating a proposal for a new organization, the National Chamber of Capital Goods Industry (CANIBICA). Because the 1960 reform to the Chambers Law required 80 percent of the firms in a given sector to petition for a new chamber, this group of industrialists officially limited the scope to capital goods, as reflected in the title, but many of the originators were from metalworking sectors as well.[16]

The proponents of CANIBICA offered a radically different evaluation of the leadership's strategy vis-à-vis the state. They assailed CANACINTRA for not sufficiently pushing the state to promote these sectors. They pointed to the gradual abandonment of the 1981 Program for Development of Capital Goods Industries, among other things, as an indicator of the chamber's failure, and they charged that the accommodationist strategy was not replicating its earlier success with regard to industrial finance or trade policy. In 1982, CANACINTRA had distanced itself from the general opposition of the business community to the nationalization of the commercial banking system, expecting that this would improve small firms' access to credit. Capital goods and metal producers who would later move into the opposition supported this position. The nationalization of the banks presented an opportunity to push for expansion of FOGAIN and thereby increase the amount of credit that was available to small firms.[17] Yet restrictive monetary policy in the early 1980s only served to heighten small firms' credit and liquidity problems.[18] Loans from FOGAIN, for example, dropped by 30 percent in real terms from 1983 to 1984. Furthermore, in 1985 FOGAIN was restructured to emphasize lending to microenterprises, and as a consequence loans to

16. The 80 percent requirement meant that this group would have to elicit the participation of others. Thus, in addition to an overview of the Mexican capital goods industry and a litany of criticisms of CANACINTRA, the original proposal, signed by a coordinating commission of thirty-nine industrialists, included a call for additional industrialists to join as founding members of the new chamber.

17. Horvath (1991, 71–72), examining FOGAIN data, notes that nonelectrical-machinery producers were one of the areas with the greatest increase in loans in the late 1970s.

18. See Maxfield 1990, 153–62 for a discussion of the impact of the bank nationalization on the availability of commercial loans in the 1980s. NAFIN-SPP-INEGI (1988, 36) emphasizes small firms' difficulties in obtaining credit from public sources as well. See also Águilar 1982.

small and medium-size industrial firms continued to drop throughout the decade (Horvath 1991, 83–84).

Moreover, from the dissidents perspective PRONAFICE was anything but a success. Even if PRONAFICE did not introduce thorough liberalization, the document indicated that the promotional policies toward the capital goods sector would be eliminated. Capital goods and metalworking firms, which had benefited from the industrial strategy of the 1970s that encouraged vertical integration, were immediately threatened by the de la Madrid government's plans to "rationalize" industrial production in the early 1980s. Although PRONAFICE did not indicate a radical shift in trade policy across the board, it directly affected producers from these sectors, who accused the chamber of inadequately defending their interests.

Beyond their own dissatisfaction with PRONAFICE, the dissidents argued that the program itself had no staying power. No sooner was the schedule of gradual liberalization announced that, in a March 1985 letter of intent to the International Monetary Fund (IMF), the Bank of Mexico and the Secretariat of the Treasury promised "a complete revision of trade policy" in order "to reduce the level of protectionism."[19] Soon thereafter, license coverage was significantly reduced. In July 1985, in the face of inflationary pressures and balance-of-payments difficulties, the de la Madrid government abruptly moved to liberalize trade, removing licensing requirements from a wide range of industrial sectors, particularly intermediate and capital goods.[20] Whereas in June 1985, 92.2 percent of domestic production and 83.5 percent of imports were covered by import licenses, by the end of the year only 47.1 percent of production would be granted this form of protection and nearly two-thirds of imports would enter the country free of permit requirements. The following month, de la Madrid announced that his administration was studying the possibility that Mexico would enter the GATT, calling for the Mexican Senate—where the PRI had all 64 seats at the time—to advise whether Mexico should apply for membership.

The bottom line, from the perspective of this dissenting group, is that at the same time as CANACINTRA's leadership was celebrating its accomplishments with the PRONAFICE negotiations, protection was largely removed from the capital goods and metal sectors, and the supposed accomplishments of PRONAFICE had vanished before the ink on the document had dried. So

19. *Journal of Commerce,* 28 March 1985. According to this article, these officials were seeking to use IMF pressure as a lever against SECOFI in order to accelerate the pace of trade liberalization.

20. See Ten Kate 1992 for a sector-by-sector breakdown of trade liberalization during this period. See also Lustig 1998; Ros 1993; USITC 1990; and Zabludovsky 1990.

much for CANACINTRA's consultative role on the PRONAFICE commission, the dissidents argued; so much for gradual trade liberalization. The dissidents pointed to these events as indicators of the bankruptcy of the accommodationist strategy. Yet when a representative from the Metalworking Council admonished the chamber's leadership for not responding more forcefully to "crucially important changes in our government's industrial policy whose consequences will be very harmful for us," he was called before the chamber's board of directors and accused of provoking divisiveness.[21]

CANACINTRA Under Siege

The events of 1985 encouraged the dissident industrialists to generalize their grievances against CANACINTRA's leadership, and quickly the sectoral-based conflict developed into a larger dispute over the chamber's strategy for advancing the interests of its members. The dissidents' campaign would no longer be about CANACINTRA's deficiencies regarding the promotion of capital goods and metal industries, but, more generally, about what they regarded as the chamber's failed strategy for dealing with the state on behalf of the weak segment of local industry. They argued that it was not just their wing of the chamber that was suffering from the leadership's strategy, but that all CANACINTRA members (and, in turn, all micro, small, and medium-size manufacturing firms) were handicapped by accommodation. They demanded a representative who would propose active industrial and credit policies, to lead the charge for economic recovery based on stimulation of domestic manufacturing and promotion of industrial integration. Throughout the mid-1980s CANACINTRA would be riddled by this conflict.

Challenging Accommodation

Among the dissidents' myriad criticisms of accommodation, two issues in particular stand out about their challenge to CANACINTRA's strategy: the loss of autonomy and the leadership's lackluster response to alliance alternatives. Rightly or wrongly, the dissidents attributed small industry's collective weakness to the chamber's lack of independence from the state. Whereas CANACINTRA's leadership regarded accommodation as the appropriate response to weakness, these industrialists came to regard accommodation as a cause

---

21. See *La Jornada*, 5 July 1985 and 2 August 1985.

of the chamber's weakness. They believed that both the chamber as an organization and its leaders as individuals had become too tightly allied with and too heavily dependent on the state and, importantly, that these relationships impeded CANACINTRA's attempts to sustain opposition to the government. The dissidents asserted that, far from improving the representational capacity and influence of the chamber, as the leadership claimed, CANACINTRA's preoccupation with organizational preservation predisposed the chamber toward passivity. Complaining that the chamber had "wasted away," the dissidents declared that "CANACINTRA has disappeared; it has lost its presence not only among industrialists but with the destiny of the country."[22] Only a renovation of the chamber's leadership and representative strategy could arrest and correct this decay.

Whereas criticisms of accommodation were not new within CANACINTRA, the wave of dissatisfaction in the 1980s had a new foundation, in that the strategy appeared to be less successful than in the past. Recall that CANACINTRA's leadership typically could defend accommodation by promoting the chamber's success in extracting benefits for small firms. In the 1980s, however, the dissidents' criticisms of accommodation had greater calling power, because they came at a time when the capacity of CANACINTRA to extract benefits had clearly diminished, as made evident by the diminished access to credit even after the bank nationalization and the aftermath of PRONAFICE. Not only did the dissidents of the 1980s make principled arguments against accommodation; they also emphasized how few concrete and material benefits the membership was gaining from the chamber's strategy.

In addition to bemoaning a lack of independence, the dissidents criticized CANACINTRA for failing to take advantage of the new and greater opportunities for dissent that were presented by the fledgling processes of political liberalization and democratization that Mexico was experiencing in the 1980s. In the aftermath of the bank nationalization, significant portions of the business sector, individually and collectively, mobilized in opposition to the PRI. And many of the businesspeople involved in this movement expressed their opposition via the National Action Party (PAN), creating a so-called *neopanista* current within the party (Arriola 1994; Mizrahi 1994; Story 1987). The mobilization of business after the bank nationalization and the emergence of the PAN suggested that there were greater possibilities for expressing opposition and challenging the state. As a group, the small industry dissidents did not identify programmatically with much of the *neopanistas'*

22. *La Jornada*, 18 December 1985.

agenda—again, the dissidents had expected to benefit from the bank nationalization, for example, and more generally they were alarmed by the withdrawal of the state from the economy, as was demanded by the *neopanistas*. Yet they could not help but notice that segments of the business community were expressing discontent and taking advantage of the new opportunities available for political participation. A fundamentally important lesson of the early 1980s was that the private sector could act publicly and politically, that dissent was possible and acceptable.

More generally, electoral reform in the late 1970s and the economic crisis of the 1980s led to a proliferation of new political parties and social movements.[23] It is important to underscore that even if the opposition parties were not yet capable of challenging the PRI, increased political-party competition and social-movement activity provided a more comforting environment for potentially dissenting actors. Profound changes in Mexico's political environment created new opportunities for dissent, opportunities that had for the most part not existed since the 1950s.

Thus, at the same time as the dissidents questioned the utility of CANACINTRA's strategy, they argued that the new political environment meant that alternatives to accommodation were more feasible. They felt that they could and should take advantage of opportunities presented by increased political pluralism: small industrialists should join forces with other social actors and demand accountability from the state. Continuing to bypass alliance alternatives, particularly at a time when accommodation was no longer generating satisfactory results, they argued, was an error. Democratization, economic crisis, and the state's changing economic policy orientation, then, made the opportunity costs of continued accommodation seem higher than ever.

Contesting CANACINTRA

The dissidents used the 1986 elections for the presidency of the chamber to heighten their calls for a renovation of CANACINTRA's representative strategy. In a sense, all the tensions within small industry that were produced by the economic and political conjuncture that took place during the first half of the de la Madrid presidency crystallized during this bitter and divisive campaign.

23. For a discussion of the electoral reforms in the late 1970s and their effects on party development, see Middlebrook 1986. For an examination of the social movements that proliferated during this period, see the essays in Foweraker and Craig 1990.

In November 1985, CANACINTRA's outgoing president, Carlos Mireles García (1984–86), designated Juan José Moreno Sada (1986–88), the chamber's first vice president and director of foreign trade, as his choice for successor to be elected in February in the coming year. To oppose the "official" candidate, the capital goods and metalworking councils nominated Roberto Romo Santillán. Romo, an owner of two foundries, had a history of active involvement in CANACINTRA. He had been president of the Metalworking Council and, within metalworking, president of the foundry section.[24]

The dissidents argued that Moreno, with close personal and professional ties to SECOFI and as a member of the governing PRI, would be too compromised to confront state authorities. Indeed, a number of newspapers reported early in the campaign that two SECOFI undersecretaries had instructed Mireles, the outgoing president, to select Moreno as his successor.[25] By these accounts, Moreno was a "product of the *dedazo*" (*Excelsior*, 5 November 1985), a reference to the PRI's mechanism for presidential succession, whereby the outgoing president personally selected the party's candidate. Although the specific allegations remained unsubstantiated, Moreno's close relations with SECOFI were never in dispute. Indeed, one business columnist ventured that Moreno's close ties to the state would "weigh heavily in the final decision of CANACINTRA members who have repeatedly demonstrated that they are tired of the lack of strong and independent positions on the part of the directors."[26] To be sure, questions of the official candidate's independence, and concerns with further erosion of the chamber's autonomy, polarized the campaign.[27]

The divide between CANACINTRA and the dissidents widened in the aftermath of the February 1986 elections, when Romo's supporters immediately claimed that Moreno's victory was fraudulent.[28] Among their various allegations, they charged that Mireles and Moreno used chamber funds to purchase the support of some CANACINTRA delegates, and that SECOFI manipulated the electoral process to ensure that the progovernment candidate would

24. The presence of smaller foundries in CANACINTRA while larger steel firms had their own chamber within CONCAMIN is a legacy of the bifurcation discussed in the previous chapter. Regarding the dissidents' candidate, Romo had also served as a public relations official for the chamber. In fact, he was selected in large part because of his polished media skills.

25. See *El Universal*, 5 November 1985; *Excelsior*, 5 November 1985; and *La Jornada*, 6 December 1985.

26. Herminio Rebollo Pineda, "De IP," *El Universal*, 4 November 1985.

27. "They give each other dirty looks, they shout at each other, and they even threaten each other" (*La Jornada*, 27 January 1986).

28. *La Jornada*, 26 February 1986.

win. Accused of publicly defaming the chamber, five of the dissidents were suspended and then expelled from CANACINTRA.

The conflict between the CANACINTRA leadership and the dissidents did not end with the expulsion of the opposition leaders. The dissidents immediately announced the formation of the National Association of Manufacturing Industrialists (ANIT), an association that, in Romo's words, would respond "to the yearning of many entrepreneurs to have an organization that truly represents them."[29] When granted legal registration as a civil association later in 1986, with Romo as president, ANIT claimed to have ninety-four members, and the founders of the dissident association expected a membership of three thousand by the end of the year.[30]

ANIT quickly launched a frontal assault on CANACINTRA's status as the representative of small industry in Mexico. While the 1986 election for the presidency of CANACINTRA transformed what had been a simmering internal quarrel into a struggle for the chamber's leadership, the expulsion of the dissidents and the creation of ANIT transformed this struggle into a war over which organization should represent small industry in Mexico. Suggesting that "on account of the people who have controlled and manipulated the organization for the last several years, [CANACINTRA] has stopped serving its members," Romo proclaimed that it was "necessary to throw out those things that no longer serve a purpose."[31] Indeed, the rival association, referred to by one observer as "one of the two CANACINTRAs that exist today,"[32] began working out of offices only a few blocks away from CANACINTRA's immense, ten-story office complex in Mexico City.

State Protection of CANACINTRA

CANACINTRA appealed to SECOFI for assistance in fending off ANIT's challenge, and SECOFI's intervention on the chamber's behalf stymied the dissidents' challenge. Subsequently, ANIT's ambitions of displacing CANACINTRA and developing an alternative strategy for representing small industry dissipated quickly.

Analysis of the ways in which the state helped CANACINTRA turn back the challenge from ANIT helps explain why the dissidents became so vehemently anticorporatist by the end of the decade. First, the state appears to have deployed coercive economic instruments to harass some of the dissident

29. *La Jornada,* 24 April 1986.
30. *El Nacional,* 14 August 1986.
31. *La Jornada,* 14 August 1986.
32. Alberto Barranco Chavarría, "Empresa," *La Jornada,* 7 July 1986.

industrialists and thereby stunt the growth of the fledgling business organization. Second, SECOFI officials used a set of discretionary prerogatives afforded by the Chambers Law to prevent the creation of an independent, rival industrial chamber. Third, SECOFI used another aspect of the Chambers Law to uphold the legal standing of CANACINTRA's leadership. Fourth, by denying ANIT access to policy making, state officials undermined the dissidents' efforts to represent small industry. In the following paragraphs I examine each of these in turn.

The most prominent members of ANIT found themselves subject to government reprisals, including audits, inspections, and denial of permits.[33] One of ANIT's directors maintained that government officials, at Moreno's behest, instigated labor problems in his and Romo's firms.[34] In fact, Romo eventually sold his foundries and moved to Houston, Texas, to pursue a business venture with a colleague, prompting one columnist to suggest that he was driven into exile by his enemies at CANACINTRA.[35]

Neither the accusations of government interference in the chamber's 1986 elections nor the role of the state in these industrialists' difficulties were proved, but both made important contributions to the dissidents' political formation. In the first instance, Romo's supporters attributed their electoral setback to the state's capacity to intervene in the affairs of the chamber to ensure the victory of docile leadership—a key characteristic of corporatism. Now, they saw the state using another set of instruments to help CANACINTRA. The significant point is not what the state did or did not do, so much as the dissidents' conviction that the state was helping CANACINTRA and that this, in turn, indebted the chamber to the government. As we shall see, throughout the 1980s and into the 1990s, the dissidents would attribute the lack of small industry representation not only to CANACINTRA's leadership, but also to the state institutions that encouraged docility and allowed the state to muzzle dissenting voices.

The chamber also called on the government to prevent the dissidents from creating a separate industrial chamber. With Romo out of the country, the leadership of ANIT passed to Ignacio Muñoz Peredo, another of the five dissidents expelled from CANACINTRA, who had been president of the Capital Goods Council until the split in 1986.[36] Under his leadership, the dissidents

---

33. *La Jornada,* 27 October 1986.

34. *Excelsior,* 2 January 1987.

35. *La Jornada,* 24 November 1986.

36. Although Muñoz Peredo did not officially become president of ANIT until March 1987, he had assumed the role of de facto leader much earlier as a consequence of Romo's absence.

renewed their efforts to create CANIBICA, a separate chamber for capital goods (and metal) industries, in a campaign that had begun, haltingly, when the eventual leaders of ANIT were still members of CANACINTRA.[37]

CANACINTRA objected to the CANIBICA project for multiple reasons. In the first regard, the chamber did not wish to see a constant source of criticism and attacks become legitimated through the granting of official chamber status to the dissidents. ANIT caused CANACINTRA officials serious public relations problems. Not only were the dissidents determined to publicly embarrass the chamber and its leadership; they were equipped to do so. The leaders of ANIT had been quite active and had risen to prominent positions within the organization: as presidents of sections and councils, and members of the executive board, they had become familiar with the inner workings of the chamber. Their criticisms could be damaging were they to emanate from an officially recognized industrial chamber that might compete with CANACINTRA for membership and government attention. However, ANIT's criticisms were much more manageable as long as CANACINTRA's leadership could dismiss them as the ranting of a small association formed by a group of dissidents disgruntled by their frustrated bid for power.[38]

Most important, the creation of this new chamber threatened CANACINTRA's membership base. A significant amount of CANACINTRA's membership consisted precisely of small firms in the capital goods and metal sectors. As we have seen, the 1970s and 1980s witnessed a proliferation of firms in these sectors, most of which were obligated to join CANACINTRA.[39] Recall that the Chambers Law required chambers to be comprehensive, for *all* firms in a given sector to be members. A new chamber for the capital goods and metal sectors would significantly decrease the size of CANACINTRA's membership and cause a serious drain on the organization's revenues. Fearing such a drain on its revenues, then, CANACINTRA opposed the dissidents' plan to form their own chamber.

37. The dissidents also requested, unsuccessfully, that the Chambers Law be changed to abolish compulsory membership. The contradiction between these two strategies of challenging the Chambers Law while simultaneously working within the corporatist framework is discussed below.

38. In fact, concerned with the damage that the dissidents' criticisms were having on the image of CANACINTRA, the chamber's leadership also appealed to other business organizations to repudiate ANIT (*La Jornada*, 18 May 1987).

39. Using the data from Figure 5, and subtracting the approximately 16.5 percent of the firms that were based in the states of Jalisco and Nuevo León and thus not required to join CANACINTRA, the remaining total of more then twenty-three thousand small firms in these subsectors amounted to roughly 30 percent of CANACINTRA's reported membership at the time.

CANACINTRA appealed to SECOFI to prevent the dissidents from creating a separate industrial chamber, arguing, correctly, that CANIBICA failed to meet the criteria for chamber formation stipulated in the Chambers Law. In particular, the dissidents lacked the support of 80 percent of the firms in their sectors, even with the proposed chamber's scope officially restricted to capital goods. Thus, the dissidents' movement to create a separate chamber was stillborn, and if ANIT were to compete with CANACINTRA for members, it would have to do so as a voluntary industrial association.

In addition to harassing the dissident leaders and blocking authorization of CANIBICA, the third way in which the state intervened in this conflict on behalf of CANACINTRA was by authorizing a change to the chamber's statutes that removed doubts regarding the legal standing of a number of high-ranking officials. When the dissidents contested the February 1986 election results, they challenged not just Moreno's victory in the presidential contest but the legality of the chamber's entire executive board. They argued that the election results violated the chamber's own statutes, which made two years the maximum amount of time that any individual could serve on CANACINTRA's executive board. With their electoral victory, Moreno, two of his vice presidents, and the treasurer would allegedly be exceeding these limits.[40] More than a year later, the chamber's general assembly was considering a modification of the statutes. The new statutes proposed by Moreno would clarify the ambiguity regarding term limits and deflect such criticisms in the future.[41] According to the Chambers Law, the interpretation of CANACINTRA's statutes, and thus a ruling on the legality of the chamber's executive board, was to be resolved by SECOFI; and the revised statutes also required SECOFI approval as well.

The dissidents, of course, would not remain passive bystanders in what might otherwise be a technical legal issue between CANACINTRA and SECOFI. ANIT was engaged in a battle with CANACINTRA over who represented small industry. It was a battle that the dissidents were losing: they had been weakened by the harassment to which they were subjected and by their

40. In fact, in the week prior to the election, Romo's campaign had formally requested that SECOFI invalidate Moreno Sada's slate of candidates on these grounds, prompting one observer to write that "everything seems to indicate that Roberto Romo Santillán will defeat Juan Jose Moreno Sada by default" (Alberto Barranco Chavarría, "Empresa," *La Jornada,* 19 February 1986). The dissidents also argued that 113 of the 190 representatives to the chamber's board of directors were in violation of the chamber's statutes (*El Sol de México,* 24 April 1986).

41. CANACINTRA's statutes prohibited any individual from serving on the board for longer than two consecutive years. The revisions reworded this article to state that no individual could serve for longer than two consecutive years *in the same position.*

inability to form a separate chamber. The controversy over CANACINTRA's statutes, then, was a chance to weaken the chamber in return. ANIT's leaders believed that if they could persuade SECOFI to overrule CANACINTRA and prevent the chamber from making these changes, they could then get SECOFI to recognize the legitimacy of their own grievances against the chamber. In their challenge to CANACINTRA as the representative of small industry, this promised to be the boost they needed.

ANIT called for SECOFI to reject CANACINTRA's proposed changes. In a full-page letter published in a Mexico City newspaper, they argued that Moreno's attempt to reform the statutes was a recognition that their own claims were accurate—that the president and the executive board were indeed serving in violation of the chamber's statutes. The letter concluded with a statement that summarized many of the dissidents' organizational grievances: "We express our complete repudiation of the current 'leadership' of CANACINTRA headed by MORENO SADA, which in addition to not representing the interests of industrialists, has become an important obstacle for the formation of specific organizations. We emphasize once again our support for the imputations of Mexican industrialists, who by law, are obliged to belong to this chamber."[42]

Once again, with the Chambers Law leaving SECOFI as referee in this dispute, CANACINTRA officials appealed for help; and once again, the government intervened on behalf of the chamber. The legality of CANACINTRA's executive board was upheld, and the chamber's revised statutes were approved.[43]

By the beginning of 1988, ANIT's challenge to CANACINTRA had come and gone. The chamber's quasi-official monopoly on the representation of small industry was intact. The outcome of the conflict was confirmed with the dissidents' announcement in November 1987 that they would not participate in the upcoming CANACINTRA elections. After having their external challenge to CANACINTRA defeated, some of the dissidents advocated making a renewed effort to gain control of the chamber organization from within by launching another campaign for the chamber's presidency. Moreno's term was to end in February 1988, and the dissidents had given serious consideration to presenting a candidate to challenge Moreno's chosen successor, first vice president Jorge Kawaghi Gastine (1988–90).

The dissidents' decision not to challenge Kawaghi further reduced CANACINTRA's willingness to challenge the new direction of economic policy. The opposition had presented strong candidates in the 1984 and 1986

---

42. *El Universal,* 28 April 1987, uppercase emphasis in original.
43. *Diario Oficial,* 21 January 1988.

CANACINTRA elections. Indeed, Romo's 1986 campaign had provided a source of internal pressure on CANACINTRA's leadership to continue opposing trade liberalization.[44] Now, as a result of the dissidents' decision to leave the chamber entirely, the likely challengers to the official leadership were gone: Kawaghi, unlike Mireles and Moreno before him, faced no opposition to his bid for the presidency. In fact, as of the beginning of February 1988, CANACINTRA had not published a single campaign bulletin for an election that was to be held later that month—a striking contrast with the 1986 campaign. Without any internal challenge, CANACINTRA lacked electoral, member-driven pressures to represent small industry.[45]

To summarize, CANACINTRA, under siege from ANIT, appealed to the state for organizational protection; and the state responded, using a variety of instruments to help the chamber ward off the dissidents' challenge. ANIT faced stumbling blocks as its leaders became burdened with economic troubles at their firms, and the creation of a separate industrial chamber failed. At the same time, CANACINTRA's leadership was upheld by the reformed statutes, and the chamber retained its virtual monopoly on the official representation of small industry to the state.

ANIT's Decline

By the end of decade, ANIT was no longer "one of two CANACINTRAs that exist," as it was labeled in 1986. Despite its leaders considerable organizational efforts and the public relations storm they created, the dissident association never neared its stated goal of three thousand members. ANIT would remain active throughout the 1980s and 1990s, but it would not rival CANACINTRA; it would not gain the capacity to represent small industry in the Mexican political economy.

44. Responding to criticisms that the chamber did not fight hard enough in defense of small industry, Moreno's supporters consistently cited CANACINTRA's opposition to entering the GATT as proof that the chamber did indeed fight for its members. See, for example, La Jornada, 25 February 1986.

45. It is also worthwhile to note the individual incentives facing CANACINTRA's top leadership. Moreno, upon leaving the chamber, was hoping to be named as a PRI candidate for member of Congress from his home state of Oaxaca. Sure enough, in March 1988, less than one week after completing his term as chamber president, Moreno was made official candidate by the PRI. Kawaghi, invested in a chain of photo-development stands that were located inside subway stations throughout Mexico City, depended on the state for this prized concession. In short, neither the outgoing nor the incoming leaders had incentives to challenge policy makers. To the contrary, the absence of opposition made confrontation decidedly undesirable.

Not surprisingly, the failure of ANIT's challenge to CANACINTRA prompted many industrialists to return to and remain within the official chamber. This includes industrialists who participated in the effort to create CANIBICA and, importantly, it includes many who had supported the dissidents and were enthusiastic about ANIT but waiting on the sidelines pending resolution of the conflict with CANACINTRA. However disappointed many were with CANACINTRA, at least the official status of the chamber offered these individual industrialists some degree of access to policy makers and means for resolving particular problems affecting their own firms, and in the difficult economic context of the 1980s there was no shortage of problems for small firms. ANIT could offer precious little in this regard.

Analysis of ANIT's decline sheds light on how small firms' core attributes—in this case the difficulties of collective action—increase the difficulties they face in establishing independent and reliable mechanisms of representation. In a previous era, as we saw in Chapter 2, when efforts to create new chambers outside CANACINTRA failed, the leaders of such initiatives typically created new voluntary associations. Yet this strategy was significantly more difficult for the small industrialists who attempted to create CANIBICA and settled for ANIT. Small firms in the capital goods and metal industries remained legally obligated to continue paying their dues to the official chamber, which was still CANACINTRA. ANIT, in contrast, would struggle to build an independent membership base. Although many simply refused to pay their membership dues to CANACINTRA and aligned with ANIT, not all potential members could be expected to engage spontaneously in such civil disobedience and collective action.[46]

Collective Action and the State

One way that business organizations attract and retain members is by providing services. To the extent that consumption of such services can be restricted exclusively to members, they can serve as selective incentives for participation and prevent free-riding. In the case of business organizations, the provision of technical and managerial assistance and market information may serve as selective incentives to induce potential members to join the organization. To be sure, ANIT had originally intended to provide an array of such services. In its original effort to attract members, the organization claimed

---

46. The sanctions for those who did not pay their annual membership dues included fines, blocking of permits, and forfeiture of the right to conduct business with the public sector.

that it would provide market research and analysis, and it promised to offer members seminars in management training. Yet with its leaders under siege and resources diverted to the campaign against CANACINTRA, ANIT lacked sufficient resources to expand the association via the provision of services.

In addition to providing services, another benefit that business organizations provide members is access to policy making. Business organizations that provide members with access to state officials depend to a degree on the state for recognition.[47] ANIT, as a new organization that was attempting to gain recognition, was especially dependent on the state. A typical pattern of development for fledgling business organizations is to begin as "minimalist organizations" that try to win concessions on a specific policy issue. Through these concessions, the organization can attract members with concrete benefits. In a sense, fledgling business organizations can use the state to provide a "multiplier" effect (see Hardin 1982, 121; van Waarden 1992, 535). Yet ANIT did not benefit from this effect, as it was unable to represent small industry to any extent in any official manner, being consistently denied access to policy-making forums. Lack of access, in turn, deprived the fledgling organization of the tools to attract and retain members.

The comparative degrees of access to the state merits further elaboration. CANACINTRA also needed access to the executive, and the chamber fought determinedly to retain this privilege. Yet while CANACINTRA leaders would come to feel that weakness and contingent access to policy making left them with little room for dissent, ANIT was locked out altogether. The dissident, rebel association was not recognized by the government as a representative of small business and subsequently was deprived of any direct input into public policy. In Mexico, the centralization of decision-making authority in the executive gave policy makers discretion over whom they wished to consult; and whether the issue was tax policy, monetary policy, or trade policy, state officials demonstrated little tolerance for a confrontational organization whose few members lacked substantial market power.

Unable to provide concrete services and lacking access to the state, ANIT sought to attract members by essentially doing what its leaders accused CANACINTRA's leaders of fearing: publicly articulating small industrialists' grievances with the rapidly changing economic conditions and their lack of input into policy making. Thus, ANIT turned to the media. Regular press

47. As van Waarden explains, "[R]esources such as membership, finance, manpower, information, participation in actions, loyalty and discipline have to be obtained from the firms in the domain. From the [state], associations require recognition, access and concessions; in short, influence" (1992, 522). See also Schneider forthcoming 2004.

conferences provided the dissidents with the opportunity to gain publicity for their views, and they used the attention they received to consistently criticize economic policy and the quality of small industry representation.

The heavy reliance on the media would have important consequences for ANIT's organizational development. First, the service provided by the media campaign was entirely nonexcludable, susceptible to massive free-riding. ANIT was claiming to "represent" Mexican small industrialists, but its form of representation did not commit the members to anything. Nor for that matter did the media strategy depend on the contributions and participation of the "represented." So long as there remained enough interest and resources among the most active militants to continue with the media campaign, they could do so, regardless of the actual size of the group's membership.

The second effect of ANIT's reliance on the media was financial, in that it was quite expensive for the dissident group to keep itself in the public eye this way. Reporters seeking information on small industry, or searching for small industrialists' perspective on a given public policy issue, turned to CANACINTRA and its extensive research and public relations departments. ANIT was rarely sought out by the press, and as a result it had to force itself into the media. Yet as a small, unofficial, and marginal organization, ANIT lacked the sort of status that could allow it to draw attention to itself simply by calling a press conference at its offices (which it eventually relinquished). Instead, the typical strategy that evolved was to invite journalists to a morning breakfast–press conference, held in the banquet room of a hotel. This was an effective way to essentially buy press coverage—many journalists attend for the meal—but, of course, renting hotel space and providing meals is expensive. Similar to the phenomenon that Nylen (1992) found in Brazil, then, the new form of independent collective action by small business in Mexico was based on—and severely limited by—the resources and commitment of a core group of dedicated militants.

The Changing Character of Dissidence

Beyond limiting the association's growth potential, ANIT's inability to access the state and provide concrete benefits to its members affected the character of its membership base. The most active industrialists, the ones who regularly participate in their chambers and take advantage of the chamber's resources, were the individuals who were also the most likely to return to CANACINTRA. This tendency occurred across sectors, importantly, including the capital goods and metalworking sectors, which had served as the base of the dissident movement. What began to emerge between CANACINTRA and ANIT, then, was a size-based split within the category of "small" industry. The firms at the upper end of the category (e.g., medium-size firms, having between 101 and 250 employees) were more likely to participate in the official chamber, while the activists in ANIT were typically owners of more marginal small (16–100 employees) and micro firms.[48] To be sure, the active firms within CANACINTRA were not "big" firms—they lacked the resources and power of the industrial firms that dominated CONCAMIN, for example— but they tended to have more resources than the dissident activists. In that sense, the sectoral distinction between ANIT and CANACINTRA became blurred, and the most salient cleavage by the end of the 1980s related to size.

The experiences of the 1980s also changed the dissidents' perspective toward the state and corporatism. The Chambers Law and compulsory membership had always been a point of tension among the dissidents. As we have seen, they attempted to convert ANIT from an association to an industrial chamber that would have been governed by the Chambers Law. Despite the controls that official status might have entailed, attaining state authorization was regarded as the most effective way of attracting members and expanding the organization. Yet ANIT also had a self-proclaimed mission of reforming the Chambers Law. In particular, the dissidents sought to abolish Article 5, which made membership compulsory.[49] In fact, in the mid-1980s, at an early stage of organization-building, the dissidents attempted to recruit members to ANIT by advertising the association's objectives as those of creating sector-specific chambers *and* repealing the Chambers Law.[50] In their challenge to CANACINTRA, then, the dissidents were simultaneously trying to repeal and benefit from the Chambers Law. By the end of the 1980s, this contradiction was resolved in favor of the anti–Chambers Law current. The efforts to create a separate chamber had failed, CANACINTRA's unrivaled status as the representative of small industry had been firmly retained, and the dissidents blamed the corporatist Chambers Law for each of these grievances.

48. Note that the sizes are not stable, in that many firms move between categories as their number of employees change. Most of the leaders of ANIT were owners of medium-sized firms that by the 1990s had become small or micro as they lost sales and subsequently reduced their workforce.

49. From the time the dissidents from CANACINTRA founded ANIT in 1986, they demanded that the law be repealed (See *El Universal,* 14 August 1986); and each August the association would celebrate its anniversary as another year "in defense of free association."

50. As early as April 1986, before ANIT was officially formed, the dissidents proclaimed that they would create separate chambers *and* challenge the constitutionality of the Chambers Law. See *El Sol de México,* 24 April 1986.

The way in which the leaders of the dissident movement saw their challenge to CANACINTRA defeated served to radicalize them over the issue of corporatism. Those dedicated militants who continued to work in ANIT also came to resent the Chambers Law more than ever, since it was now seen not only as the cause of CANACINTRA's lack of autonomy, but also as the reason for their own inability to create a more autonomous organization. Whereas, in the immediate aftermath of ANIT's split from CANACINTRA, repealing the Chambers Law was attractive simply as a means to undermine CANACINTRA, by the late 1980s repealing the Chambers Law would become an end in and of itself. Quite simply, ANIT was born anti-*CANACINTRA,* but the manner in which they lost the conflict with the official chamber made the dissident small industrialists anti*corporatist.* As we shall see in the following chapter, democratization, which contributed to the emergence of the dissident movement in the 1980s, allowed this anticorporatist movement to flourish in the 1990s.

Conclusion

The mid-1980s was a period of ongoing economic crisis and change in the Mexican political economy. The near bankruptcy of the economy in 1982, the subsequent recession, and the inability of the de la Madrid government to renew a cycle of economic growth meant that small firms would operate in an economy marked by declining public-sector demand, low levels of consumer purchasing power, and reduced availability of credit. The crisis, and subsequent pressures, also encouraged the de la Madrid government to abandon decades of developmentalist economic policies and move toward an economic model that would rely on international markets to allocate resources. For small firms, responding to the decline of the domestic market and the state's withdrawal from the economy presented daunting challenges.

The mid-1980s was also a period of incipient democratization. Although the ruling PRI's national electoral hegemony remained intact, the party would begin to face regional electoral challenges. And the state's inability to provide for many citizen's basic material needs prompted new forms of social protest. By making alternative forms of political participation appear to be safer, more feasible, and more productive, democratization encouraged many small industrialists to question the utility of CANACINTRA's state-centered strategy of accommodation. By any estimation, even that of the leadership, accommodation was less fruitful than it had been in the past. But a strategy generating reduced benefits was even more open to criticism in light of potentially new opportunities for alternative ways of dealing with the state.

This chapter has revealed how economic crisis, neoliberalism, and democratization exacerbated a set of long-standing conflicts within CANACINTRA. Capital goods and metal producers took a set of sectoral-based grievances regarding the chamber's position vis-à-vis the state and built a movement that questioned the entire representative strategy of the chamber. Although the state would intervene in the ensuing conflict and preserve CANACINTRA's unrivaled status as the representative of small industry, the conflict would have lasting effects on the Mexican political economy.

Finally, it is worth noting some of the important similarities and differences that the movement of dissident small industrialists, analyzed in this chapter, shares with the small business opposition that Mizrahi (1994) observed in the northern state of Chihuahua. In both cases, smaller firms lacking market power and unable to protect their assets with capital flight invest more resources into political activism. Those lacking "exit" invest in "voice" (Hirschman 1970). An important difference, however, has to do with sectoral and geographical factors. The main source of business activism in Chihuahua came in the commercial sector. The commercial firms in the North, in contrast with smaller industrial firms in the center, did not depend on state intervention (e.g., trade protection, government purchases, and consumption subsidies) to the same degree. Nor, because of geography and distinct organizational histories, did they have the same history of tight collaborative relations with the Mexico City–based executive. The Chambers Law called for commercial chambers to be established on a *regional* basis. Unlike industrial chambers, which for the most part were national and narrowly sectoral (CANACINTRA of course providing an important partial exception), commercial chambers were state- and city-based. The commercial firms' principal grievances regarded abuse of state power, and their longer trajectories of autonomy from Mexico City made strong opposition to the state and PRI relatively natural.

The dissidents in ANIT emerged facing a different set of economic and political incentives and constraints. They had an interest in assailing the state not for abusing its power, but to the contrary for its not using its power to protect them from international competition. Moreover, for small industrialists in and around Mexico City, dealing with the state was always an issue, the important questions concerning the appropriate strategy. The dissidents, like CANACINTRA, struggled over the best way to interact with the state. Thus, the legacy of working within the state mattered, not just for CANACINTRA but for dissidents too.

It is important to underscore, then, how ANIT went from competing *within* institutions to fighting *over* institutions. The dissidents' initial challenges to CANACINTRA conformed to the rules of the game that were established by the corporatist framework: they competed for leadership positions within the organization; they attempted to redirect the chamber's strategy for dealing with the state; they moved to create an official, industrial chamber; and they appealed to the state to use the faculties of the Chambers Law for regulating CANACINTRA's statutes. In short, the conflict played itself out almost exclusively according to the ground rules established by the Chambers Law. Failure to displace CANACINTRA within the corporatist framework, however, motivated the dissidents to dedicate their resources to a campaign to dismantle business corporatism; and in the late 1980s the dissidents would lead a broad coalition to reform the Chambers Law. This campaign, and the effects of the ensuing conflict over corporatism, are analyzed in the following chapter.

FOUR

Democratization and Diminished Representation
Institutional Transformation and Political Exclusion

The late 1980s and early 1990s were a period of sweeping political and economic change in Mexico. Although the PRI managed to retain the presidency in the July 1988 elections, the presidency of Carlos Salinas de Gortari (1988–94) would be a watershed event in Mexican politics. Growing opposition to the regime, expressed by increasingly combative parties and the continued growth of social movements, produced a series of electoral and judicial reforms. The neoliberal economic model was consolidated in this period as well. By 1994, import barriers had been reduced significantly, foreign investment had been deregulated, most state enterprises had been privatized, and Mexico had negotiated and joined the North American Free Trade Agreement (NAFTA) with the United States and Canada. The focus of this chapter is the effects of democratization and neoliberalism on the representation of small industry.

The momentous political and economic changes that Mexico underwent in this period unleashed two projects to reform the institutional framework of business representation. Democratization prompted Mexico's largest and most internationalized firms to spearhead a plan to establish a new system of state-business interaction. In what can best be conceptualized as a "project from above," business elites and state officials sought to reform business corporatism and create a policy-making environment that was compatible with and supportive of the neoliberal economic model. This project from above consisted of new mechanisms for representation being created by leading firms and of the state's recognizing organizations dominated by business elites as authoritative. The ensuing patterns of business representation and government-business interaction were most evident in a series of tripartite economic pacts and the negotiation of NAFTA.

At the same time as democratization inspired a reconfiguration from above, however, the institutional framework regulating government-business interaction was also coming under siege from below. Democratization provided fertile ground for a wide-ranging coalition of business dissidents to undertake a protracted and well-publicized campaign to abolish what they assailed as "business corporatism." The anticorporatist movement, spearheaded by the small industry dissidents in ANIT, had as a centerpiece the elimination of compulsory membership in business chambers and a fundamental reform of the Chambers Law. The dissidents' campaign against corporatism made the Chambers Law, the central piece of legislation regulating business organizations, a prominent issue in Mexican politics. The threat that compulsory membership might be removed revealed CANACINTRA's organizational dependence as never before.

CANACINTRA subsequently found itself in a dilemma, caught in the crosswinds of institutional contestation, between a project from above to modernize corporatism that would marginalize the organization and an equally threatening project from below to abolish corporatism. Squeezed between these two very different, yet equally threatening, projects to transform state-business interaction, CANACINTRA fought to retain the status quo. The chamber's defense of compulsory membership, and more generally its active engagement in the conflict over institutions, greatly reduced its capacity to represent. Thus, just as economic conditions became the most threatening to small industry, CANACINTRA become the most subservient. Democratization had unleashed a conflict over political institutions that left CANACINTRA paralyzed.

The domination of state-business interaction by organizations that were controlled by Mexico's most elite firms, the paralysis of CANACINTRA, and the weak representative capacity of ANIT had profound effects on small industry representation in this period. Although the difficult environment increased the importance to small firms of having an agent to defend their interests, CANACINTRA found its capacity to represent small firms significantly restricted. The chamber's leadership was aware of the threat that neoliberal economic policies presented for small industry. CANACINTRA made numerous public statements to this effect and released multiple studies documenting the dire consequences that trade and investment liberalization, for example, were having on small industry.[1] Yet while chamber officials quietly expressed concern about these consequences, they never directly challenged the government, and CANACINTRA resolutely avoided allying itself with other disaffected social actors.

This explanation of small industry's response to neoliberalism adds an important institutional twist to arguments that small industrialists did not oppose trade liberalization because they regarded it as part of a larger, anti-inflationary strategy that they welcomed. For example, Pastor and Wise (1994) attribute small firms' virtually silent response to "asymmetrical information," arguing that collective action problems prevented small firms from gathering and disseminating adequate information that would allow them to properly distinguish between these different elements of policy. To be sure, lack of information may have affected the orientation of many individual small industrialists—but not that of their representatives. The leaders of CANACINTRA had sufficient information and were aware of the threats that liberalization presented for small industry, yet they chose not to act on what they knew.

Nor was the lack of response a result of a lack of opportunity. Opposition parties debated the merits of NAFTA, and the early 1990s saw the emergence of a variety of social movements that rose up in protest against the direction of economic reform. Dissent, though perhaps not effective opposition, was possible and visible—the problem for small industry in this period was not authoritarianism. To the contrary, it was a set of political conflicts that were unleashed and intensified by democratization itself that left the chamber paralyzed in the face of threatening neoliberal economic reforms. The outcome was that small industry representation, which had already declined in the 1980s, reached a historic low. CANACINTRA was seemingly locked into a representative strategy that was producing only the most minimal of returns to its members.

The chapter consists of three sections. The first is an analysis of the project from above, spearheaded by big business and the state to "modernize" corporatism and restructure state-business interaction. In the second section, I examine the anticorporatists' project to abolish business corporatism. The third section has as its focus CANACINTRA's responses to the challenges of neoliberalism in the context of intense institutional contestation.

1. For example, Victor Manuel Terrones, CANACINTRA's president from 1994 to 1996, reported that 4,724 small manufacturing firms had closed their doors from 1992 to 1994, at a loss of seventy-five thousand jobs (Terrones López 1994). See also the analysis of CANACINTRA official Gilberto Ortíz Muñíz (1992) and the numerous studies produced by the chamber's Center for Economic Studies.

Big Business, the State, and the Modernization of Corporatism

Beginning in the late 1980s, Mexico's largest and most internationalized firms assumed a prominent, collaborative role in policy making.[2] Although virtually all analysts of this period call attention to the role of associations dominated by big business and the new business-government coalition in explaining policy-making patterns and the consolidation of the neoliberal model, the relationship between these changes and the broader process of democratization have been left largely unexplained.[3]

The new form of interest articulation was unprecedented in terms of its organizational form, as associations dominated by the country's largest firms came to monopolize business representation and use broad, multisectoral organizations to interact with policy makers. Big business's strategy in this period had a distinctly institutional focus, in that business elites were not merely trying to change policies but instead attempting to reform the economic policy-making process. In addition to advocating for substantive policy changes, such as securing broader and deeper property rights, reducing regulation, and liberalizing trade and investment regimes, Mexico's leading firms sought to restructure the institutional framework that guided state-business interaction.

Big-Business Strategy

To understand the reconfiguration that state-business institutions underwent in the late 1980s and early 1990s, it is worthwhile to underscore three important characteristics that distinguish big business from small business in the political arena. First, large firms can more easily avail themselves of strategies of both "exit" and "voice" (see Hirschman 1970, 1981), while voice is typically the only instrument available to small firms. Second, within the realm of voice, large firms are typically less constrained by state institutions that regulate associative activities. Thus, as we have seen, big business adapted to corporatism by forming voluntary associations that operated outside the Chambers Law (see Chapter 2), while small industrialists'

---

2. The literature on the role that business associations dominated by big business played in policy making during the Salinas period is immense. See, among others, Luna 1995b; Tirado 1998; Tirado and Luna 1995; Schneider 1997; Thacker 2000; B. Heredia 1995, 1996; Alba Vega 1996b, 1996a; Valdés Ugalde 1996; Concheiro Bórquez 1996; Bensabat Kleinberg 1999; Johnson Ceva 1998; and Elizondo 1993.

3. See, as an exception, B. Heredia 1995.

attempts to do so were much less successful (see Chapter 3). Third, large firms not only have greater capacity to evade and circumvent institutionally imposed restrictions on interest articulation; they also have a greater capacity to alter existing institutions.

Each of the distinguishing characteristics of big business is important for understanding the events analyzed in this chapter. Protracted economic crisis and depressed investment levels throughout the 1980s increased the highly indebted Mexican government's vulnerability to the exit power of capital. And as numerous observers have shown, big business used exit and the persistent threat of exit, along with the promise of repatriating flight capital, to apply an extraordinary amount of pressure on the state for policy change (Mahon 1996, chapter 4; Thacker 2000, chapter 3).[4]

In addition to using exit to press for policy change, however, big business also exerted pressure on the state with voice. A critical change of the 1980s was Mexico's most elite and internationalized firms coming to commandeer the Business Coordinating Council (CCE), the private sector's peak, umbrella organization, created in 1975. The establishment of the CCE altered the landscape of business organizations, for it integrated the network of official corporatist chambers and confederations with Mexico's most important independent associations. The organizations that are members of the CCE, which cover virtually all economic sectors, are the Mexican Bankers' Association (ABM), the Mexican Association of Insurance Institutions (AMIS), the Confederation of Industrial Chambers (CONCAMIN), the Confederation of Chambers of Commerce (CONCANACO), the National Agricultural Council (CNA), the Mexican Employers' Confederation (COPARMEX), and the Mexican Businessmen's Council (CMHN).[5]

The CCE, under the control of Mexico's largest firms, came to monopolize business representation: the CCE would represent the private sector during the making of the tripartite economic pacts that formed the central aspect of economic policy-making during the Salinas period, and in the 1990s a related organization created by the CCE for foreign trade monopolized the

4. For discussions of capital flight and estimates of the dollar value of accounts held abroad by Mexican citizens, see Lessard and Williamson 1987, Dornbusch 1990, de Murguía 1986.

5. The Mexican Bankers' Association (ABM), a founding member, was replaced after the 1982 bank nationalization by the Mexican Stockbrokers' Association (AMCB). When the commercial banks were reprivatized in 1991–92, the ABM rejoined the CCE, giving the peak organization eight members, and the AMCB changed its name to the AMIB (Mexican Association of Securities Institutions). In 1999 CON-CANACO withdrew from the CCE after a conflict over leadership. For analyses of the CCE, see Luna and Tirado 1992; Tirado and Luna 1995; and Schneider 2002.

private sector's representation for NAFTA negotiations. Thus, in the late 1980s, big business combined exit and voice strategies and thereby began "to exert double-barreled pressure on the state" (Thacker 2000, 36).

To understand the full impact of these events, it is important to recall that big business always combined exit and voice—the "double-barreled" application of both exit and voice was not unprecedented. What was new in this period, and what would profoundly affect the entire network of business representation, was that big business's use of voice had a distinctly institutional focus. The CCE was not combining exit and voice strategies simply to secure new policies. Rather, economic crisis, the move toward neoliberalism, and democratization encouraged Mexico's largest firms to embark on a campaign of institutional reform, whereby they would restructure the entire framework for business-government interaction.

To distinguish the new elements from elements of continuity, we can conceptualize big business's voice strategies according to two dimensions. One dimension regards the extent to which business is *reacting* to government policies or is acting *proactively* to shape policy. A second dimension regards the nature of strategy in terms of form, the extent to which business projects its interests *narrowly* or in a *coordinated* multisectoral fashion.[6] Prior to the late 1980s, there were very few instances of coordinated, proactive interest articulation on the part of big business in Mexico. Rather, voice on the part of big business tended to be narrow when proactive and only coordinated when reactive. Figure 6 illustrates the typology of big-business strategies, with the entries in each cell providing examples of the respective modes of action.

Big business engaged in intense interaction with the state in a proactive fashion throughout the postrevolutionary period. Indeed, a variety of sector-specific associations were created to engage with the state in precisely this way. This includes organizations that were formally outside the corporatist framework, such as those representing the banks (ABM) and insurance firms (AMIS), but also the heterogeneous set of sector-specific chambers and voluntary trade associations. A key characteristic of these organizations was that they tended to be controlled by and to represent the interests of sectors with minimal numbers of firms (e.g., financial services) or, in the case of more populated sectors, a select group of the largest and

---

6. On business strategies more generally, see Haggard, Maxfield, and Schneider 1997. While many authors use the term *encompassing,* I prefer *coordinated,* because many actors are not taken into account by supposedly "encompassing" organizations, as discussed in Chapter 1. In fact, many peak associations are designed in a way that makes them explicitly nonencompassing in a vertical sense.

	Reactive	Proactive
Narrow	Individual (e.g., capital flight)	Sectoral associations
Coordinated	COPARMEX, CCE (1975–85)	CMHN, CCE (post-1985), COECE

Fig. 5   Big-business activism in twentieth-century Mexico

most important national and transnational firms (e.g., the National Association of the Chemical Industry [ANIQ]).[7]

Although big firms managed to minimize the constraints of corporatism and secure access to the state on their own terms, the informal arrangements that prevailed suffered from being unreliable. That government-business interaction was ad hoc meant that the state might act without consulting big business. Unreliability, and the ensuing sense of vulnerability to "arbitrary" state action, was particularly worrisome in the context of the 1917 constitution's vague guarantees of protection of private property rights (see Elizondo 1992) and the PRI's formal alliance with organized labor (see R. B. Collier 1992). In short, though the post-Cárdenas governments were only "revolutionary" in rhetoric, the constitution gave the state the means to be revolutionary in substance, and the alliance with labor could provide the motivation to do so.

Big business responded in a pair of ways to the unreliability of a consultative framework in which they lacked routinized access to the state. First, to insure against the government's capacity to implement arbitrary policy changes, big business preserved the ability to exit by pressuring the state to minimize exchange controls and retain a comparatively open capital account (Mahon 1996, chapter 3).[8] Second, in the instances when the state "violated" the implicit agreement to consult big business, business elites typically supplemented the use of capital flight with coordinated and reactive mobilizations against the state (Tirado and Luna 1986; Luna, Tirado,

7. Even CONCAMIN, the confederation to which all official industrial chambers and most voluntary associations belonged (the former through compulsion, the latter by choice), retained a comparatively low profile relative to these associations.

8. Mahon's argument, with its emphasis on not only the use of capital flight but also the application of pressure to make sure that capital flight would remain an easily deployable instrument, takes us beyond the standard accounts of capital flight and disinvestment as business responses to episodes of "populist" policy making (see Dornbusch and Edwards 1991; and Arriola 1988). This is a critical distinction, for it suggests that exit power is not an inherent and immutable characteristic of capital, but one that depends on the existence of exit destinations and the absence of exchange controls to impede exit. See also Winters 1994. .

and Valdés 1987; Guzmán Valdivia 1961; Bravo Mena 1987; delli Sante 1979). Thus, as numerous observers have noted, close and amiable relations between the state and business were punctuated by episodes of intense conflict.[9] The principal organization behind coordinated and reactive mobilizations was COPARMEX, and then in the mid-1970s the CCE.

Importantly, these episodes of reactive and coordinated business mobilization tended to be followed by a quick return to more narrow and proactive strategies. The recurrent pattern featured a collective response on the part of business in reaction to threatening government initiatives (real or rhetorical), securing the desired substantive outcome (typically putting a brake on actual reforms or forestalling proposed reforms), and then demobilizing. Rarely would coordinated and reactive mobilization produce new mechanisms of consultation to facilitate ongoing proactive interest articulation; and even when such new consultative mechanisms did emerge, they tended to be short-lived.[10]

Big business broke the pattern of reaction-demobilization in the late 1980s and embarked on a project to restructure government-business interaction—to "modernize" business corporatism. This project from above, spearheaded by Mexico's largest firms, entailed an effort to create a new framework for state-business interaction and consultation built on information, predictability, and transparency (see Schneider 1997).

The Mexican Businessmen's Council (CMHN) was the driving force behind this change in big business strategy. The CMHN, founded in the early 1960s, has a membership of thirty-five to forty of the wealthiest businesspeople in Mexico. Membership, by invitation only and subject to unanimous approval of the existing members, is consciously restricted to representatives of Mexico's largest economic groups.[11] Although CMHN members played a critical role in founding the CCE in the 1970s (Schneider 2002), until the mid-1980s the CMHN rarely acted as a business organization in terms of aggregating interests and serving as an agent or intermediary for a collective set of interests. Rather, it was simply a conduit for individual members to establish contacts,

9. There exists an extensive literature on the periodic mobilizations of big business in the postrevolutionary period, with most analysts examining episodes of conflict during the presidencies of Cárdenas (1934–40), López Mateos (1958–64), and Echeverría (1970–76). See, among others, Mártinez Nava 1984; Arriola 1981; Luna 1992b; Luna, Tirado, and Valdés 1987; and Tirado and Luna 1986.

10. To provide but one example, the mechanisms for government-business interaction established in the mid-1970s, in response to business mobilization and the emergence of the CCE, part of the "Alliance for Production," were nowhere to be seen in the debate over entering the GATT in 1979–80.

11. As one observer concluded, "[W]ithout question [the CMHN] is the most elitist of the major organizations" (Camp 1989, 167). See also Ortíz Rivera 2000; and Schneider 2002.

articulate their individual concerns, and resolve their particular problems.[12] Membership in the CMHN provided business leaders with a mechanism for maintaining close and frequent, though informal, personal contact with key policy makers, including cabinet secretaries and the president.[13] As one member described the CMHN's meetings with President de la Madrid, "[E]ach member of the council will use that as an opportunity to ask the president for an individual meeting. In other words, what the council has become is *a channel for individuals to make contact with the president rather than to represent the interests of the private sector as a whole*" (Camp 1989, 170; emphasis added).

In the mid-1980s, however, the CMHN commandeered and transformed the CCE. Not only did the CMHN essentially form a cartel within the CCE, with control over four of the organization's seven votes (its own, plus those of AMIS, the Mexican Stockbrokers' Association [AMCB], and CONCAMIN), but the CMHN also bankrolled the organization, providing 90 percent of the income (see Ortíz Rivera 2000; Luna and Tirado 1992; Schneider 2002).

Most important, the CMHN converted the CCE from an instrument that had been used to unite business against the state into a peak organization that would collaborate with the state. Under the CMHN's tutelage, the CCE secured a quasi-official role in designing and implementing economic policy. This new role featured routinized interaction in official settings with Mexico's most important policy makers. The remarkable feature of big-business strategy in the late 1980s and early 1990s, then, was not the use of a voice strategy per se, but rather the new form of big business's voice strategy. Mexico's largest firms were now interacting with state officials proactively, in a coordinated fashion.

Importantly, the timing of this institutional strategy can be attributed to both the emergence of neoliberalism and the process of democratization. The liberalization of trade and investment policies, and the subsequent negotiation of NAFTA, increased the importance of ongoing state-business communication. While a changed economic model provided the rationale for restructuring corporatism, democratization increased the motivation for doing so. For the first time, the 1988 elections presented a challenge to PRI

12. In fact, CMHN's own origins conform to the general pattern described above. The council was created in reaction to the reformist rhetoric (if not policies) of President López Mateos and as an instrument with which big business could improve foreign investors' view of the Mexican economy (Ortíz Rivera 2000).

13. Although such unofficial meetings are difficult to track with certainty, CMHN members were reported to meet with cabinet officials on a weekly basis and with the president on a biweekly basis (Camp 1989, 169). Schneider (2002, 90) reports that the CMHN's core activity was a closed, monthly lunch with high-ranking government officials.

domination. Electoral competition potentially gave PRI leaders the incentive to appeal to the party's mass bases, precisely the sort of actions that traditionally alienated big business. Moreover, increased party competition, and the likelihood of growing opposition power in the legislature, threatened to dilute business power.

The State and Big Business

The change in big-business representative strategy was not an entirely endogenous process. To the contrary, the Mexican government welcomed and encouraged the fundamental changes that were occurring within the ranks of business organizations and worked with the CMHN and CCE to develop new consultative mechanisms (Schneider 2002).[14]

The state's facilitation of big-business organization was evident in a series of tripartite economic pacts and the NAFTA negotiations. In December 1987, with inflation spiraling out of control following an outflow of capital and the devaluation of the peso, the de la Madrid government announced a tripartite Economic Solidarity Pact (PSE). The PSE aimed to arrest the underlying inflationary expectations by reducing the fiscal deficit (principally through spending reductions and public-sector price increases), placing a ceiling on wage and price increases, and increasing the scope and speed of trade liberalization.[15]

The government recognized the CCE as the official representative of business in the PSE, which Whitehead argues "provided the focus, the rationale, and the machinery" for the new pattern of government-business interaction (Whitehead 1989, 186; see also Roxborough 1992a; Kaufman, Bazdresch, and Heredia 1994). Moreover, while the PSE was initially introduced as an emergency measure in December 1987 by the outgoing de la Madrid administration, the pact was renewed throughout 1988 and then regularized during the Salinas presidency.[16] Under Salinas, the tripartite economic pacts

14. Democratization and economic liberalization also prompted big business to build new institutions in Argentina and Brazil as well, though with less success. Schneider (forthcoming 2004) attributes these differences to the responses of the Argentinean and Brazilian states. The effects of these processes on small industry representation in the two South American countries are examined in Chapter 6.

15. Later versions of the pact would also peg the exchange rate to the U.S. dollar. For discussion of policy components of the economic pacts, see Lustig 1998; and Aspe 1993.

16. Combining an apparent obsession with acronyms with a poetic use of homonyms, in 1989 Salinas renamed the Pacto de Solidaridad Económica, or Economic Solidarity Pact (PSE) as Pacto de Estabilidad y Crecimiento Económico, or Pact for Stability and Economic Growth (PECE) and then in 1992 changed the name again, to Pacto para la Estabilidad, la Competitividad, y el Empleo, or Pact for Stability, Competitiveness, and Employment (PECE).

became the principal policy-making forum. Virtually all important decisions regarding economic policy were made in the context of the pact, particularly in the meetings of the *comité de seguimiento* (Aspe 1993, 22–23; Kaufman, Bazdresch, and Heredia 1994, 387).

The Salinas administration also used the occasion of NAFTA to develop new consultative mechanisms in concert with big business. In 1990, as the government was preparing for the negotiations, though still before the goal of a trade agreement was announced, Secretary of Trade Jaime Serra Puche encouraged business advocates of the neoliberal economic model to present the government with a single interlocutor for foreign-trade consultation. Seeking to incorporate the private sector into the NAFTA process, and taking the economic pacts as a model for state-business collaboration, the Secretariat of Trade and Industrial Development (SECOFI) invited the CCE to form a specialized, foreign trade unit to represent Mexican business (Thacker 2000, 142).[17] The CCE, in turn, responded by establishing the Coordinator of Foreign Trade Business Organizations (COECE), which integrated the handful of export-related business organizations into a single body. Although this new coordinating body remained formally subordinate to the CCE, state officials transformed it into the most important Mexican business organization in the negotiation of NAFTA by granting it a de facto monopoly of representation in what was the most visible and important issue of economic policy of the early 1990s.[18]

That state officials would actively participate in constructing a new framework for government-business interaction is not surprising, given the new economic model. The Salinas government's expressed commitment to economic "modernization" was explicit in the emphasis on the importance of big business. As Salinas remarked in his first State of the Nation *informe* in 1989, "[I]n today's competitive world what we need are large corporations capable of competing with large multinational firms" (cited in B. Heredia 1996, 144–45). Indeed, it is worth emphasizing the broader array of rhetorical changes that accompanied the economic policy changes. Under Salinas big business would no longer be politically stigmatized for an association with foreign capital. Rather, economic "modernization" and the broader

---

17. In fact, the state had been encouraging this sort of coordination and unification for years. As early as 1986, the Mexican government had pleaded for export-oriented organizations to unify. Speaking to the annual ANIERM convention, then secretary of trade Hector Hernández Cervantes noted that "it is easier to have a single interlocutor than to have five or six, as is the case with CEMAI, the U.S.-Mexico Chamber of Commerce, CONACEX, ANIERM, etc. I believe that you should make an effort to unify yourselves in this respect" (*Mercado de Valores,* 3 February 1986, 107).

18. For detailed analyses of COECE, see Alba Vega 1996b; Luna 1992a; Puga 1993b; Rubio 1992; Thacker 2000, chapters 5–6; and Gallardo 1994.

program of integration implied by NAFTA meant that the owners and managers of Mexico's largest firms came to be regarded in an almost heroic light, as the crusaders leading Mexico's insertion into the "First World."[19]

More broadly, the changed state role from that of owner and active participant in economic activity to a more subsidiary one as facilitator called for a new relationship with big business (Evans 1997a, 1997b). Officials in the Salinas government were more than ready to transform their contacts with big business from personal and informal meetings and meals to formal policy-making sessions. While the government had responded to a confrontational and reactive CCE by attempting to marginalize it from policy making, the remade and proactive CCE and COECE were enthusiastically embraced.[20] The state seized the opportunity to develop and consolidate a new working relationship with big business by granting monopoly of representation to the CCE, for the economic pacts, and then COECE, for NAFTA.

To summarize, then, the rapid economic change of the Salinas period was accompanied by a project to "modernize" business corporatism. This project from above featured an effort on the part of both big business and the state to construct a new framework for interaction: big business responded to the potential uncertainty of democracy by securing a reliable, routinized, and stable role in policy making; and a group of technocratic state officials responsible for economic policy, and dependent on private investment after a protracted investment crisis, anxiously sought to gain private-sector support. Together, they developed new sets of consultative mechanisms to provide certainty and predictability in economic policy management. The new relationship would be evident in the continuation of the tripartite economic pacts and the NAFTA negotiations. Both featured intense collaboration between the state and elite private-sector proponents of the neoliberal model.

Corporatism Transformed

The new corporatist arrangements featured the exclusionary characteristics that O'Donnell (1977) labeled "bifrontal," in which business becomes

---

19. In contrast, throughout most of the postrevolutionary period the government worked to keep its tight relationship with big business "behind closed doors," fearing the political repercussions of appearing too close to a distinctively "nonrevolutionary" actor. See Ortiz Rivera 2000, 7, citing interview with ex-president López Portillo.

20. Contrast the paths of two CCE presidents: Manuel Clouthier, president from 1981 to 1983, was the PAN's gubernatorial candidate in the state of Sinaloa in 1986, and the PAN's presidential candidate in 1988. Claudio X. Gonzalez, president from 1985 to 1987, participated actively in the 1988 Salinas campaign and later served as President Salinas's special adviser on foreign investment from 1988 to 1994.

integrated into the state apparatus while the state penetrates and controls weaker social sectors. It is important to emphasize the extent to which the bifrontal characteristics were reflected not only between classes but also *within* the business sector. For the new policy-making arrangement to be effective, dissenting actors within business would have to have limits placed on their access to the state. Indeed, the new mechanisms for government-business consultation ensured that not all of the private sector would be heard.

The new pattern of government-business consultation simultaneously magnified the interests of large firms and marginalized the dissenting voices of smaller ones. Small industry, for example, was not directly represented in the negotiation of the economic pacts, as the private sector was represented by the CCE. Although the CCE's membership consisted of seven organizations, representing virtually all sectors of Mexican business, small industry was represented indirectly, through CONCAMIN (of which CANACINTRA is a member). The CCE's internal structure contributed to the overrepresentation of large firms by allocating votes equally according to member organizations (Luna and Tirado 1992). For example, organizations with a handful of large firms had the same vote as those with tens of thousands of smaller firms. And many of Mexico's largest firms were prominent members of multiple associations within the CCE.

The importance of COECE during the drafting of NAFTA further accentuated the elite domination of business representation. COECE, like the CCE, was dominated by a fraction of internationalized, export-oriented firms that strongly supported NAFTA (Thacker 2000). COECE was not designed to provide state officials with a wide array of opinions on the relative merits of the free trade agreement: its mission was to fine-tune NAFTA, not debate it. According to COECE's director, Juan Gallardo Thurlow, the organization aimed "to *support* the efforts of the official government negotiators in the definition of the terms to be negotiated" and "to *support* SECOFI's free trade negotiating office to achieve the best possible trilateral agreement that takes into consideration the interests of the Mexican private sector" (Gallardo 1994, 137, emphasis added). In fact, as a way to solidify its monopoly on business representation in NAFTA, in 1991 COECE requested that all other business organizations refrain from public declarations regarding the negotiations (Alba Vega 1996a, 155; Luna 1992a).

The mechanics of COECE's operations and interaction with trade officials further served to limit small industrialists access to the state. For example, as the negotiations between Mexico, the United States, and Canada progressed, COECE underwent a process of internal reorganization to replicate the structure of the trilateral negotiations, replacing its sectoral divisions with six-member units corresponding to each of the official issue-areas.[21] In the process of reorganizing COECE from approximately 120 divisions to fewer than twenty teams, the elite-dominated leadership of the CCE and COECE appointed approximately two-thirds of the new representatives (Puga 1993b, 67–68). Although the reorganization left COECE in a position to become more actively involved in the negotiations than originally expected, even to the extent of its accompanying SECOFI negotiators to the trilateral meetings and consulting with Mexico's representatives before and after each bargaining session, it also served to reduce representation. As COECE's participation increased, so too did the amount of time and resources required.[22] Members paid their own ways to meetings and negotiations without compensation, and the taxing negotiating process further raised the threshold for participation. This marginalized small firms in two ways. First, the requirements of time and travel were particularly onerous for smaller firms. With fewer resources and smaller managerial staffs, small firms were less able to remain involved in the intense negotiations. Second, when members resigned—and the turnover rate after just a year of negotiations exceeded 70 percent—their replacements again were appointed by the directors of the CCE and COECE (Rubio 1992, 125–27; Puga 1993b, 68).

In sum, while both the CCE and COECE purported to represent the "general" interests of Mexican business, and were regarded by the state as doing so, both were dominated by Mexico's most elite firms. They are "peak" associations, but they are only partially encompassing. They are encompassing in a horizontal sense, in that they are multisectoral, but they are not encompassing in a vertical sense. In fact, they were explicitly designed to be nonencompassing in this sense, to stifle dissenting voices. Thus, Kaufman, Bazdresch, and Heredia (1994) conclude, the prominent role given to the CCE in the pacts "magnified the interests of large financial-industrial groups that were in a reasonably good position to absorb the costs of economic liberalization" (391). Likewise, Thacker (2000) concludes that "the most active participants [in the NAFTA consultations] were those who supported the basic idea of NAFTA, and those from the largest firms and groups.

---

21. Some were broad sectors (e.g., agriculture, services, transportation) and some were specific manufacturing sectors (e.g., automobile, textiles), but mostly these divisions were thematic (e.g., dispute resolution, intellectual property, rules of origin, safeguards). See Maxfield and Shapiro 1997; and Cameron and Tomlin 2000.

22. During the NAFTA negotiations, COECE participated in 3,056 meetings with government officials (Alba Vega 1996a, 58).

Very often, these two categories overlapped, resulting in an alliance between new state and big business elites to negotiate the free trade agreement with the United States and Canada" (166).

The transformation of corporatism had profound implications for small industry. Small industrialists as individuals tended to be filtered out on account of the process and intensity of government-business collaboration. Moreover, the new pattern of government-business consultation, in which the state recognized the elite-dominated CCE and COECE as the legitimate representatives of business, marginalized small industrialists' organizations too. CANACINTRA, a nonvoting member of the CCE, had minimal influence over the contents of the economic pacts; with or without the chamber's ratification the pacts would be signed and implemented.[23] Likewise, with or without CANACINTRA's ratification, the Salinas government was moving ahead with NAFTA. The chamber, in sum, was marginalized on account of the decidedly *nonencompassing* characteristic of the peak business organizations that had obtained quasi-official status. And ANIT, once again, was thoroughly excluded. As Adolfo Valles, the president of ANIT (1991–93), lamented,

> [I]t is worrisome that in the face of NAFTA two groups have been formed in Mexico: on one side the institutional group, represented by the trade authorities, and nourished with information, studies, and monographs of the COECE; and [on the other side] the legislative, consisting of the chambers of senators and deputies, together with small and medium businessmen, who have not been properly notified about the proposals because they do not have any direct input into the process and the discussions (*Excelsior,* 16 June 1991).

Institutional Contestation from Below

Just as big business responded to neoliberalism and democratization by seeking to reformulate government-business interaction, so too did a faction of weaker firms. As a result, the late 1980s and early 1990s witnessed the institutional framework that structured business association under siege, not just from above but from below as well, as a wide-ranging coalition of business dissidents embarked on a protracted and well-publicized "anticorporatist" campaign to reform the

23. In interviews, a number of CANACINTRA officials remarked that the tendency to convene extraordinary sessions of the pact's *comité de seguimiento* increased under Salinas, and chamber officials frequently were not notified of these meetings until the last minute.

Chambers Law and eliminate compulsory membership to business chambers. In this section I examine the development of the broad anticorporatist movement and the ensuing episode of institutional contestation.

The growth of this movement of the weak was facilitated by democratization. We might expect this movement of weak actors protesting an alliance between the state and big business to fizzle, but instead the movement gained strength throughout the early 1990s. Political parties seeking instruments to dismantle corporatism—widely regarded as a pillar of PRI domination—seized the issue. And an increasingly independent judiciary, also a product of democratization, provided fertile ground in which the movement could flower.

The Transformation of Dissidence

By the late 1980s ANIT had undergone a transformation, from a fledgling business organization that sought external support in its attempt to represent small industry, to the leader of an anticorporatist movement committed to the abolition of the Chambers Law. ANIT turned to the media to criticize the state of small business representation and wage war on what it criticized as "business corporatism" (*corporativismo empresarial*). Holding regular press conferences, the dissident group called repeatedly for reform of the Chambers Law.[24] The group's rallying cry was that compulsory membership violated the Mexican constitution and the Universal Declaration of Human Rights, to which Mexico is a signatory. In addition to giving press conferences, ANIT organized a series of public forums for analysis of the Chambers Law, forums that had the stated objective of developing a revised law to be submitted to the Mexican congress.[25]

The leaders of ANIT were successful in their use of the media and began to attract significant public scrutiny. An important breakthrough occurred in February 1989, when *Expansión,* a leading business magazine, featured an exposé on the small business dissidents and likened their campaign to reform the Chambers Law to the struggle of "David versus Goliath."[26] The article itself brought the dissidents more press coverage, as their assertion that nearly

24. Rubén Barrios Graff (president from 1989 to 1991) held weekly press conferences, and Adolfo Valles Septién (1991–93) attempted to do the same (Puga 1992, 42). Since 1993, ANIT held its press conference the last Thursday of each month.

25. The first of these public meetings was held in Mexico City in January 1988, followed by similar events in Guadalajara and Monterrey.

26. "Microindustriales: De la disidencia a la organización," *Expansión,* 15 February 1989.

twenty thousand businesspeople throughout the country were refusing to pay membership dues was reported by a prominent business columnist in *La Jornada* (26 March 1989). Thus, through their careful use of the press, they managed to keep themselves and the Chambers Law in the public eye; and as early as July 1989 rumors began to circulate that officials in SECOFI would convoke a "forum of popular consultation" to consider changes in the law that it would present to Congress in November that year.[27]

The broadening of the dissidents' campaign, evolving from anti-CANAC-INTRA to anticorporatist, allowed them to tap into a wider perception in the Mexican business community that business organizations were failing as representatives (Hernández Rodríguez 1991). Many businesspeople who had nothing to do with CANACINTRA had their own grievances with the system of business organization and representation. For example, three-quarters of the small firms and half the medium firms questioned in a 1992 survey found that joining an association was not useful, but fewer than half the firms interviewed were actually members of CANACINTRA (NAFIN-INEGI 1993, 46). Small firms' political dissatisfaction went beyond CANACINTRA.

The sense of underrepresentation was exacerbated by the economic dislocations of the 1980s and early 1990s, and, critically, by the exclusionary pattern of peak, state-business consultation. Many came to resent the monopoly of representation assumed by (and granted to) the CCE and COECE, organizations dominated by the most elite actors in the private sector. As a technocratic group of policy makers worked closely with a select group of elite firms, it appeared that the agreements that were reached suffered from inadequate consideration of how the effects of such accords would fall unequally throughout the private sector. This perception and the ensuing resentment had been augmented by the comments of Agustín Legorreta, prominent financier, CMHN member, and CCE president (1987–89), who remarked that economic policy was negotiated "by the president of a presidential country with a small, very comfortable group of 300 people who make the important economic decisions in Mexico" (Valdés Ugalde 1997, 220, citing *Unomásuno*, 19 May 1988).[28]

---

27. *La Jornada*, 19 July 1989. The dissidents' use of the press also brought them some, albeit limited, attention from the academic community. See, for example, the first sentence of Mexican political scientist Cristina Puga's monograph on small business representation in Mexico: "The curiosity awakened by the political activity of [ANIT], which since 1989 led a visible and well directed media campaign in defense of the country's small industrialists, was the origin of this project" (1992, 11). See also Luna 1995a.

28. See also "Los 37 más ricos del país descartan la democracia y se adueñan del trato con el gobierno," *Proceso*, 27 November 1989.

The dissidents from ANIT took these concerns about representation and framed them in terms of corporatism. The dissidents argued that compulsory membership gave the official organizations too much independence from their members. Whereas ANIT's grievances in its early years were typically directed toward CANACINTRA, by the end of the 1980s and in the early 1990s the dissidents advanced more generalized criticisms of how corporatism distorted representation. Thus, the complaint that organizations such as CONCAMIN and CANACINTRA ratified the economic pacts without consulting their members were framed not simply as criticisms of these organizations, but as symptoms of larger pathologies that stemmed from the Chambers Law. These organizations did not have to consult their bases, the dissidents argued, because compulsory membership guaranteed their revenues.

ANIT successfully tapped into this wider base of dissent to construct an alliance against the Chambers Law. The dissidents collaborated with other associations that, like ANIT, opposed the corporatist regulations of business organization. In particular, many regionally based industrial associations shared this resentment of the official chambers and confederations. Although these associations can join CONCAMIN and take advantage of the confederation's services, like the sectoral trade associations they are not allowed to vote, since only officially recognized *chambers* can be full, voting members of confederations. Sure enough, many regional associations became bothered by the lack of representation that came from their second-class status within CONCAMIN.[29] In short, just as the dissident small industrialists objected to CANACINTRA's failure to adequately represent their interests, many leaders of regional associations in CONCAMIN came to complain of a lack of representation in the confederation.

By the early 1990s, then, the founders of ANIT were at the core of a broad, anticorporatist coalition. They appealed to individuals in other associations, encouraging them to stop paying dues to official chambers, expanding the movement well beyond the participation of the small industrial firms that had grievances with CANACINTRA in the 1980s. And by establishing links with regional associations, ANIT built a broad heterogeneous movement that included a wide array of associations from a mix of sectors and regions.[30]

The anticorporatist coalition became increasingly active in the 1990s, with continued press conferences, forums, newspaper announcements

29. *Expansión,* 15 February 1989. See Hernández Rodríguez 1991 and Luna and Tirado 1992 for more complete discussions of how the activity-based pattern of interest representation in the industrial sector left regional groups underrepresented.

30. I analyze the development of this movement in more detail in Shadlen 1997, chapter 5.

(*desplegados*), and the drafting of an initiative to reform the Chambers Law that it submitted to Congress. By 1992 it had succeeded in making the Chambers Law a prominent public issue. Its media campaign received significant attention, and many official organizations felt compelled to undertake studies and lobby responsible officials in the executive.

Democratization and Institutional Contestation

Democratization is critical for understanding the growth and trajectory of the anticorporatist movement in this period. The leaders of this movement were fringe members of the business community, and they faced considerable obstacles. After all, state officials and major business organizations dominated by Mexico's largest firms were hostile to this movement, which if nothing else was disrupting the peaceful, harmonious period of government-business relations. The anticorporatists were weak actors facing powerful opponents, and in another political setting their campaign would likely have died before it ever got off the ground, but democratization provided new opportunities for advancing their cause. In particular, democratization increased the incentives for opposition political parties to pay attention to and promote the anticorporatists' campaign, and democratization gave rise to an increasingly active and independent judiciary (Domingo 2000) with the capacity to rule on the issue of compulsory membership.

Opposition political parties seized on the issue of business corporatism as a way to expand their constituencies. To the extent that the dissidents were fighting for "democratization" of the business sector, their struggle was no longer simply a conflict between capitalists, but one with broader appeal. The message was no longer specifically about small business representation, but now addressed the more general question of the ability and right to form associations free from state constraints. To that end, in the early 1990s, both the National Action Party (PAN) and the Party of the Democratic Revolution (PRD) proposed legislative initiatives to reform the Chambers Law and eliminate compulsory membership.[31]

The most immediate boost to the anticorporatist movement came not from political parties, but rather from the judiciary. In July 1992, the Supreme Court declared the Chambers Law to be unconstitutional, on the grounds that compulsory membership to business chambers violated Article 9 of the Mexican

31. For discussion of these proposals and the parties' shifting positions on the Chambers Law and compulsory membership, see Shadlen 2000, 95–97.

constitution, which guarantees each individual freedom of association. In the particular case before the court, the owner of a hospital in the state of Durango protested the fine that he received for refusing to join the National Hospital Chamber, and he requested an *amparo,* a court-ordered injunction that protects individuals from the state. After having his initial petition for an injunction denied by a district judge in February 1991, the plaintiff appealed to the Supreme Court, which ruled in his favor in July 1992.[32]

The 1992 ruling marked the beginning of the protracted death of the Chambers Law. The writ of *amparo* grants legal protection to individual plaintiffs against acts of executive power that violate individuals' constitutional rights, but this protection is provided only on a case-by-case basis. That is, the court provides an injunction to protect the individual plaintiff without establishing a generalized precedent. Laws against which courts have issued injunctions remain in force, and all other individuals seeking protection must file for their own *amparos.*[33] Only when a law is declared unconstitutional five times by the Supreme Court is a generalized precedent established, one that makes the law effectively unenforceable. Not until October 1995 was the precedent established, after incessant petitioning for injunctions by dissident businesspeople and long delaying on the part of the state (SIID 1996).

Although the July 1992 ruling was but the first step in what would be a long, drawn-out legal process, it marked an important turning point in the dissidents' campaign against the Chambers Law. By granting the injunction, and thereby declaring that the Chambers Law was unconstitutional, the Mexican Supreme Court provided the anticorporatists with a legal foundation on which to support their grievances. In March 1992, ANIT president Adolfo Valles had filed a complaint with the National Human Rights Commission (CNDH), claiming that the Chambers Law violated his constitutional right of free association. The CNDH responded that it could not help, that Valles was not complaining of the abuse of authority or the misapplication of a law, but rather about a law itself, and thus it was out of the CNDH's jurisdiction. The CNDH only had responsibility in cases in which public officials violated citizens' rights by acting outside their legal obligations; the officials in this case, who were demanding that delinquent firms pay their chamber dues—the officials who Valles complained were violating his constitutional rights—were following their legal obligations by

---

32. See "La rebelión de los empresarios," *Expansión,* 30 September 1992.
33. Bailey describes the *amparo* as "a court-ordered writ which combines aspects of *habeus corpus* and injunction" (1988, 198 n. 14).

enforcing Article 6 of the Chambers Law. However, since Mexican law gives citizens the right to request a court-ordered injunction in instances when even the legal execution of the law is prejudicial, the CNDH encouraged Valles to request such an injunction and thus allow the Mexican Supreme Court to judge whether or not the Chambers Law was constitutional.[34] The July 1992 ruling, then, demonstrated that this was a fruitful path.

It is worth noting that the plaintiff who received the first *amparo* was not affiliated with ANIT. However, the dissidents were quick to integrate this judicial strategy for combating corporatism into their own campaign, which until that time had been based principally on press conferences and meetings with legislators; and they became actively involved in many of the ensuing cases that followed the July 1992 ruling. In fact, a lawyer connected to one of the firms in the movement offered legal services to businesses that were threatened with sanctions for violating the Chambers Law, their offense being that they had not paid their membership dues.

The Supreme Court ruling also provided an aura of imminent change. In the first regard, the 1992 ruling was followed by a proliferation of requests for injunctions. In Mexico City alone it was estimated that more than one hundred requests for injunctions were received by September 1992 (*Expansión*, 30 September 1992).[35] In addition, the strong wording of the decision, in which one of justices referred to the chambers and confederations as "fascistic," suggested that the Court was prepared to make additional such rulings and ultimately abolish the network of official chambers and confederations. Indeed, in September 1992, the Court made a second ruling against the Chambers Law. Moreover, rumors quickly began to circulate that SECOFI was preparing a revised Chambers Law that did not include compulsory membership; and, according to one newspaper, the revised law would be presented in the Chamber of Deputies by the end of 1992.[36]

The storm around the Chambers Law prompted a number of official business organizations into action. They denounced the Supreme Court's ruling, undertook studies to evaluate the Chambers Law, embarked on public relations campaigns in defense of compulsory membership, and began to deploy

34. Correspondence from Jorge Madrazo (inspector, CNDH) to Adolfo Valles, 22 April 1992.

35. Reports differ, however, on how many cases were actually heard by the court. *El Financiero* (23 September 1992), for example, put the number of pending cases at fifteen.

36. The quote from the justice was published in "La rebelión de los empresarios," *Expansión*, 30 September 1992. The report of the revised law was published in *El Economista*, 12 August 1992. For a review of various positions on compulsory membership and the Chambers Law, see "Posiciones antagónicas en la IP ante la próxima Ley de Cámaras," *El Economista*, 20 July 1992.

their political resources to lobby officials in SECOFI. In a series of public declarations, a number of major business organizations emphatically rejected any reform of the law that would eliminate compulsory membership.[37] Typically, they exalted the importance of corporatism for policy-making coordination, insisting that without compulsory membership and the Chambers Law, the government would not have been able to negotiate the economic pacts or NAFTA. CONCAMIN, for example, asserted that in the making and implementation of the economic pacts the state "relied on the chambers and confederations to transmit the negotiated decisions, a situation for which obligatory affiliation played a role of primary importance" (CONCAMIN 1992, 8).[38]

Institutional Contestation, CANACINTRA, and Small Industry Representation

The conflict over corporatism was particularly challenging for CANACINTRA. On the one hand, chamber officials acknowledged (and concurred with) many of the criticisms of the prevailing arrangements for business representation. CANACINTRA was clearly a marginal participant, a bit player, in the emerging pattern of government-business consultation (see Ortíz Muñiz 1992, 312). In fact, there could hardly be better evidence of CANACINTRA's dilemma than the rhetoric and attacks of ANIT itself. The dissidents consistently criticized CANACINTRA for being unrepresentative at the same time as they assailed the economic policies negotiated by peak associations such as COECE and the CCE. Yet everyone knew that CANACINTRA was not, by any stretch of the imagination, a peak organization. The fact of the matter is that ANIT's attack on the NAFTA negotiations and the exclusionary nature of government-business consultation could equally well have been made by CANACINTRA.[39]

37. See *El Economista*, 12 August 1992; and 18 August 1992. The unity of the official business organizations in defense of compulsory membership and the Chambers Law was not new in 1992. When the dissidents in ANIT began to publicly challenge the Chambers Law in the late 1980s, for example, the official organizations responded in a similar way (e.g. *La Jornada*, 11 September 1989). What was new in 1992, however, was the considerable amount of resources that they would expend to fight against the change in the law.

38. As one CONCAMIN official commented in defense of the law, "I can just see the government trying to go ahead with the pacts and NAFTA without our participation. They would have to go out to Reforma and ask whoever passed by: 'Are you a businessman? What do you think about our plan?'"(*Expansión*, 30 September 1992, 94). Reforma is a major avenue in the heart of the financial district in Mexico City.

39. Just as José Colín's critiques of political economy in the 1950s could have been made by CANACINTRA as well. Indeed, in both cases, the critiques articulated by outspoken dissidents *were* made by the chamber, internally.

On the other hand, the campaign against the Chambers Law threatened to destroy the organization altogether. Among official business organizations, CANACINTRA had perhaps the most to lose from the removal of compulsory membership. Not only did its membership consist principally of small firms, which increased the difficulties of collective action and the importance of compulsory membership, but the chamber was extraordinarily dependent on membership dues for revenues.[40] CANACINTRA received approximately 90 percent of its budget from obligatory membership dues (Hoeckle 1993); and according to a CANACINTRA study, 60 percent of the chamber's members complained about paying their dues, calling such payments "an additional tax."[41] Chamber officials feared that the removal of compulsory membership could precipitate a 40–60 percent decline in membership. The combination of an extraordinarily high percentage of its revenue coming from membership dues, low participation rates, and a generalized sense of dissatisfaction with the chamber's performance made voluntary association a frightening prospect.

Caught in the crosswinds of institutional contestation, between a "modernizing" project from above and an "abolitionist" project from below, CANACINTRA fell back on its corporatist traditions. The chamber would have preferred a third path, to "formalize" corporatism by heightening the role of *official* organizations in government-business consultation (CANACINTRA 1992). Formalization was regarded as a way to square the circle, to protect CANACINTRA both from the marginalization produced by the project from above and from the hemorrhaging of membership and revenues implied by the project from below. To that end, CANACINTRA fleetingly joined forces with CONCAMIN in a project that would have extended compulsory membership to firms in the financial sector and stipulated, by statute, a consultative role for *official* organizations (CONCAMIN 1992). Yet the movement to formalize corporatism was short-lived, as the most powerful actors in CONCAMIN were committed to the modernizing project; and, in contrast to the abolitionist campaign, formalization found few allies in civil society or among political parties.[42]

---

40. The other official organization with a similar membership base was CONCANACO. Not surprisingly, the commercial confederation was among the most outspoken defenders of the Chambers Law.

41. *La Jornada,* 9 October 1992.

42. The dissidents charged that CONCAMIN and CANACINTRA's "formalization" proposals amounted to efforts to blackmail government authorities, "telling them that if they continue to grant the chambers and confederations compulsory membership, the government will be able to continue to count on their unconditional signature for everything it wants" (letter from Ignacio Muñoz Peredo to CONCAMIN, January 1993).

Lacking the strength to impose formalization, CANACINTRA ended up siding with the modernizationists against the abolitionists. Because CANACINTRA attached the highest priority to preserving compulsory membership, it became essential for the chamber to distinguish itself from those associations that wanted compulsory membership removed. It did not matter to chamber officials that ANIT's criticisms of the emerging system of state-business interaction were accurate, for what the dissidents proposed was even more threatening. It is also important to note the role of the CCE, which was not regulated by the Chambers Law but did not actively oppose compulsory membership. Ultimately, the CCE would not invest resources either to defend or to reform the Chambers Law; and it certainly would not endorse the campaign of the hypercritical anticorporatists. Thus, the CCE—an organization with an entirely different history, membership, and trajectory—became a convenient and temporary ally for CANACINTRA on the issue of the Chambers Law.

Defending Corporatism

CANACINTRA embarked on a vigorous campaign in defense of compulsory membership. Chamber officials lobbied President Salinas and joined the other official organizations in denouncing the Supreme Court's ruling on the Chambers Law. CANACINTRA criticized the Supreme Court ruling and defended the constitutionality of the law, maintaining that the constitution allows the state to impose limits on free association in order to satisfy public objectives and the general interest (CANACINTRA 1992; CONCAMIN 1992).

CANACINTRA also staked out a position in defense of corporatism as the most appropriate arrangement for securing small industry representation. In October 1992 the chamber presented President Salinas with a detailed, twenty-eight-page document that defended the Chambers Law as the key to its own ability to serve as representative of small industrialists.[43] According to CANACINTRA (1992), the structure of Mexican politics and the particular impediments to organization among small firms made compulsory membership essential. Far from depriving small industrialists of representation, CANACINTRA argued, compulsory membership and the Chambers Law provided firms with representation that they would otherwise not have. CANACINTRA maintained that the Chambers Law served the interests precisely

43. The study was written explicitly in response to the controversy over compulsory membership. At the same time the chamber submitted a similar document in defense of compulsory membership to the Chamber of Deputies.

of the small firms that "by themselves lack the capacity to present their needs to government authorities."[44] Rapid removal of compulsory membership would only further weaken the chamber and, subsequently, further reduce small industry representation.

CANACINTRA invested considerable resources in developing and disseminating its defense of corporatism. The basis of the chamber's argument was threefold: (1) small firms need organization, (2) compulsory membership is necessary for securing organization, and (3) corporatism is necessary for making sure that organizations represent small firms.

First, the chamber emphasized the importance of organization for representing small industry. Since the nexus of policy making remained the executive branch, rather than the legislature, where small firms might have more voice on account of their numerical weight, organizations were as essential as ever (CANACINTRA 1992, 16). Second, CANACINTRA emphasized the importance of corporatism for overcoming an inherent disinclination toward association. That is, CANACINTRA suggested that in the absence of compulsory membership, most business organizations would simply disappear, because Mexicans lacked the essential culture of association.[45] Finally, CANACINTRA argued that only organizations with compulsory membership could be sure to represent all the members, regardless of size. To quote:

> We are convinced that obligatory membership is wise and correct, since it forces the directors of the chamber to represent the interests of the entire sector, and to work with the members to establish a relationship that allows them to count on true representation to public authorities. This would be impossible in voluntary associations, which only represent the economically most powerful actors that form the association and—as experience teaches us—impose their own interests. It should be evident that the only way to have generalized representation is counting on the registration of everyone. (CANACINTRA 1992, 23–24)

44. *El Nacional*, 22 July 1992 (similar statements can be found in virtually every Mexico City newspaper on this date). See also the comments of CANACINTRA official Gilberto Ortíz in *La Jornada*, 9 October 1992.

45. In the United States, CANACINTRA argued, "citizens have greater conscience of participation in organizations; it is enough to point out that among the economically active population in the U.S., it is calculated that each individual participates in around seven associations, counting among others their participation in athletic, business, professional, civic, religious, neighborhood, and charity associations, a situation in which our country does not come anywhere near close to matching" (CANACINTRA 1992, 16–17).

CANACINTRA and Neoliberalism

It is in the context of these dual challenges to corporatism that we need to consider CANACINTRA's representative strategy in the early 1990s. The economic policy changes of this period posed even more fundamental challenges for small manufacturers than did those of the preceding period. The deepening of trade liberalization, in the context of an overvalued currency and tight monetary policy, led to a flood of imports. Although currency devaluations had partially muffled the effects of trade liberalization in the mid-1980s, in subsequent years small firms producing for the domestic market would feel the full brunt of import competition. Whereas imports accounted for 21.3 percent of total supply of manufactured goods in 1985, by 1991 this figure had grown to 35.4 percent (CEESP 1993).

The chamber's strategy for representing its members on economic policy, however, became wrapped up with and inseparable from its strategy for protecting the organization in the changing political environment. As much as the modernization of corporatism from above threatened and marginalized CANACINTRA, the abolitionist project from below severely limited CANACINTRA's alternatives. SECOFI had extended numerous organizational, financial, and legal concessions to help CANACINTRA fend off the challenge from ANIT, and the chamber was dependent on this organizational protection for its ability to stay intact. Moreover, the debate over the Chambers Law in the 1990s exacerbated this dependence. The state had delivered organizational protection to CANACINTRA principally through the corporatist framework, and the protracted debate over the Chambers Law raised the possibility that this framework, especially compulsory membership, could be removed. The controversy over corporatism, then, greatly increased CANACINTRA's dependence on the state.

The precarious organizational position reinforced the chamber's accommodationist strategy. This is not a case of small firms lacking information (Pastor and Wise 1994) or the small firms' organization simply withholding information from its members. CANACINTRA's leaders were informed and alarmed, but, as always, they chose to express their concerns through safe channels—to voice their opposition cautiously and to avoid alliances with other actors who shared their grievances. As always, the chamber expressed concern without mobilizing opposition. All decisions about how to respond to economic policy and policy making were made in the context of the fight over the Chambers Law. Indeed, throughout the NAFTA negotiations, and throughout the consolidation of the neoliberal model under Salinas more generally, the imminent threat of a revised Chambers Law hung over the heads of CANACINTRA's leadership, in its own words, "like the Sword of Damocles."

Conclusion

In the late 1980s and early 1990s, democratization unleashed a set of conflicts over political institutions, and these conflicts ultimately paralyzed CANACINTRA and further reduced its capacity to represent small industrialists. In this chapter I have discussed big firms' project to remake business corporatism from above and the project on the part of a coalition of small firms to abolish corporatism from below. Given the contrasting resources of the two sets of protagonists, there is little reason to expect that the anticorporatist coalition would have much success. That it did was in large part a result of democratization. The changed political environment increased opportunities for dissent, made parties available as new political sponsors, and made a judicial strategy more propitious than in the past.

Both the modernizing project from above and the abolitionist project from below were threatening for CANACINTRA. Tight collaboration between the state and horizontally—though not vertically—encompassing organizations left little space for participation in policy making. The chamber thus had every reason to oppose the remaking of state-business relations, and it even launched a fleeting—but unsuccessful—effort to formalize corporatism. As always, however, CANACINTRA's highest concern remained organizational preservation. The modernizing project was problematic, in that it severely reduced the chamber's access to the state, but the abolitionist project, entailing the end of compulsory membership, was, for CANACINTRA, much worse. It was a nuclear strike, and it was to be averted at any cost. Thus, CANACINTRA sought to protect the organization, and once again, organizational protection entailed suppression of small firms' interests in key issues of economic policy. CANACINTRA did not represent, because it could not represent.

The subordination of small industry in Mexico's peak business organizations combined with the hyperaccommodationist posture of CANACINTRA to produce a system of state-business relations that neglected small industry. Not surprisingly, with small industry lacking access to policy makers and the capacity for interest articulation, it received minimal attention from policy makers in the Salinas administration. No one fought for small industry credit, for example, and industrial integration was left to the market. Small firms were never the driving force behind economic policy, but in the 1990s, as Mexico became more democratic, small firms had less representation than ever before.

FIVE

Orphaned by Democracy

Small Industry Representation in Contemporary Mexico

The first year of the presidency of Ernesto Zedillo Ponce de León (1994–2000) was marked by deep economic crisis, following the collapse of the peso in December 1994. The crisis produced an outburst of social protest and activism, allegations of corruption and criminality involving prominent PRI officials, and continued violence and mobilization in the state of Chiapas. Zedillo, who emerged as the PRI candidate only after the March 1994 assassination of Salinas's chosen successor, responded to rising popular discontent with the acceleration of key political reforms.

Under Zedillo, critical institutions affecting both association-based and party-based channels of interest representation underwent significant reform. In 1995 the increasingly independent Supreme Court made its fifth ruling against compulsory membership, at last establishing a legal precedent that would signal the end of the 1941 Chambers Law. The Court's ruling triggered a renewed legislative conflict over the Chambers Law, and soon thereafter the law was replaced by new legislation that eliminated compulsory membership, the 1997 Law of Business Chambers and their Confederations (Arriola 1997).

The electoral arena underwent dramatic change in this period as well. Zedillo, over the objections of many in his party, agreed to a major electoral

I thank Tim Power for suggesting this title. This chapter draws heavily on material presented in Shadlen 2002.

reform in 1996. This reform, which marked the culmination of the slug-gish process of piecemeal liberalization that had begun in the 1980s, brought an end to the hegemonic party system and paved the way for the PRI to suf-fer unprecedented electoral setbacks (Klesner 1997b; Becerra, Salazar, and Woldenberg 1997). In the 1997 midterm elections, opposition parties gained control of the national legislature, defeating the PRI, and in 2000, the PAN's Vicente Fox won the presidency.

These major political changes created new challenges and opportunities. Organizations that had long depended on compulsory membership would have to adjust to the new environment, while other actors saw promise in the opening of new political space for mobilization. Likewise, the end of PRI domination of the Chamber of Deputies meant the legislative branch of gov-ernment would no longer be a simple rubber stamp for the president's pro-grams. Instead, and for the first time in modern Mexican history, the national legislature and opposition parties would have the potential to serve as mech-anisms of interest representation. To be sure, the PRI retained significant power in this period—most important, the presidency, which it would not lose until the 2000 elections. Yet Mexico's protracted process of democ-ratization indisputably crossed critical thresholds during the late 1990s: the realms where associations and civil society organizations (CSOs) operate fea-tured a remarkable degree of pluralism, and the electoral arena became sig-nificantly more competitive.

Paradoxically, democratization in the late 1990s did little to arrest the decline of small industry representation that had begun in the previous decade. To the contrary, and notwithstanding the removal of constraints on association—constraints that had reduced autonomy and raised barriers to dissent—and the emergence of increased competition among political parties, small industry's capacity to participate in politics continued to diminish in this period. The removal of obstacles to representation does not guarantee representation. Indeed, analysis of small industry representation via associations, CSOs, and political parties illustrates how small firms' dis-tinct political and economic characteristics make them poorly equipped to exploit the opportunities of democracy.

In the first section of this chapter I analyze the declining capacity of interest associations. The removal of compulsory membership—the princi-pal corporatist concession under the 1941 Chambers Law—would reveal small industry's collective action problems as never before. CANACINTRA was unable to adapt to the new environment, and its subsequent decline left small industry representation in the hands of Mexico's peak organizations, which were dominated by big business, or an unstable transnational alliance of weak and ineffectual small business associations.

In the second section, I examine the capacity of CSOs to fill the gap left by the decay of associations. I suggest that the basic difficulties small firms confront in establishing reliable mechanism of representation are manifest in the realm of civil society too. The analysis focuses on the advances in and pitfalls of ANIT's efforts to establish alliances with the wide array of social protest movements that proliferated in the wake of the 1994–95 economic crisis. Although participation in CSOs brought small business increased visibility, it also revealed a set of tensions that are not easily overcome. Not only are small firms peripheral actors in these broader organizations, but their interests conflict with the core of the movements, and increased participation threatens to reduce accountability to the firms they supposedly represent.

In the third section I examine the new opportunities for small industry representation produced by electoral democratization. To this point the analysis has been focused on the effects on representation of small firms' difficulties in overcoming the impediments to collective action. I consider in this chapter the effect of small firms' other core characteristic, limited electoral resources, by examining the role of political parties as mechanisms of representation. Opposition parties began the Fifty-seventh Legislature (1997–2000) with ambitious plans for policy development, and they convened extensive hearings with the goal of writing new legislation for small business. Yet the effort failed, definitively, as the initiative never even passed from the level of committee to be debated and acted upon by the full congress. Analysis of this failed project illustrates the unreliability of parties as representatives of small industry. As the case study reveals, the bill failed not simply on account of the natural give-and-take of legislative politics, but, rather, because none of the three parties took seriously its commitment to represent small business. Each party systematically subordinated the interests of small firms to the interests of other, more important, constituencies.

Associations Without the State

Although compulsory membership to chambers would not be officially terminated until January 1997, the establishment of legal precedence in 1995 made that aspect of the Chambers Law effectively unenforceable. Because individual plaintiffs could obtain injunctions without going through long court

battles, firms stopped paying membership dues and SECOFI stopped sanctioning violators. The days of compulsory membership to chambers were over.

The demise of compulsory membership, in the context of broader economic and political changes, provoked a reevaluation of CANACINTRA's relationship with its members. The chamber's strategy to recruit and retain
members had traditionally been oriented more toward the state than toward
the firms that composed the membership. The reasons for this orientation
derived from the nature of the post–World War II developmentalist policy-
making regime and the corporatist institutions. Since CANACINTRA had access
to the state agencies that made crucial economic policy and regulatory decisions such as in the issuing of import licenses, for example, small firms lacking individual clout depended on the chamber to act as their agent. And
because the Chambers Law made membership compulsory, the relationship
between the chamber and its members was asymmetrical: small firms needed
CANACINTRA more than the chamber depended on the membership.

Each of these conditions underwent significant change in the 1990s. The
neoliberal model implied a fundamental transformation of corporatism. The
replacement of import licenses with tariffs, for example, clearly deprived
CANACINTRA of an important concession that it had been able to deliver to
members. Also, the new pattern of state-business consultation that emerged
in the late 1980s and 1990s, featuring close collaboration between policy
makers and peak organizations that were controlled by Mexico's largest firms,
meant that CANACINTRA had less access to the state and was less able to
deliver a service of providing voice.[1] Finally, the end of compulsory membership, first de facto and then de jure, meant that CANACINTRA would have
to attract members on a voluntary basis. The refusal of the Zedillo administration to uphold compulsory membership, either judicially via the Supreme
Court or administratively by sanctioning firms that violated the Chambers
Law, meant that the chamber was no longer assured of members and
membership dues. By the mid-1990s, then, the economic model and the
transformation of corporatism, including the elimination of compulsory
membership, made it more difficult for CANACINTRA to attract small firms
while at the same time made it imperative to do so.

Preparing for Voluntary Association

The leaders of CANACINTRA attempted to reform the chamber. In addition
to the unsuccessful external strategy to formalize corporatism and forestall

---

1. See the discussion in Chapter 4.

reform of the Chambers Law, examined in the previous chapter, CANACIN-
TRA had an *internal* strategy to adapt to the new political economic environment. A confidential "Immediate Action Program," prepared at the highest levels of the organization, served as a guiding document for organizational
reform in the mid-1990s.[2]

The cornerstone of CANACINTRA's reform program entailed the provision
of more services, and particularly services for which the chamber could charge
fees.[3] By providing a wider array of services to small firms, CANACINTRA
hoped to make membership so desirable that firms would choose to join on
a voluntary basis. And by charging for such services, the chamber aimed to
generate an additional source of revenue. Diversified revenues might
make the organization less dependent on the state, for the simple reason that
the existence of alternative sources of revenue reduce vulnerability to the
removal of state support.[4]

CANACINTRA thus embarked on an ambitious program to increase the
quality and variety of services that it provided. The chamber expanded its
training courses, for example, and it worked with state agencies to open a
special office where firms could take care of regulatory paperwork and taxes
in a single visit (*ventanilla única*).[5] The chamber put additional resources
toward facilitating members' access to credit, developing a Center for Financial Support to Industry (CAFI), which rented space within CANACINTRA to
a pair of commercial banks. CANACINTRA also began to develop a satellite-
based videoconferencing system (Satelitel) that would link the chamber's
delegations throughout the country. In addition to facilitating communication, the new system could be used for interactive training seminars—not
only by the chamber but also by large firms working with their suppliers.
CAFI and Satelitel are good examples of services that were designed to accom-
plish each of the chamber's goals set out in the Immediate Action Program:

2. This document, prepared in the final months of the presidency of Vicente Gutiérrez Camposeco
(1992–94), is included in the bibliography as CANACINTRA 1994.

3. The chamber also sought to gain additional revenue by selling more advertising in CANACIN-
TRA publications and by renting excess office space.

4. Thus, the Immediate Action Program emphasized the diversification of resources through the
provision of chargeable services as an essential measure to "diminish the vulnerability of CANACIN-
TRA to a possible change in the [Chambers] Law" (CANACINTRA 1994, 3). At another point, the program stressed the need "to specialize in providing chargeable services in order to reduce the financial
vulnerability that comes from the concentration of income on membership dues" (CANACINTRA
1994, 32, point 12).

5. It should be noted that while not all these services were new, even the preexisting programs
such as the *ventanilla única* were expanded significantly and treated with a new sense of urgency as the
loss of compulsory membership became imminent.

they would make members more appreciative of the organization by responding to important concerns, credit in the case of CAFI and training in the case
of Satelitel; and they would diversify revenues and reduce dependence on
membership dues, since CANACINTRA would receive rent from the banks and
commissions from financial intermediation facilitated by CAFI, and it would
charge for use of Satelitel.[6]

Crisis, Decay, and Diminished Representation

At the same time that the end of compulsory membership made the need
to find new revenue sources more essential than ever, however, the chamber
found itself less capable of responding to the challenge. The deep economic
crisis that followed the 1994 devaluation of the peso led to widespread bank-
ruptcies. Many of CANACINTRA's members ceased to exist, and many of those
that did not close their doors conserved scarce resources by suspending their
chamber membership. In addition, CANACINTRA's tepid response to the rapidly changing economic environment during the late 1980s and early 1990s
had led to widespread discontent on the part of the membership; and the
economic crisis only aggravated the damage already done to the chamber's
legitimacy among small manufacturers. The combined result of the crisis
and the continuing loss of stature was that fewer firms voluntarily paid their
membership dues.

When compulsory membership was officially terminated at the end of
1996, CANACINTRA's membership plummeted. Rather than gaining or even
retaining members, the chamber underwent massive hemorrhaging. After
decades of continued membership growth, the chamber entered into a rapid
and precipitous tailspin. From nearly ninety thousand firms in the late 1980s,
CANACINTRA's membership shrunk to approximately fifteen thousand by
1997. Figure 7 illustrates the dramatic decline. While membership rebounded
in 1999–2000 in the context of economic recovery, it remained at a lower
level than in the 1960s. The decline is particularly sharp when membership
is measured as a percentage of all manufacturing firms. Whereas CANAC-
INTRA's membership accounted for 10 to 15 percent of all manufacturing
firms in the mid-1950s and, following the 1960 reform of the Chambers

---

6. This is the tip of the iceberg. Other innovations included a program to allow members to apply
a portion of their membership dues toward up to 30 percent of the cost of a variety of services. More
interesting investments included the purchase from SECOFI of the National Industrial Development Lab-
oratories (LANFI) and coinvestment with SECOFI in the Technological Transfer Unit (UTT).

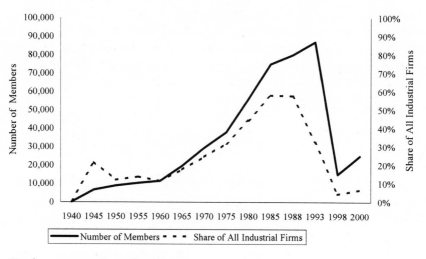

Fig. 6   CANACINTRA's membership
Source: CANACINTRA's 1961a; Garza 1993.

Law, rose to nearly 60 percent of all firms by the 1980s, by the end of the 1990s fewer than 5 percent of all manufacturing firms belonged to the chamber, the lowest share since the 1940s.

The loss of so many dues-paying members left CANACINTRA in serious financial difficulties, precisely the sort of revenue crisis that the leadership had sought to avert with the Immediate Action Program. In fact, the decline in membership—as dramatic as it is—greatly understates the gravity of the problem. It was not simply that small firms would no longer join the chamber; the end of compulsory membership meant that *large* firms would no longer be compelled join either. It is important to recall that while CANACINTRA historically has been the representative of small industry, officially it included many large firms. The dominant pattern of postwar association analyzed in Chapter 2 featured large firms leading efforts to create sector-specific organizations separate from CANACINTRA. What we saw was that when groups of industrialists sought to form their own sector-specific chambers, CANACINTRA routinely lobbied state officials to block authorization. At times CANACINTRA's calls were unheeded, and new chambers were formed, taking away significant numbers of firms. The more dominant pattern after the 1960 revision to the Chambers Law, however, was that rather than creating new chambers, large firms formed their own voluntary trade associations.

To understand the effect on CANACINTRA of this pattern of association, and the effect of the subsequent change, three critical points need to be underscored. First, the large firms that created their own associations essentially abandoned CANACINTRA, leaving the chamber to smaller firms that typically did not join these voluntary associations. Second, officially these firms had to remain as dues-paying members to CANACINTRA (membership to voluntary associations could only be complementary to, not in lieu of, membership to chambers). Third, CANACINTRA's progressive dues schedule meant that these larger firms provided a significant share of the chamber's revenues. The end of compulsory membership altered this pattern. Because large firms with representation outside CANACINTRA—the ones that had essentially financed and abandoned the chamber—no longer had the legal obligation to join, CANACINTRA could no longer count on this source of revenue.

Finally, the financial crisis was worsened by the fact that the strategy to invest in services had not just failed to create new sources of revenue, but had backfired. Many of the projects, such as Satelitel, entailed large investments, and to finance these investments the chamber had borrowed significantly. Yet the recession reduced the demand for the services. Thus, in the wake of the 1995 crisis, investment in services turned out to be quite costly: participation diminished at the same time as the chamber's debt-servicing obligations ballooned. In fact, CANACINTRA had taken out large loans against its Mexico City office building, and in the wake of the crisis the chamber, like many businesses and families, risked losing its "home" to its creditors (Rangel Flores and Fuentes Vivar 1999).

To stave off its creditors, CANACINTRA downsized. It cut back on the services it provided, reduced its staff and payroll, and moved into a smaller part of its building to make more office space available on a rental basis. Indeed, part of the ground floor, once the center for service provision, was rented as a retail outlet for Telmex, Mexico's leading telecommunications firm, while the remaining portion and mezzanine were converted into a branch of Sanborns, a department store and restaurant chain.[7]

Ultimately, CANACINTRA failed to make the transition from being a business association built for developmentalism to an association capable of thriving under the neoliberal model, a difficult transition that was further

7. Telmex and Sanborns are both owned by Grupo Carso, the economic conglomerate controlled by Carlos Slim, Mexico's wealthiest businessman. The irony of Carlos Slim's now serving as the primary source of revenue for CANACINTRA is matched only by the irony of CANACINTRA's regularly renting advertising space on the roof and sides of its building to some of the same foreign firms whose prominence in Mexico the chamber had strongly criticized in the recent past.

complicated by the removal of compulsory membership and economic crisis. The chamber's efforts to construct a new and financially sound relationship with the membership were unsuccessful. It continued losing members and its financial situation worsened considerably.[8] The financial crunch created a vicious circle: the chamber lacked members and resources, and without a membership base it lacked resources to invest in services that could increase membership in a time of voluntary affiliation.

Importantly, the chamber's principal problem by the late 1990s was no longer that dependence on the state and concern with organizational preservation led to the subordination of members' members' concerns—the problems associated with corporatism. Rather, with the removal of compulsory membership the problem was that CANACINTRA, quite simply, became irrelevant. It would not disappear, but it was left lingering in a state of decay, with diminished representative capacity and minimal access to the state.

CANACINTRA's declining role in Mexican politics meant that a bigger share of the burden for representing small industry fell on the shoulders of the Confederation of Industrial Chambers (CONCAMIN), of which CANACINTRA is a member.[9] While CONCAMIN was historically dominated by large Mexican and transnational manufacturing firms, it took a greater interest in small industry in the 1990s. It held a series of forums on small industry, and as we shall see, it participated actively in a project to write legislation for small industry development. Yet CONCAMIN was also marginalized by the new pattern of state-business consultation, which gave a prominent role to peak organizations such as the CCE. Thus, even as CONCAMIN became more responsive to the concerns of small industry, it had scarcely more capacity than CANACINTRA to represent this segment of capital.

As discussed in the previous chapter, small industrialists were marginalized from the new pattern of state-business interaction, which was dominated by organizations such as the CCE and COECE. Of course, virtually all business organizations, including those dominated by big business, such as the CCE, claim to represent small firms. The question, however, is not whether peak organizations call for helping small firms, which they invariably do, but the extent to which they will defend the interests of small industry when

8. One observer, noting CANACINTRA's dwindling membership and deepening financial crisis, remarked that the chamber was on the verge of "extinction" (José R. Martínez Bolio, "Pequeña empresa," *Excelsior*, 10 March 2000).

9. CONCAMIN also suffered from the loss of compulsory membership, but it was better able to withstand the storm because it had always depended to a greater degree on the noncompulsory contributions of voluntary associations.

these interests enter into conflict with the interests of larger firms. This distinction, between simply making statements on behalf of a social actor and actively promoting its interests over the interests of others, is of crucial importance in examining Mexico's new peak and "encompassing" organizations. For it is at moments of conflicting interest that having an advocate becomes most crucial and that the lack of representation becomes most clear.

The fundamental issue of how the CCE reconciles conflicting interests is evident in the organization's approach to industrial policy. Industrial integration may be driven by the autonomous investment decisions of leading firms, but postwar history has also demonstrated the important role the state can play in encouraging linkage between large and small firms (Amsden 2001; Wade 1990). Some regulations will be resisted by larger firms that would prefer lower-cost or higher-quality sources of supply that may be available in foreign markets. The real crux of representation, then, comes down to the capacity and willingness of an organization to fight for promotional policies that specifically help small firms even if doing so places constraints and short-term costs on bigger firms. Such was the role that CANACINTRA played for decades, but neither the chamber nor CONCAMIN are able to fight these battles in the new political-economic environment. Peak organizations dominated by Mexico's largest firms serve as an unreliable substitute.

Furthermore, even when the interests of small and large firms are entirely compatible—when the challenge is not conflict reconciliation but rather interest coordination—peak organizations dominated by large firms provide unreliable representation. As discussed in Chapter 1, the concerns of smaller firms tend to be different from those of larger firms. To be sure, large firms may not be threatened by the sorts of demands that are made by small firms. To the contrary, large firms would stand to benefit from small firms—which are potential suppliers—having better access to credit and technology. Such improved access could enable these small firms to be more productive and better equipped to integrate into broader chains of production. But lobbying has costs; and for organizations controlled and dominated by large firms, the costs of lobbying on behalf of small firms has to be weighed against the costs of operating without a dynamic sector of small firms. Individual firms may look out for their own suppliers and clients, but at an organizational level these incentive are less salient. The result is that Mexico's peak organizations consistently express support for small firms, but such firms remain a low priority. In sum, the interests of smaller firms remain subordinated in Mexico's new network of business associations.

A Transnational Response to National Weakness

In response to CANACINTRA's decay and the subordination of small firms' interests within Mexico's peak organizations, a number of associations have emerged to fill the gap. One such group is ANIT. As we have seen, ANIT's principal problems throughout the late 1980s and early 1990s were lack of access to state officials and to key state concessions that were available under the corporatist framework. Thus the peripheral association was unable to sustain its challenge to CANACINTRA and remained marginalized from policy making.

ANIT's fortunes did not change with the transformation of corporatism. To the contrary, ANIT suffered from even more intense collective action problems than did CANACINTRA, as it lacked the institutional foundation of the latter organization. ANIT, for example, could not count on the benefits of inertia, where some firms continued to associate simply because they always had. The removal of compulsory membership evened the playing field, so to speak, but at a low level.

To compensate for this weakness and isolation, in the late 1990s ANIT joined forces with similarly frustrated and dissenting small business groups throughout Latin America. ANIT led Mexico's delegation to the initial meeting of the Latin American Business Forum in Porto Alegre, Brazil. The 1997 meeting, convened by the Brazilian Association of Business for Citizenship (CIVES), an activist group of industrialists based in São Paulo, was also attended by Argentina's Assembly of Small and Medium Business (APYME). The 1997 meeting was followed by an October 1998 meeting convoked by ANIT in Mexico City, and another in Managua, Nicaragua, in February 2000.

The product of this transnational collaboration, the Latin American Association of Micro, Small, and Medium Firms (ALAMPYME), amounts to a coordinated attack on what is regarded as a process of economic integration that victimizes small firms throughout the region. The declarations of each meeting emphasize the dire effects of "market fundamentalism" and advocate replacing the dominant neoliberal model with one that prioritizes poverty reduction, a "just" distribution of income, and economic development based on stimulation of the domestic market. Not surprisingly, ALAMPYME's calls for economic reactivation are based on industrial integration and extensive support of small industry.

The transnational route to interest articulation is more interesting for the size-based grievances it reflects than for representative capacity per se. To be sure, ALAMPYME provides small firms a voice in periodic and sporadic moments of transnational mobilization against the course of economic policy in Latin

America.[10] Yet there is little ongoing communication between the three organizations, particularly between the two South American members and ANIT. Each member acts in the name of the alliance, but typically without consulting the other delegates. Although the members convene international meetings and issue statements of solidarity, the real work that remains to be done is at home. In the case of ANIT, acting in the name of ALAMPYME gives it a fresh ring, but there is very little "Latin America" in ALAMPYME in Mexico. It is another name for the same confederation of dissident Mexican associations, led by ANIT, that have attempted to establish new representative channels for small business since the 1980s. Representation, ultimately, remains a local affair. And as participants in a local affair, whether it is ANIT or ALAMPYME, these associations continue to operate with very little access to policy makers and other channels of authority. They have not been able to compensate for the decay of the network of official business organizations.

Searching for Allies: Small Industry and Civil Society

That the late 1990s witnessed declining representation for small industry was the result not only of the diminished capacity of business associations, but also of the inability of civil society organizations (CSOs) to fill the gap. In this section I analyze the crisis of small industry representation that became manifest in the realm of movements and CSOs.

The collapse of the peso in January 1994 and the government's response to the ensuing economic crisis generated widespread protest and opposition throughout Mexico.[11] Furthering the discontent was the perception that the Zedillo government's response—which included enacting spending reductions, increasing the national sales tax, and accelerating privatization and liberalization schedules beyond Mexico's international commitments— appeared to be imposed as conditions of U.S. and International Monetary Fund assistance. The result was the emergence of a broader array of protest against the neoliberal model, some new and some building on long-standing trajectories of social mobilization.[12]

10. Indeed, CIVES called the initial meeting explicitly as a parallel to the "São Paulo Forum," and ALAMPYME constituted itself as the "business workshop" of the regional conference.

11. According to a 1996 survey conducted by the newspaper *Reforma* (15 January), 59 percent of those interviewed said NAFTA had brought no benefits whatsoever in its two years of existence.

12. See Foweraker and Craig 1990; Cook 1996; Williams 1996, 2001; and Bruhn 1997a for analysis of social movements produced by protracted economic crisis.

With regard to small industry, the economic crisis appeared to vin-
dicate many of the criticisms that ANIT (and others) had been making
of economic policy and economic policy making since the 1980s. And
the Zedillo government's response to the crisis only served to sharpen
their criticisms. In March 1995, for example, ANIT president Raymundo
Artís (1993–95) denounced the government's stabilization package and
called for the resignations of the top economic policy makers, including the secretary of finance, the secretary of trade, and the director of the
Bank of Mexico.[13]

Economic crisis and the emergence of CSOs also presented ANIT with
opportunities to establish new sets of alliances and integrate into broader
networks of social protest. Democratization, as we have seen, presents actors
with new alliance alternatives and opportunities for this sort of coalition-
building. In the case of CANACINTRA, of course, first the commitment to a
strategy of accommodation and later the chamber's intensified dependence
on the state had foreclosed this route. Because ANIT, in contrast, operated
with significantly more autonomy from the state, it could, in the words of
one of the organization's key leaders, embark on an intense outreach program to "make friends with half the world" and establish links with various sources of opposition in Mexican politics.[14]

Thus, in addition to establishing transnational alliances, ANIT responded
to the crisis of the 1990s by participating in broad networks of economic
and political protest within Mexico. Throughout the late 1990s, ANIT
worked with a variety of organizations that challenged the government's
management of the economy. These included debtors' organizations, such
as El Barzón, and broader antineoliberal organizations, such as the Mexican Free Trade Action Network (RMALC).[15] Throughout the 1990s,
ANIT joined these sorts of organizations in a variety of activities, including mobilizations in defense of debtors' rights, campaigns in protest against
the neoliberal model (including the negotiation of a trade agreement with
the European Union), and publications to disseminate economic alternatives.[16] Small firms also became actively involved with broader and more

13. *La Jornada,* 31 March 1995.

14. Interview with ANIT president Adán Rivera (1997–2001), Mexico City, 23 June 1997. See
Shadlen 2000 for an explicit contrast between the political strategies of CANACINTRA and ANIT.

15. For analysis of the debtors' movement, see Williams 2001; and Senzek 1997. For analysis of
RMALC (and the anti-NAFTA social mobilization more generally), see Arroyo and Monroy 1996; and C.
A. Heredia 1994.

16. See Arroyo and Monroy 1996; RMALC 1997; and CASA 1998.

transformative "citizenship" movements such as Alianza Cívica, Causa Ciudadana and Movimiento Ciudadano para la Democracia.

Representation and CSO Participation

In Chapter 1, I examined a set of underlying tensions that strain the relationship between small industry and CSOs. In general, the common interests in increased consumer purchasing power and expansion of the domestic market must be balanced against sharply different perspectives regarding state regulations. As a result, alliances between small industrialists and popular movements have historically been short-lived and tenuous, flourishing during times of economic crisis (when the urgency and immediacy of the situation overshadows the differences) and deteriorating as crisis subsides.[17]

To the extent that these underlying tensions are managed, however, serious problems continue to exist regarding the representation of small industry. The reason for this is that CSOs, in general, are not equipped to provide the sort of representation needed by small industry. To be sure, the transformative projects of many CSOs could facilitate improved representation for small industrialists, especially if such projects were to redress power asymmetries within the private sector and improve the political institutions that affect small firms' capacity to organize and mobilize. But short of societal transformation, and regardless of the prevailing political-economic environment, small industrialists need a representative to advocate on their behalf, even if at the margins of policy. Under either developmentalism or neoliberalism, both of which encourage industrial giantism via the consolidation of large-scale conglomerates, small firms need an agent to do their bidding with the state. This is precisely the representation that CANACINTRA supplied throughout most of the postwar era—and that it lost the capacity to provide in the 1990s.

In Mexico, CSOs have neither the structure nor the position within the national political economy to provide this sort of representation for small firms. Key concerns of small manufacturers, such as industrial integration and improved access to credit, are not featured prominently on the CSOs' agendas. Nor are the CSOs consulted by politicians and state officials on issues of public policy that affect small firms. Participation in CSOs brought Mexican small industry new allies and increased the sector's public visibility. That much is undeniable. Yet the degree to which this avenue is fruitful for securing continuous, reliable representation is questionable.

---

17. O'Donnell's (1978) discussion of postwar Argentina captures this pattern wonderfully.

Not only do CSOs have questionable capacity for representing small industry, but small business organizations' participation in broader transformative movements risks further weakening of their own representative capacity. Although CSOs present small firms with opportunities to obtain visibility and potentially regain voice, the price of visibility and voice is loss of control over the content of the message. Associations such as ANIT are peripheral members of CSOs in Mexico, and few key day-to-day concerns of small business are important to most CSOs. ANIT is a resource for RMALC and Alianza Cívica, for example, but it appears to have little influence within these organizations. Rather than the interests of small firms being subordinated to those of larger firms, then, as is the case within Mexico's powerful peak business organizations, within CSOs the interests of small industry are subordinated to other movements and members of civil society. Thus, small firms' fundamental difficulties in securing durable representation—difficulties that have been examined throughout this book in the realm of business associations—are also present in the domain of civil society.

Of course, there is no a priori reason why groups such as ANIT cannot pursue multiple tracks—seek to deepen democracy with CSOs while also representing small firms at the margins. Yet in Mexico this pattern of activism has weakened the already scarce representative capacity of associations. The simple reason for this is that as associations dedicate more resources to broader transformative projects, they risk losing touch with their own core members. ANIT, for example, despite more than fifteen years of sustained activism, lacks an organizational structure to facilitate communication with members and to aggregate interests within the organization. The association is not any more in touch with small firms' interests and needs than CANACINTRA is or was. Indeed, there is little evidence, from surveys or firm-level interviews, that many industrialists are familiar with ANIT. Owners and managers complain about the lack of representation they receive from their chambers, but few appear to recognize that another association has attempted to represent them. For all ANIT's efforts—alone, with similar groups in Latin America, and with its allies in Mexican civil society—it has not been able to fill the gap created by CANACINTRA's decay. Analysis of CSOs and small industry in Mexico lends at least partial support to Hagopian's (1998) concern that movements, while capable of drawing societal attention to important issues, have doubtful capacity to represent in lieu of interest associations and political parties.

Legislating Industrial Policy:
Parties and the Representation of Small Industry

At the end of the 1990s, political parties and the national legislature became potentially valuable for representation. National midterm elections in 1997 gave a coalition of opposition parties a majority of seats in the Chamber of Deputies, the lower house of Mexico's congress. The PRI, though still the largest single party, no longer had a majority in the lower house. With congressional control stripped from the long-dominant PRI, the legislature would no longer serve as the executive's rubber stamp. Parties in the Fifty-seventh Legislature had unprecedented capacity to bargain on behalf of constituents and legislate.

In this section I will analyze a failed effort on the part of political parties to design new legislation for small firm development. The proposed initiative was a project of the Commission for Industrial Development, which was created in 1997 with ambitious goals of legislative action. The commission immediately concerned itself with the plight of small firms. There was an announcement at the founding meeting of the commission, for example, of the creation of a Subcommittee on Micro, Small, and Medium Firms, which called for the legislature to develop a promotional strategy targeted directly and explicitly at smaller firms.[18] The text of the subcommittee's Proposed Working Program emphasized that promotional instruments for small firms "must be differentiated from any industrial policy applicable to big firms. The supports and facilities made available for small firms cannot be the same as those made available for big firms, for their circumstances, deficiencies, needs, and priorities are totally different."[19] Notwithstanding these lofty goals, the end product of the commission's work was an extraordinarily weak initiative that could not even muster enough support (or interest) to be presented to the full chamber for debate and vote.

That many of the proposals the commission would hear were watered down and that the Fifty-seventh Legislature failed to produce new legislation do not necessarily mean that small firms lacked representation. After all, legislative politics in democracies are full of compromise and trade-offs. As discussed in Chapter 1, being represented does not guarantee getting what you want. What this case study, reveals, however, is that none of the

18. "Acta de Instalación," *Gaceta Parlamentaria,* 9 October 1997.
19. "Propuesta de Programa de Trabajo," 4.

parties took seriously its role of representing small industry. Neither the PAN, the PRI, nor the PRD objected to helping small firms, of course. To the contrary, deputies from all parties professed concern. But they did so when it was safe, when doing so would not step on others' toes. When push came to shove, however, each of Mexico's three principal political parties systematically subordinated the interests of small firms to the interests of other—more important—constituencies and to broader party strategies. In this instance, the "proof" of small industry lacking representation is not in the result, but rather in the process.[20]

Debating Small Industry Support

Over the course of nearly three years of hearings, the commission heard numerous diagnoses of the difficult challenges faced by small firms along with proposals for assisting such firms (Comisión de Patrimonio y Fomento Industrial 1998a, 1999). Participants at the forums pointed to persistent deficiencies in Mexico's industrial sector, notwithstanding the growth of exports and the general economic recovery that had begun in 1997. Although Mexico's largest firms had adjusted to international competition since the late 1980s, small firms continued to lack the internal resources and state support needed to adjust and compete, with the result being increased import intensity, the widespread bankruptcy of small firms, the disruption of productive chains, and, ultimately, a process of industrial polarization.[21]

Numerous participants used the forums to urge legislators to take the opportunity to supplement the government's "horizontal-functional" industrial policies with more activist and promotional instruments to help small firms integrate into productive chains. Briefly, horizontal-functional policies treat all sectors equally. Rather then promoting sectors, or even clusters of firms within a sector, the state dedicates itself to correcting for market failures owed to information gaps, to improving communication, and to building trust among firms. Thus, for example, government agencies provide market analysis and sponsor trade fairs that promise to establish

20. Because the proposed bill analyzed in this section was never debated in the full legislature, and because no law was passed, little documentation exists in the official records of the Chamber of Deputies and there was only scant press coverage. The analysis is based on the commission records that have been released (Comisión de Patrimonio y Fomento Industrial 1998a, 1998b, 1999), internal communication within the legislature, and extensive interviewing of the actors involved.

21. For detailed examinations of the effects of liberalization on Mexico's industrial structure, see Dussel Peters 1997, 2000. Scholars who explicitly focus on small firms include Dussel Peters (2001); de María y Campos (2002); Haar, Leroy-Beltrán, and Beltrán (2003); and C. Garrido (2002).

contact between potential suppliers and customers. Horizontal-functional policies also entail the provision of training in business administration (e.g., bookkeeping, payroll, and inventory management), and helping small firms prepare applications for credit.[22]

To be sure, many small firms do need precisely this sort of support. Yet many analysts suggest that the horizontal-functional approach is not sufficient and needs to be combined with direct promotion.[23] Such promotion can consist of "selective industrial policies," common during the developmentalist era; and promotion can consist of less distortionary and more market-conforming "demand-driven" programs of concentrating government procurement. Legislators in Mexico were not being advised to abandon the horizontal-functional approach, but rather to supplement it.[24]

Some of the most detailed proposals for renovating Mexico's industrial policy along these lines came from organizations such as CANACINTRA and CONCAMIN. Since the early 1990s, CONCAMIN had called for more activist industrial policy (see CONCAMIN 1991b); and in 1996 it began to collaborate with CANACINTRA and prominent Mexican academic economists in advocating explicit instruments to support smaller local firms and promote industrial integration. These instruments would include subsidized credit, fiscal incentives for the creation of interfirm consortia and to encourage small firms to adapt new technologies and equipment, set-asides in government purchasing, and investment in industrial parks and infrastructure.[25] The centerpiece of the proposal was the creation of a Small Business Institute. The institute, modeled after the Small Business Administration in the United States, was envisioned as an autonomous agency responsible for coordinating and promoting all governmental action in the area of small firm development, in addition to channeling resources directly to such firms.

22. For analysis of such policies in Mexico, see Mendez Martínez 1996; Valdés Gaxiola 1994; Ruíz Duran 1993; and Máttar Márquez 1991.

23. The literature on small enterprise development is enormous and continues to grow. Tendler (1997, 108–15) provides a concise overview of the debate regarding different approaches to small firm development, including useful references. See also Sengenberger, Loveman, and Piore 1991; Humphrey and Schmitz 1995; Ruíz Durán 1994; and Muñoz 1996a.

24. Wade's (1990) seminal analysis of postwar industrialization in East Asia provides an excellent description of the relationship between horizontal-functional and activist approaches. Although *Governing the Market* is best known, rightly, for its emphasis on the role of an active state in channeling resources into new sectors and thus reshaping a country's industrial profile, Wade is careful to show the synergy between these two approaches to industrial policy. See also Lall 1996.

25. See the presentations of CONCAMIN and CANACINTRA in Comisión de Patrimonio y Fomento Industrial (1999, 21–49).

It is worth stressing how broader changes in Mexican political economy affected CANACINTRA and CONCAMIN's representative strategies. Although the chamber and confederation historically directed their energies toward the executive branch, the new pattern of state-business consultation discussed in Chapter 4, which featured state officials collaborating closely with big-business-dominated peak organizations such as COECE, CCE, and CMHN, meant that these organizations lacked reliable access to the president and key members of the economic cabinet. The 1997 elections, which created a congress that for the first time might serve as a policy-making arena, and which included a commission that appeared prepared to legislate industrial policy, then, presented a new opportunity for interest articulation, an opportunity that the associations were keen to exploit in light of the end of compulsory membership and the transformation of corporatism.

Despite the extensive consultation and the proposals presented, the final draft of the initiative that the commission considered at the end of the 1997–2000 legislative session was quite modest. It ultimately amounted to a legislative codification of the status quo, placing significantly greater emphasis on improving the implementation and administration of existing horizontal-functional policies than on designing and developing new, supplementary policy instruments. Although the revised initiative still called for the creation of a Small Business Institute, it assigned the agency a much less prominent role. Nor did the initiative constitute *industrial* policy, as it was designed to help all small firms, regardless of activity.[26] To understand how a commission that, at the outset of the legislative session, appeared committed to using its new powers to assist small firms would end up producing such a weak initiative, and why not even this weak initiative would leave the commission and be debated by the full Chamber, it is important to examine the strategies of Mexico's three main parties.

Party Strategies and Small Industry

A critically important role in the fate of the legislation was played by the National Action Party (PAN), which held the presidency and one of the three secretariats on the commission. The PAN rejected contentions that a new development approach was necessary. As a result, the commission turned out to be infertile territory for the development of activist policies.

26. This change was reflected in the title—whereas participants in the forums and consultations contemplated a law for the development of small industry, the proposed initiative was titled the "Law for Development of Small Firms."

Underlying the PAN's antipathy toward industrial policy was the nature of the party's ties to business. Since the early 1980s, the active participation of business leaders, particularly from the north of Mexico, had brought the PAN substantial financial resources and contributed to the professionalization of the party (Arriola 1994; Mizrahi 1994; Chand 2001). Importantly, the new leadership came largely from organizations such as the Confederation of Chambers of Commerce (CONCANACO) and its local chambers of commerce, and the multisectoral Mexican Employers' Confederation (COPARMEX).[27] These organizations opposed channeling public resources toward the *industrial* sector, and their representatives insisted throughout the negotiations that the law be about small *business* rather than industry.[28]

Under the influence of these segments of business, the PAN's leadership maintained that the government's existing programs simply lacked coordination and were administered in a dispersed and wasteful fashion throughout various state agencies. Opposition to channeling public resources for industrial policy meant that the more expensive policies advocated in the commission's hearings, such as subsidized credit and government investments in industrial parks and infrastructure, were rejected. Instead, the party simply sought to streamline the operation of existing programs. With better coordination through an agency such as the Small Business Institute, commission president Juan Bueno Torio argued, the government's existing programs could be made more effective.[29]

The PAN's position on industrial policy illustrates the problematic relationship of small firms with political parties. Small industrialists lack sufficient resources to play an important role within the PAN. As a result, they were subordinated to other business constituents and their calls for activist industrial policies were generally rebuffed.

In addition to its being viewed as reflecting the interests of a particular business constituency, the PAN's position should be understood in the context of the party's negotiating strategy. Although the legislation could pass in the commission and the full Chamber of Deputies without the PRI's support, the PRI's majority position in the Senate meant that its participation would

27. Recall that the Chambers Law stipulated that commercial chambers be regional, rather then sectoral (as was the case with industrial chambers). The chambers of commerce in CONCANACO are state- and city-based. COPARMEX, which operates outside the Chambers Law, also has a regional structure, based on local Employers' Centers (Centros Patronales).

28. Interview with Ing. Bernardo Ardavín, ex-president of COPARMEX, 11 June 2001. See also Comisión de Patrimonio y Fomento Industrial (1998a, 69–72).

29. *El Financiero,* 16 August 1999. Interview, 5 June 2001, Mexico City.

be necessary. To gain the PRI's support, however, the bill would first have to obtain the support of the executive, to which the legislators remained subordinate. And the executive was overtly skeptical of the entire project, concerned that the introduction of new policy instruments would compromise Mexico's commitments under NAFTA and the trade agreement being negotiated with the European Union. Officials from the Trade Secretariat (SECOFI) subsequently rejected the proposals for activist industrial policies, consistently reiterating their faith in the current programs.[30] Negotiating with the executive thus contributed to the initiative being markedly weak in comparison to the sorts of policies entertained in the commission's hearings.

Although the watered-down initiative was less offensive to SECOFI, the PAN was nevertheless unable to gain the support of PRI deputies. In the midst of the 2000 elections, party officials were reluctant to support a project that had become closely identified with Bueno Torio and the PAN. The PRI's presidential candidate, Francisco Labastida Ochoa, had his own proposal, one that was similar in most dimensions with the initiative that Bueno Torio wrote in consultation with SECOFI.[31] As one PRI deputy on the commission explained, the problem was not that they did not like the initiative per se, but that it was not *their* initiative.[32]

Nor did commission president Bueno Torio obtain the support of the Party of the Democratic Revolution (PRD), the other major opposition party in the legislature. Neither the PRD's national party leadership nor the legislative delegation took an interest in the low-profile debate over the initiative. Unlike other initiatives addressed in the Fifty-seventh Legislature that the PRD seized on to assail the governing PRI and the nature of neoliberal policy, such as the appropriate level of the national value-added tax and banking reform, this project did not energize party officials, who saw little opportunity in it.[33] Small business was not an important enough constituency to compel the party leadership to develop any sort of strategy around the initiative.

With the PRD leadership on the sidelines, the party's position became defined by the individual deputies on the commission. Here, it was Pedro

30. See, for example, the statements of Secretary Herminio Blanco, in Comisión de Patrimonio y Fomento Industrial 1998a; of Undersecretary Decio de María, in Comisión de Patrimonio y Fomento Industrial 1999; and of Undersecretary Raul Ramos Tercero, in *El Financiero*, 10 February 2000. Nor did SECOFI officials share the commission's concern with creating a Small Business Institute to oversee and coordinate programs, as such a function was, purportedly, already performed by the Intersecretariat Commission on Industrial Policy (CIPI).

31. Labastida's proposal was also directed toward small *business* rather than small *industry*.

32. Confidential interview, 1 June 2001, Mexico City.

33. For discussion of the legislative politics of tax and banking reform in Mexico, see Shadlen 1999.

Salcedo, a former president of ANIT (1995–97) and the PRD's secretary on the commission, who single-handedly led a campaign against the initiative. Salcedo, a small manufacturer from the capital goods sector, was elected from a congressional district in Mexico City.[34] Because legislators in Mexico have small budgets and reduced staffs, they come to depend more on party leadership and other deputies who have specialized expertise on given issues. In this case, most members of the PRD delegation were unfamiliar with the details of what was being proposed. With the leadership neither participating in the commission's work nor even signaling a preference, Salcedo—himself a small industrialist—became authoritative and ultimately defined the PRD delegation's position.

Salcedo's opposition is best understood in the context of ANIT's longstanding conflict with CANACINTRA. Although the 1997 Chambers Law had officially terminated compulsory membership, it included a new obligation that all firms must register in a national business directory, called the SIEM. And the new law made registration obligatory via the existing network of chambers. In other words, a firm that had been a member of CANACINTRA, for example, would no longer have to pay membership dues to the chamber, but it had to register with the SIEM via the chamber. This clause enraged the anticorporatist dissidents, who regarded it as an end run around the legal battle they had won.[35]

Salcedo's legislative agenda was centered around ANIT's campaign to abolish the new Chambers Law, eliminate the SIEM, and ultimately create new political space for new associations. From the first meeting of the commission in October 1997, Salcedo had declared that the legislative body would welcome the participation of *voluntary* associations, such as the network of organizations with which ANIT had allied in the 1990s; and throughout the legislative term he regularly used his position as secretary on the commission to integrate the subject of the Chambers Law into forums on industrial policy and virtually every issue that he encountered.[36] Such was Salcedo's

34. Salcedo's 1997 candidacy, for which he and other ANIT leaders lobbied extensively to obtain, was part of a concerted strategy by ANIT to increase the ties between small industry and the PRD (Shadlen 2000).

35. Although chambers were allowed to retain a portion of the SIEM registration fees, the registration fees themselves were significantly less than chamber membership dues had been. This may have been an implicit subsidy, but it was an extraordinarily small one that in no way compensated for the loss of compulsory membership.

36. See, for example, the Acta de Instalación, *Gaceta Parliamentaria*, 9 October 1997. See also the statement on the Chambers Law that is included in the proposals of the Subcommittee on Industrial Policy (Commission de Patrimonio y Fomento Industrial 1998b).

unwavering commitment to this issue, above all others, that journalists came to refer to him as "el diputado del SIEM."

With regard to the small business initiative, Salcedo's opposition was rooted in the central role of managing the Small Business Institute, which the proposal, even the watered-down version presented by Bueno Torio, potentially gave to organizations such as CANACINTRA. The institute was to be managed by a governing board that would be controlled by official business organizations.[37] These organizations, and not voluntary associations such as ANIT and ALAMPYME, were designated as the official partners and collaborators of the institute, and they would have control over the institute's resources. Salcedo and ANIT regarded the Small Business Institute as another way for the chambers and confederations to replace the state subsidies they had lost with the elimination of compulsory membership.[38] Thus, Salcedo adamantly refused to support the PAN's initiative, and the remaining PRD deputies—following Salcedo's lead—either opposed the proposed legislation or simply abstained.

In summary, Mexico's political parties demonstrated a lack of commitment to small industry in the Fifty-seventh Legislature. The PAN held years of hearings on an initiative to promote small industry and watered it down to satisfy different and more important business constituents and to make it palatable to trade officials. The PAN was in charge of the commission and appeared to be taking its job seriously, and the PAN has made much ado about the importance of small firms, but when it came to representing the sector's interests against those of other constituencies, the PAN abdicated.

Importantly, neither the PRI nor PRD, both of which rejected the PAN's bill, did so on programmatic grounds. Nor did either party attempt to improve the project, building on the activist proposals of CANACINTRA and CONCAMIN. Were small industry an important constituency, either party could have held Bueno Torio's feet to the fire and compelled the PAN leadership to develop activist—or even nonactivist—legislation in line with the commission's stated goals. The PRI, however, did not take its legislative role seriously: it made no effort to deepen ties with these weakened organizations that were struggling to represent small industry, and it treated the commission's work with disdain. PRI legislators instead responded to signals from the executive and then the party's 2000 presidential candidate,

37. According to Articles 6 and 7 of the proposed initiative, four members of the governing board would come from the executive branch, and five members from "accredited" chambers and confederations.

38. See, for example, ANIT's press release of 30 September 1999, criticizing the draft version of the initiative for the role given to CANACINTRA and CONCAMIN.

preferring to retain the status quo and not challenge the big-business-led free trade coalition. To be sure, some individual PRI deputies advocated a more assertive role for the legislature, but this faction was blocked by the party leadership. For example, the party's original secretary on the commission, Mauricio Rossell (also the original coordinator of the Subcommittee on Micro, Small, and Medium Firms), was the leader of a splinter group within the PRI delegation that called for a reform similar to the more activist proposals that CANACINTRA and CONCAMIN proposed. Yet Rossell was quickly removed from his position as secretary; and over the course of three years, five different deputies were rotated through this position.

Nor would the PRD push more forcefully for the promotion of small firm. The bill was unimportant to the party leadership, and this lack of interest left matters up to Salcedo and ANIT. Salcedo made no effort to develop an improved bill, as that would have entailed collaborating with CANACINTRA, ANIT's long-standing enemy. In addition to illustrating the difficulty of establishing links between parties and small industry, the case of the failed initiative provides further evidence of how democratization can unleash conflicts (in this case between CANACINTRA and ANIT) that exacerbate the already difficult process of small firm representation. As in the debate over NAFTA in the early 1990s, examined in Chapter 4, CANACINTRA and ANIT were in agreement on the fundamental issues. These two organizations ought to have been allies on the proposed legislation considered by the Commission for Industrial Development. Yet it is important to emphasize that a more concerned PRD leadership could have forced Salcedo to put aside this sectarian struggle. The problem was that in the final analysis, neither the PRD, the PAN, nor the PRI regarded small industry as a valuable constituency.

In a postscript to this section, it is worth noting how little changed in the first years of the administration of PAN president Vicente Fox (2000–2006). One of Fox's first moves, in February 2001, was to create an Undersecretariat for Small and Medium Firms, to which he appointed Bueno Torio as secretary. The office, housed in the new Secretariat of the Economy (SECON), formerly SECOFI, essentially creates the watered-down version of the Small Business Institute that was proposed in Bueno Torio's final initiative. The low-profile undersecretariat operates with minimal resources and minimal staff, and it lacks the autonomy to develop more activist policies toward small firms. The bureaucratic change gives a new home to the limited horizontal-functional approach to small enterprise development that has been the norm since the mid-1980s.

Conclusion

Small industry's representation continued to decline in the 1990s, notwithstanding the removal of legal obstacles to interest aggregation and political participation. Whereas corporatism presented small firms with the challenge of dealing with the consequences of dependence on the state, the elimination of compulsory membership brought into stark relief the difficulties of establishing organizational cohesion among small firms. CANACINTRA lost the capacity to act as small firms' agent, and no other representative—neither alternative business associations nor civil society organizations—filled the vacated space. Fragmented, and lacking an authoritative organization with a national presence, small industrialists lost regularized access to the state. Their interests were subordinated—to those of large firms within an emerging network of business associations based on voluntary association, and to those of other movements in broader social alliances.

To be sure, this period witnessed the massive proliferation of new associations representing diverse segments of business. One 1999 estimate put the number of associations claiming to represent small firms in one manner or another at approximately three hundred.[39] The issue is not the number of associations, however, but the capacity of these associations to represent. The new organizations that emerged tend to be unstable. They suffer from even more intense resource limitations than does CANACINTRA, and they tend to rely on the dedication and commitment of a few committed leaders.[40]

The final years of the decade also brought about new opportunities for interest articulation via political parties. Increased electoral competition produced an awakened congress, which included a commission that appeared to be prepared to legislate industrial policy. Business associations that found themselves weakened in Mexico's new political economy, which featured state officials collaborating closely with a set of voluntary-based peak organizations dominated by the country's largest firms, were keen to exploit the new opportunities. As we have seen, CANACINTRA and CONCAMIN participated actively in the commission's hearings. Yet these organizations were rebuffed by parties that were committed to other segments of business. In fact, the only "small business" association with close access to parties in the Fifty-seventh Legislature was ANIT, via Salcedo and the PRD. Yet the extent to which ANIT itself is representative of and accountable to small firms is highly questionable.

39. *Diario de Yucatán,* 21 May 2000.
40. See Nylen 1992 for similar findings in the case of Brazil.

Ultimately, democracy provides opportunities for new forms of social protest and political participation (Smith and Korzeniewicz 1997), but not necessarily ones that small firms can exploit. The irony, of course, is that the previous authoritarian regime, which so many actors (including small business owners) struggled to topple, presented significantly more fertile terrain for small industry representation. Under the executive-branch-dominated corporatist regime, small industrialists had to sacrifice autonomy to secure political voice and access, but they did manage to retain voice and access. In contrast, as Mexico has democratized and small industrialists have gained autonomy, the price of autonomy has been marginalization and, increasingly, irrelevance. The case of Mexico suggests that because small firms suffer from a set of political characteristics that make representation difficult, simply removing barriers to representation may not be sufficient. In a setting in which actors purportedly have equal access to policy makers, small industry remains disadvantaged.

Finally, the lessons revealed in this chapter have important implications for future development policy and policy making in Mexico. In the 1980s, during the transition from a developmentalist economic model to a neoliberal model, that the expected "winners" within the business community would attempt to marginalize the expected "losers" and lessen the latter's capacity to obstruct reforms is hardly surprising. Larger firms that anticipated benefits from more open-ended integration into the international economy allied with state technocrats to build a "free trade coalition" (Thacker 2000), and this coalition pushed for and then consolidated the neoliberal model. Small industrialists, who had voiced active support for developmentalism and generally lacked the resources to adjust to the pending changes, were not included in this coalition.

By the mid-1990s, however, the neoliberal model itself was no longer in question.[41] The most salient issues in Mexican political economy were no longer implementing and consolidating neoliberalism, so much as redressing the inequities and deficiencies of the new model. Current debates about policies toward small business, for example, are conceived not in terms of development strategy, but rather in terms of what have been labeled "second-generation reforms" (Pastor and Wise 1999). The discussion of the Small Business Development bill analyzed in this chapter, a case study of

---

41. Note, for example, that the Zedillo government's response to the 1995 financial crisis was not to question the merits of neoliberal reform, but to deepen the reforms. This can be contrasted with de la Madrid's initial response to economic crisis in 1982.

the legislative politics of second-generation reform, demonstrates this: virtually none of witnesses who testified to the Commission on Industrial Development were calling for a fundamental reshaping of Mexico's strategy of economic development. Many were, however, calling for new approaches to developing and regulating credit and product markets and, ultimately, to constructing new mechanisms for market governance (Snyder 2001).

The successful implementation of market-completing, second-generation reforms depends on a number of factors, including more effective governance and increased participation (Tendler 1997; Evans 1996). The link between representation, participation, and second-generation reform will be discussed further in the following chapter. For now, it should simply be noted that markets and market governance require information, not only horizontally between firms but also vertically between firms and the state, and generating such information may depend on bringing more actors into the policy-making process. Yet participation, like representation, must be problematized, not taken for granted. Without the ability of weak actors to secure reliable representation—without the ability to make sure that their interests and concerns are articulated, heard, and taken seriously in policy-making circles—second-generation reforms are likely to stumble.

SIX

Representation, Participation, and Development

In a 1979 report on Mexico, the World Bank argued that because small firms have generally weak lobbying capacity, an important step toward helping such firms would be to replace import licenses with tariffs (1979, 49). The logic of the Bank's argument is clear enough: systems where benefits are allocated according to lobbying capacity are likely to favor those with greater political resources.[1] That economic policy and the policy-making regime benefited large firms in postwar Mexico is indisputable. Again, to repeat a point made in Chapter 2, developmentalism was a strategy of economic "giantism," and the complex process by which licenses were granted clearly played to the strengths of larger firms with more resources to invest in working the system. But the World Bank's logic neglects the distinct challenges that some actors face in securing representation. The rather naive presumption is that in the absence of instruments that allocate access to one group more than another, opportunities to interact with policy makers will be more evenly distributed. Furthermore, the Bank neglects the importance of representation in any economic policy regime, developmentalist or neoliberal.

The experience of the subsequent decades in Mexico reveals these critical deficiencies in the World Bank's logic. The replacement of the license system with uniform tariffs did not equalize influence within the industrial sector, but, to the contrary, contributed to the drastic weakening of small

1. In a similar vein, an entire literature on rent-seeking criticizes discretionary state interventions for encouraging business organizations to seek narrow and particularistic benefits rather than policies that promise to raise welfare more generally. See Olson 1982; and Krueger 1974.

industry. The elimination of licenses removed an invaluable resource for organizational development and cohesion. Yes, licenses encouraged rent-seeking; but they also provided organizations with tools to smooth internal dissent and retain solid membership bases. In the absence of such resources, the 1980s and 1990s witnessed the fragmentation of small industry into a multitude of tiny and ineffectual associations. Lacking organizational cohesion, small firms' interests routinely became further subordinated to the interests of better organized and more powerful social groups.

In this book we have seen how small industrialists' core sociopolitical characteristics make securing representation difficult. Small firms face intense collective action problems, on account of group size, resource constraints, and spatial dispersion—all of which combine to create atypically strong incentives for free-riding. Small firms also lack sufficient electoral resources to serve as political parties' core constituencies; and because the interests of small firms often conflict with those of actors that do have such resources, small firms tend to be subordinated within electoral coalitions. An important lesson to be learned from the present study is that interest aggregation and articulation is as difficult as it is essential for many actors, and what might appear to be a level playing field brought by a minimal state, in both economic and political senses, might make representation *more* difficult.

A key element of this book has been the argument that these issues are not static. Although economic and political weakness make obtaining reliable representation an uphill battle in virtually all contexts, the struggle is more difficult in some settings than in others. Variation in political and economic conditions makes different attributes of small industry more or less salient and consequential. In this chapter I consider the extent to which the analysis presented here can be generalized, and I discuss the implications of the study for our understanding of contemporary democracy and economic development.

I begin by reviewing some of the principal findings of the Mexican case, emphasizing the important ways that democratization complicated small industry representation. We then turn from longitudinal to cross-national comparison, examining the politics of small industry representation in two of Latin America's other large, industrialized countries, Argentina and Brazil. The third section returns to the theme of economic development, centering on the importance of small industry—and small industry representation—for responding to the major economic and social challenges facing developing countries in the twenty-first century.

The Rise and Decline of Small Industry Representation in Mexico

Although small firms' core characteristics make representation difficult, the precise challenges vary with changing political and economic conditions. In Mexico's authoritarian, executive-dominated regime, for example, a problematic relationship with political parties had little consequence. Instead, what mattered were actors' capacities to obtain access to the state officials working in the executive branch. In the case of small industry, the regulation of business associations by a corporatist framework that included compulsory membership meant that the high barriers to collective action could be overcome as well. Thus, as we saw in Chapter 2, corporatism provided opportunities for small industrialists, organized in CANACINTRA, to project their interests and secure an important role in Mexico's post–World War II political economy.

Democratization in the 1980s and 1990s unleashed a set of conflicts that reduced small firms' ability to secure effective political representation. As was pointed out in Chapter 3, democratization raised the perceived opportunity costs of a statecentric strategy. CANACINTRA's accommodationist strategy to secure representation for small industrialists, which entailed suppression of members' interests, nonconfrontational approaches to the state, and explicit disassociation from regime opponents, may have appeared prudent in an authoritarian setting. However, democratization made this posture appear unnecessarily conservative. With new forms of social protest emerging throughout the country, new avenues and mechanisms of interest articulation opening, and new alliance partners becoming available, it is not surprising that some began to question the trade-offs involved in accommodation. Moreover, because the more fertile and permissive political terrain emerged during a time of diminished access to state resources and declining returns to the dominant strategy, the likelihood of profound conflict over strategy was even greater. Thus, the new opportunities presented by democratization, combined with the introduction of both political and economic uncertainty, magnified the challenges of organizational cohesion.

A brief comparison of the disputes about accommodation in the 1950s and the 1980s highlights the importance of political context. Both periods saw the emergence of dissident movements. In the 1950s, José Colín, a disillusioned ex-president of CANACINTRA, sought to broker an alliance between small industry and a set of opposition movements that were challenging the ruling PRI. More recently, in the 1980s, a set of disaffected industrialists who left the chamber and created an alternative association, ANIT, attempted to displace CANACINTRA. In both instances, the chamber's response was to move closer to the state, and in both instances the challenges subsided.

The aftermath of the unsuccessful challenges to accommodation present more differences than similarities, however, for the backlash against accommodation in the 1980s was significantly more resilient. While José Colín's challenge sputtered, the movement led by Roberto Romo, Ignacio Muñoz Peredo, and others would have lasting effects on the Mexican political economy. Even after the challenge to CANACINTRA was thwarted, the dissidents in ANIT were able to build a broader movement that challenged long-standing corporatist institutions.

That CANACINTRA's accommodationist strategy was producing different results in the two time periods provides a partial explanation for why dissent collapsed in the 1950s and expanded more recently. The state was no longer providing useful concessions for CANACINTRA to share with its members in the 1980s. Because the benefits accruing to accommodation were not what they once were, the ability to rationalize loss of autonomy in terms of material results was reduced. Nor could CANACINTRA avail itself of material benefits to lower the incentives for dissent. Instead, the chamber dealt with its antagonists by prevailing on the state to use the corporatist apparatus to undermine opposition. Whereas CANACINTRA had relied on the state to protect it against the organizational initiatives of big business in the 1950s, it was now relying on the state to protect it against its own—against a dissenting wing of small industrialists. And because accommodation provided fewer tangible material benefits, CANACINTRA resorted to a more coercive response to dissent, which, not surprisingly, provided the dissidents with further grievances against both CANACINTRA and the state.

But why did dissent *flourish* in the face of coercion and repression? The differences in benefits produced by accommodation is not a sufficient explanation for the different trajectories of dissent. A key factor in explaining the intensification and persistence of dissent in the recent period is democratization. Without an enabling political environment, the leaders of ANIT would not have been able to transform a quarrel over CANACINTRA's organizational strategy into a full-blown conflict about political institutions. But democratization made new political allies available, and it also made feasible a judicial strategy to seek reform of the corporatist framework. Democratization also inspired organizations that were controlled by Mexico's largest firms to construct new, exclusionary mechanisms for state-business consultation, and the ensuing arrangements further spread dissent within the business community and contributed to the growth of the anti-corporatist movement. None of these conditions was available to nurture Colín's earlier movement.

Ultimately, by introducing a period of intense institutional contestation, democratization weakened CANACINTRA and made the chamber less representative. While big business's project to transform corporatism unquestionably reduced CANACINTRA's capacity to work with the state on behalf of small industry, the dissidents' challenge to compulsory membership paralyzed the chamber. The protracted conflict over corporatism seriously restricted CANACINTRA's options for responding to the dramatic economic policy shifts of the Salinas period. CANACINTRA, thus, did not mobilize opposition when it could have in the 1980s, and it could not mobilize opposition when its own leaders believed it should have in the 1990s. But this was not for lack of opportunity. The problem for small industry was not authoritarianism. The political conflicts unleashed by democratization itself had paralyzed the chamber in the face of threatening neoliberal economic reforms.[2]

But CANACINTRA's paralysis was not the only effect of democratization on small industry. The removal of compulsory membership in the 1990s replaced weakness and subservience with disintegration and fragmentation. Intense collective action problems made it difficult for alternative associations to emerge and fill the gap left by CANACINTRA's decay. ANIT embarked on a broad, ambitious search for allies—internationally and within Mexican civil society—but despite increased activism in the late 1990s, the association remained unable to represent small industrialists in a meaningful way. The dissidents could destroy CANACINTRA, but they could not replace it.

Contrasting the analysis in Chapter 2 with that in Chapters 3, 4, and 5, then, we see two self-reinforcing dynamics—but with opposite currents creating upward and downward spirals, respectively. Under developmentalism and authoritarianism, accommodation allowed CANACINTRA to overcome dissent, stabilize the organization, and increase representative capacity. In the context of neoliberalism and democratization, notwithstanding the initial victory over ANIT in 1986–87, accommodation ultimately radicalized dissent, spurred a vibrant anticorporatist movement, and gave rise to a set of political conflicts that would significantly weaken the chamber and reduce small industry representation.

---

2. The paralysis in CANACINTRA, and the subsequent decline in small industry representation, are clearly perverse effects of a movement that originally emerged as an effort push for stronger and more forceful representation.

Nor was small industry able to compensate for its losses in the associational arena by securing more representation in the electoral. While the failed legislative initiative to design a program for promoting small industry is only a single event, it provides key insights into how the interests of small firms become subordinated within electoral coalitions. Mexico's principal political parties all expressed great concern with small business, but neither the PRI, nor the PAN, nor the PRD was prepared to advocate on behalf of the sector and advance a strategy of industrial promotion. Each party instead subordinated small industry to other constituents and broader party strategies. The important lesson here is not that the bill did not pass—after all, plenty of bills get stalled in legislatures around the world—but how and why the bill died in committee. No party took the job of representing small industry seriously. While in this book I have placed primary emphasis on the challenges that small industrialists face in the realm of associations, the case study presented in Chapter 5 points to serious difficulties that small firms have in securing reliable representation through political parties as well.

To summarize, regime change altered the relative significance of small industry's core characteristics and made representation more difficult. While small firms were able to exploit opportunities that were available in the authoritarian regime, they were less able to take advantage of the new sets of opportunities presented by democratization in the 1980s and 1990s. The problem for small industry in Mexico would not be underdeveloped democratic institutions, but rather the effects of democratization on the sector's strategies for securing representation.

Comparative Perspectives: Small Industry Representation in Argentina and Brazil

Mexico, of course, is not unique in experiencing democratic transition and economic liberalization simultaneously. To the contrary, such dual transitions were common in the later decades of the twentieth century, as the third wave of democracy coincided with the age of economic globalization. To this point, the analysis of how these changes affect the representation of small firms has been organized around a study of postwar Mexican political economy. This section complements the longitudinal analysis with cross-national comparisons, analyzing business politics in postwar Argentina and Brazil.

Business in both Argentina and Brazil was also subject to corporatist regulations on interest association. Yet the political reactions to corporatism, and the nature of the institutions themselves, led to distinct patterns of business organization. In this section I examine business politics in these two countries, paying special attention to the role of associations in representing small industry. The comparative analysis illustrates the differential effects of corporatist institutions (both between capital and labor and within the business sector), and underscores both the importance of the state for small firms' ability to overcome obstacles to collective action, and the difficulties that small firms have in taking advantage of the opportunities presented by democratization.

Corporatism and Anticorporatism in Postwar Argentina

In 1953, President Juan Perón expanded corporatist legislation into the business sector, with a revised Law of Professional Associations (LAP).[3] The new framework established a hierarchical structure of business organizations with compulsory membership. The LAP created a pyramid of four levels, with sector-specific chambers integrated into federations, which were incorporated into national confederations of industry, commerce, and agriculture, this entire structure topped by an economy-wide peak confederation.

A critically important aspect of Perón's corporatist project was that it was designed to strengthen a segment of capital that was politically supportive. Perón's rule was marked by sharp conflict with Argentina's largest firms, organized in the Argentine Industrial Union (UIA). In fact, Perón closed the UIA in 1946, and in 1953, under the auspices of the LAP, the UIA was legally disbanded.[4] At the same time, Perón embraced a project led by smaller firms, mainly from the interior of the country, who held a series of conventions with the desire of forming organizations that would increase their representation in national politics.[5] Under Perón's tutelage, these various organizations merged to create the General Economic Confederation (CGE). Perón's new corporatist framework raised the CGE, which was explicitly pro-Peronist, to the top of the official hierarchy, making this

3. Perón, secretary of labor under the 1943–46 military government, was elected president in 1946 and reelected in 1951. He was overthrown by a military coup in 1955.

4. Mainwairing refers to the action against the UIA as "an attempt—partially successful—to displace the traditional industrial bourgeoisie" (1986, 5). For detailed discussions of Perón's relationship with the UIA, see also Kenworthy 1972; Cuneo 1967; Freels 1968; Teichman 1981; Lewis 1990; and Manzetti 1993.

5. Brennan 1998, 90–91; Seaone 2003, chapter 3; Cuneo 1967; Freels 1968.

confederation—controlled by the weaker segment of local capital—the most important business organization in the country. As a consequence, in the remaining year's of Perón's government, no other business group had as much access to policy makers as did the CGE.[6] With the LAP imposed as a means by which to consolidate the new, supportive organization's domination of business politics and to strengthen the weaker segment of capital at the UIA's expense, the antipathy of big business toward Perón was quickly joined by a rejection of corporatism as well.

The events following the September 1955 military coup, in which Perón was deposed and after which sent into exile, had important, lasting effects on the trajectories of business organizations in Argentina. The military reversed Perón's biases, repealing those aspects of the LAP that applied to business, reinstating the UIA's legal standing, and outlawing the CGE.[7] Then, the return of civilian politics in 1958 precipitated a rebirth of the CGE, as President Arturo Frondizi relegalized the organization.[8] Yet, importantly, other aspects of the LAP that had existed briefly in the early 1950s remained suppressed. Neither the civilian regimes nor the military governments that ruled in postwar Argentina restored the corporatist framework created by Perón. Compulsory membership was eliminated, so firms could join whatever chambers or associations they desired; these organizations were free to affiliate (or not affiliate) with other organizations and confederations; and no institutional framework provided organizations with regularized access to the state.

The ensuing pattern of business association left Argentina with rival business organizations representing distinct segments of business and distinct projects of economic development. In the same sectors of economic activity, large firms typically joined organizations linked to the UIA, and small firms typically joined organizations linked to the CGE. The most salient differences between the leadership of the two were not in terms of sector, but rather in the size of firms.[9] The UIA became the voice of the

---

6. On the importance of CGE, see, among others, Brennan 1998; Freels 1968, 56–57; Lewis 1990, 173–74; and Teichman 1981, 150–51.

7. These measures formed a part of the 1955–58 military regime's larger strategy of "deperonization," which also entailed banning Perón's political party from national politics, a ban that would not be lifted until the early 1970s.

8. The legalization of the CGE was one element of a secretive preelection pact, which included Frondizi's promising to legalize the Peronist party and reinstate many labor leaders in exchange for Perón's support in the 1958 election.

9. Caggiano (1975, chapter 1) contrasts the leadership profiles. See also O'Donnell 1978; Szusterman 1993; Niosi 1974; Freels 1968; Cuneo 1967; Smith 1991; and Acuña 1995. Of course, individual firms could in fact affiliate with both associations, effectively hedging their bets.

larger industrial firms, both nationally owned and local subsidiaries of foreign enterprises, while the CGE was the political front for the smaller, domestic-oriented firms that sought a model of industrialization based on expansion of the domestic market.

Although the organizational profiles in Argentina were similar to those that developed in Mexico, with the CGE and UIA analogous to CANACINTRA and CONCAMIN, respectively, business organizations played a fundamentally different role in the postwar Argentine political economy. As most analysts of this period have observed, Argentine business organizations were more political organs, part of broader movements, than they were representative agents. The UIA was linked to the Radical Civic Union (UCR) and to factions of the military, for example, while the CGE remained tightly tied to the Peronist movement; and these organizations' importance rose and fell with the fortunes of their political allies.

Understanding the distinctive and politicized trajectories of Argentine business organizations requires appreciation of the countries' intense political instability and, importantly, the dismantling of corporatism. As fluid as the Mexican system was, with a proliferation of voluntary associations emerging along side the network of official chambers and confederations, business politics in Mexico appears highly institutionalized in comparison with Argentina, where business organizations were unable to count on any systematic and consistent channels to interact with policy makers. Lacking reliable access to the state, Argentine business associations had little to offer potential members. In addition, they had few incentives to develop internal systems for interest aggregation and coordination—to develop the capacities that were necessary to function as representatives. Rather, in the institutional vacuum of postwar Argentina, organizations essentially became politicized clubs of like-minded entrepreneurs.[10]

With regard to small industry, the postwar environment meant that the CGE lacked both the inducements and the constraints that provided CANACINTRA with incentives to develop the strategy of accommodation that was analyzed in Chapter 2. In fact, the CGE's representative strategy was nearly the mirror image of CANACINTRA's. Whereas CANACINTRA bypassed alliance alternatives and remained rather cautious in publicly criticizing economic policies that encouraged giantism, for example, the CGE developed a close

---

10. Schneider (forthcoming 2004), who links organization to state initiatives, argues that the inconsistent and contradictory messages emanating from an unstable political system stunted the development of Argentine business associations.

relationship with organized labor and was extraordinarily outspoken in its condemnation of economic policy. Indeed, from the time it was relegalized until it was repressed again in 1976, the CGE regularly allied with the General Labor Confederation (CGT) and the Peronist opposition to mobilize resistance to postwar economic policy. To be sure, the CGE and CGT did not always act in concert throughout this period, but at key moments the labor movement and the Peronist opposition could count on the support of small business in the formation of what O'Donnell (1978) has labeled a "defensive alliance" (see also Brennan 1998; Seoane 2003, chapter 5; Castell 1985).

In considering this period of Argentine politics, it is helpful to consider that the absence of corporatism meant that the state had a limited array of subtle instruments with which to induce business organizations to moderate their behavior. The state could not threaten to remove a benefit, such as compulsory membership, to elicit cooperative and conciliatory behavior, or make leaders of the CGE think twice about participating in the "defensive alliance." The Argentine state had one primary mechanism with which to influence the CGE's behavior—outright repression of the organization and its allies, which is ultimately what it deployed in 1976.

While the absence of corporatism created a permissive environment in which the CGE could freely engage in multiclass alliances, the apparent autonomy was double-edged. The absence of any institutionalized framework for interaction and the organization's distance from the state, except in the brief period when Perón returned to power in 1973, meant that the CGE had few opportunities to advocate on behalf of members as CANACINTRA did.[11] As a result, it had little incentive to devise reliable mechanisms with which to gather and reconcile members' positions on key issues. Nor, it would appear, was the organization compelled to formulate a strategy to project members' interests discreetly and behind the scenes with government officials. Thus, despite the political prominence of the CGE in most accounts of postwar political economy, it would be very difficult to maintain that small industrialists in Argentina secured reliable representation.

Democratization and Business Politics in Contemporary Argentina

After a period of intensely repressive military rule, from 1976 to 1983, Argentina experienced a democratic transition that introduced fresh terrain

---

11. When Perón returned to power, he appointed José Ber Gelbard, the longtime leader of the CGE, to be minister of the economy. For analysis of the CGE during this period, see Brennan 1998, 106–10; Ayres 1976; and Seoane 2003, chapters 7–8.

for business interest organization. The new environment would be significantly less politicized and more pluralist than what was witnessed in the postwar decades. Business politics would no longer feature rival organizations forming part of rival political movements that articulated distinct development projects; and, critically, organizations would be safe from government repression. No longer would associations have to worry about being outlawed, having their assets frozen, or even having their leaders imprisoned, as they did throughout the postwar period (Acuña 1995; Birle 1997).

Yet Argentine business continued to lack an institutional framework that might nourish and encourage organizational development. Whereas in Mexico the state and leading sectors of business together created a new form of business-government interaction in the course of democratization (see Chapter 4), this sort of institution- and organization-building did not occur in Argentina (Schneider forthcoming 2004). As a result, the institutional vacuum created by the dismantling of corporatism in the 1950s remained. Membership was still voluntary, and organizations could not count on routinized access to state officials. Instead, government-business interaction was remarkably ad hoc, as officials consulted with small groups of leading firms, the choice of firms depending on the issue at hand (Ostiguy 1990; Acuña 1995; Schneider forthcoming 2004).

Democratization and this more pluralist system of government-business interaction have not ushered in an increase in small industry representation. The CGE, intensely repressed during the late 1970s, has been unable to bounce back. Nor have new organizations that have emerged gained the capacity to represent small firms. In Argentina, democratization has led to more fragmentation rather than better organization and more representation. In the following paragraphs we will look briefly at the representation of Argentine small industry in the final quarter of the twentieth century.

The military regime that ruled Argentina from 1976 to 1983 crushed the CGE because of the organization's alliance with Peronism and the labor movement. All organizations belonging to the CGE were closed, and the confederation itself was again outlawed. Economic policy created an equally inhospitable environment for small manufacturers, as a combination of tight credit, currency overvaluation, and trade liberalization provoked a long period of deindustrialization. Indeed, some have argued that a principal goal of economic policy makers during the Proceso, as it is called, was to dismantle the social bases of the recurrent alliance between organized labor and small industry.[12]

12. J. M. Villareal 1987; O'Donnell 1978; Smith 1985; Canitrot 1980.

The serious economic challenges for small industry continued in the decades after military rule. The 1980s was a period of protracted economic crisis, as the government of President Raúl Alfonsín struggled to meet obligations on the large foreign debt accumulated by the military regime (Smith 1991; Kaufman 1988; Aggarwal 1996, chapter 13). Then, following the outbreak of hyperinflation at the end of the decade, the Peronist government of President Carlos Menem introduced a period of deep structural change in the Argentine economy, using the Law of Convertibility to fix the peso to the U.S. dollar while at the same time undertaking deep, comprehensive privatization and trade liberalization.[13] The economic instability and hyperinflation of the 1980s and the austerity and liberalization of the 1990s would have dramatic effects on small industry, as the country underwent a process of further deindustrialization that featured significant weakening and disarticulation of productive chains.[14] These economic conditions, added to the outright repression that was experienced under the 1976–83 military dictatorship, seriously undermined the CGE.

Nor has the new political terrain of the post-1983 democracy constituted fertile ground for the CGE's recovery. Democratization allowed for the relegalization of the CGE and its various affiliates, but the confederation has been unable to recover either its membership base or public prominence. It has become a skeleton of what it once was, maintaining essentially abandoned offices in Buenos Aires with a sparse administrative staff. The CGE, or more accurately the few dedicated leaders who keep it alive, persistently search for opportunities to work with the government and other business organizations and thus regain a public role, but such opportunities are few and far between. In addition to the difficult economic conditions that would make collective action difficult in any case, the CGE's lack of access to the state seriously reduces firms' incentives to join and participate. Ironically, the less politicized system of government-business interaction makes access to the state even more difficult for the CGE, which can no longer even count on its alliance with Peronism. In the 1990s, the remade Peronist party led by Menem had a fundamentally different base of social support from that of "traditional" Peronism (Acuña 1994; Brennan 1998; Levitsky 2001). Under Menem's leadership, the Peronists had little interest in collaborating with

---

13. In December 2001 the Convertibility Law was finally abandoned, in the depths of Argentina's worst economic crisis in the postwar period.

14. Moori-Koenig, Ferraro, and Yoguel (2002) and UIA (n.d.) specifically examine the situation of small industrial firms. Acuña (1994), and Donato (1996) discuss the effects of economic conditions on the industrial sector more generally.

and resuscitating this dying organization. No longer could the CGE count on its external ally for help in organizing smaller firms.

When the CGE is compared to CANACINTRA, it is clear that the vicious cycle discussed with reference to Mexico is even more evident in the case of the Argentina. The moribund CGE plays virtually no role in government-business relations, but without either access to the state or a stable membership base, it has been unable to reconstitute itself in democratic Argentina. Of course, CANACINTRA has also lost its external source of support: it can no longer count on compulsory membership or the political backing of the ruling PRI. But at least the chamber has a legacy of organizational cohesion that saves it from suffering quite the same fate as that of the CGE.

It was largely in response to the demise of the CGE that a new organization, the Assembly of Small and Medium Business (APYME), emerged in an attempt to represent small firms in Argentina. As indicated, the 1980s was a period of protracted economic adversity, marked by the debt crisis and the repeated failure of programs to promote macroeconomic stabilization and recovery, a time when government-business consultation was dominated by a handful of Argentina's largest firms (Ostiguy 1990). In this context, a group of small industrialists in and around Buenos Aires sought to build a new organization specifically to defend the interests of small firms.

In contrast to ANIT, APYME grew dramatically in the 1990s. It created a network of regional associations throughout the country and claims to have approximately ten thousand members.[15] Of the three founding members of ALAMPYME, discussed in Chapter 5, APYME is unquestionably the largest.

Two important factors explain this distinct capacity for collective action among this subset of small firms in Argentina: distinct origins and external sponsorship. Whereas ANIT was born in competition with an existing organization (CANACINTRA), APYME emerged explicitly to fill the gap left by the erosion of the CGE. Although these new associations in both Mexico and Argentina suffered from a lack of access, APYME, unlike ANIT, was never attacked by the state on behalf of a favored rival. The Argentine state did not stunt APYME's growth, as appears to have happened in the case of ANIT. Collective action, always difficult for small firms, is even more so in space that is already occupied. In Argentina, however, this was not as much of a problem as it was in Mexico. APYME also benefited from

15. I interviewed APYME's president twice for this project, in March 2001 and then again in June 2003. In the twenty-seven months that passed between visits—among the most trying times in Argentinean history—APYME had moved into a significantly *larger* office space in Buenos Aires, so to have room for its growing staff.

its leadership's tight relationship with the Argentine Agrarian Federation (FAA) and the support of a bank based in Argentina's long-standing movement of credit cooperatives. The FAA and Credicoop provide small firms in Argentina with the financial and administrative support that ANIT traditionally has lacked, reducing the dependence of the association on the limited resources of its leaders. This sort of invaluable "external sponsorship" has allowed small firms in Argentina to overcome the otherwise daunting challenges to collective action.

Not only did APYME's membership continue to grow, but so too did its level of activism. APYME was intensely critical of the Convertibility Law and the Menem government throughout the 1990s. And as economic conditions further deteriorated toward the end of the decade, APYME embarked on a strategy of building new alliances with a wide range of social groups that sought fundamental change in Argentina's strategy of integration into the global economy. One prominent example of this activism is APYME's participation in a series of events and protests that were organized by the Confederation of Argentine Workers (CTA), the branch of the labor movement that posed the most consistent and active opposition in the 1990s. Indeed, in late 2001 APYME joined the CTA and a wide range of Argentine social movements and CSOs to create the National Front Against Poverty (FRENAPO).

In an important sense, however, APYME has been *too* successful in filling the space left by the CGE. APYME may express the legitimate grievances of many small firms, but it has even less of a role in policy making than the CGE did. Government officials pay virtually no attention to APYME, and the association is rarely consulted on matters that concern small firms. Indeed, the association's bimonthly magazine is full of articles and photographs commemorating its leaders' participation in public events and promoting alternative strategies of development, but rarely does one come across discussions with legislators or officials from the Ministry of Economy. Nor is there much collaboration between APYME and other Argentine business organizations.

APYME, ultimately, is a political movement that operates in a world of opposition CSOs, far removed from the day-to-day issues on which small firms need representation. APYME, like ANIT, has been successful in integrating small firms into broader networks of social protest, but without gaining access to policy making. In neither case, however, has the movement-oriented strategy compensated for small industrialists' weakness in the realm of business organizations.

To the extent that any business organization represents small industry in contemporary Argentina, it is the UIA. Historically the voice of Argentina's largest and most internationalized firms, the UIA attempted to become more broadly representative in the aftermath of military rule. The newfound interest in small firms is in part a function of the intense economic difficulties faced by the industrial sector in the 1980s and 1990s. What many industrialists perceived as hostility toward the manufacturing sector in general on the part of the Menem government helped settle many of the sectarian conflicts that had long festered within the UIA (see Kait 1997). The UIA created a specialized department to address the concerns of small and medium-size industry, the Departamento PyMI, and the UIA also launched a program to gather detailed data on the performance of small firms, called the Observatorio PyMI.

Despite the recent interest in small firms on behalf of the UIA, a number of factors make this organization an unreliable representative. Most important, power is allocated in such a way as to prevent the interests of small firms from becoming urgent priorities of the organization. The members of the UIA, industrial chambers, remain dominated by larger firms. And because voting within the UIA is weighted by production, those sectors with the highest density of large firms retain control over the UIA's agenda and political strategy. The result is a marked disjuncture between the research and analysis of the UIA and its positions on many key issues of public policy. The Departamento PyMI remains peripheral within the UIA, and the interests of small firms remain a low priority for the organization.

Corporatism and Business Politics in Postwar Brazil

Patterns of business organization in Brazil were also shaped by corporatism and the nature of the postwar policy-making regime. The Brazilian corporatist framework emerged during the rule of Getulio Vargas (1930–45).[16] The Consolidation of Labor Laws (CLT) established a hierarchical network of organizations, with local, sectorally defined *sindicatos,* to which membership was compulsory; state-level federations; and national, sectoral confederations. Within industry, the National Industrial Confederation (CNI) was formally at the peak of the hierarchy. Because of the importance of São Paulo industry, the Federation of Industries of the State of São Paulo (FIESP) became the most important actor in the CNI and the leading representative of Brazilian capital.

In contrast to Argentina, where business elites rejected (and ultimately abolished) corporatism, Brazilian business elites acquiesced to state-imposed

16. On the origins of corporatism in Brazil, see Schmitter 1971, chapter 2; Leopoldi 1984, chapter 2; and Erickson 1977, chapters 2–3. The corporatist framework remained in place after the 1937–45 Estado Novo, though many controls were relaxed during the period of civilian rule that began in 1946.

regulations on associational life. An important factor in explaining these distinct reactions is that corporatism did not exacerbate intrabusiness conflicts, as it did in Argentina. Rather, the CLT was introduced with the principal objective of containing a growing labor movement. Much more than a framework for state-business interaction, the CLT was the cornerstone of the Brazilian system of industrial relations, in which the state sought to institutionalize industrial relations by channeling employer-employee conflicts through purportedly technical channels. Thus, workers were also channeled into a network of syndicates, federations, and confederations, and these official employer organizations and employee organizations would be principally responsible for collective bargaining.[17]

The importance of these very different origins and purposes of corporatism cannot be understated. Vargas did not impose corporatism on Brazilian business; rather, after initial hostility in the early 1930s, the ensuing arrangements represent what one scholar has labeled a "gauging of forces" between the state and big business (Leopoldi 1984, 371).[18] In fact, the details of the corporatist framework in Brazil emerged out of negotiations between the Vargas government and leading business organizations. As a result, in Brazil, corporatism was much less threatening to business than in Argentina. The controls imposed on labor organization and mobilization were significantly more limiting than those regarding employers: restrictions on union formation and activity were more onerous, workers had more difficulty forming associations outside the corporatist framework, and when they did they were more easily suppressed.[19] Thus, business in Brazil would not adopt a strongly anticorporatist position, for even after the Estado Novo terminated in 1945, leading sectors of Brazilian capital continued to benefit from and appreciate a set of political arrangements that brought about labor control and minimized industrial conflict.[20]

---

17. In this regard, the CLT also created a new ministry to regulate work-related issues and established a three-level labor court system to adjudicate disputes. See Erickson 1977; Mericle 1974; and Schmitter 1971.

18. Other analysts who emphasize the role of business elites in the making of corporatism include Schmitter (1971, 182); and de Castro Gomes (1976).

19. See Schmitter 1971, 117–18; Leopoldi 1984, 55–63; and Mericle 1974, 78–79. More generally, see the discussion on the differential effects of corporatism in O'Donnell 1977.

20. Not surprisingly, big business's perspective on corporatism changed under the Goulart government (1961–64), when state officials deployed the CLT to grant labor more concessions and thereby cultivate working-class support. This opposition later subsided under military rule, when corporatist restrictions were again deployed as instruments of labor control (Boschi 1978, 169–70; Erickson 1977).

To be sure, many business leaders found the regulations on organization to be onerous and formed voluntary associations outside the corporatist framework. As in Mexico, this process was most pronounced among larger firms. As internationalization produced greater differentiation within the industrial sector, larger firms in the more dynamic sectors of the economy established independent associations. These associations provided Brazilian business elites with greater flexibility in dealing with the state.[21] In fact, the state encouraged this more narrow form of business collective action by working closely with selective groups of businesses in the implementation of sectoral policy initiatives, in what came to be called "bureaucratic rings" (Cardoso 1975).

In sum, because corporatism was not associated with an antithetical political project, and because corporatism was imposed by the state not *on* big business but rather *with* big business, it did not engender the same backlash as it did in Argentina. So long as corporatism solved labor problems for Brazilian industrial elites and remained flexible enough to allow for the establishment of alternative mechanisms for interest representation, little effort would be made to abolish the CLT.

While the reactions to corporatism distinguish Brazil from Argentina, the reactions within corporatism distinguish Brazil from Mexico. As indicated, many larger firms in both Brazil and Mexico created voluntary associations that operated alongside official corporatist organizations. Yet the relationship between the two types of organizations was different in the case of Brazil, where the mission of the voluntary associations was to complement the corporatist organizations. In fact, in Brazil a division of labor developed, in which corporatist organizations addressed issues under the rubric of the CLT and voluntary associations specialized in sectoral, microeconomic areas. Thus, some scholars describe the relationship between the two types of organizations as "mutual strengthening" (Diniz and Boschi 1978), while another refers to this as a "combined corporatist" arrangement (Leopoldi 1984).

The strategy of operating within the corporatist organizations while simultaneously creating alternative forms of representation was driven by the nature of the CLT, which endowed the legally recognized syndicates, federations, and confederations with irreplaceable functions. Some activities remained outside the competencies of the voluntary associations, particularly those

---

21. Among the various analyses of Brazilian political economy that emphasize the role of voluntary associations, see those in Boschi 1978; Diniz 1989; Leopoldi 1984; Schmitter 1971; and Addis 1999.

concerning issues having to do with labor relations. Official business organizations played a key role in Brazil's system of industrial relations (Mericle 1974; Diniz and Boschi 1978). Moreover, the creation of a National Industrial Training Service (SENAI) and Industrial Social Service (SESI) strengthened the official organizations by providing them with substantial financial resources to manage (Mericle 1974, 79–80; Leopoldi 1984, 411–14).[22]

The complementary roles of these two different types of organizations gave industrial elites something of a stake in both. As a result, even when large firms formed their own voluntary associations, they did not entirely abandon the official organizations. To the contrary, the corporatist organizations and the parallel voluntary associations tended to share office space and administrative personnel, and they usually had the same leadership (Diniz and Boschi 1978, 175–78; Nylen 1992, 111–14).

The ensuing pattern of business organization had important implications for small industry. As noted, corporatism was more constraining for labor than for business—but within the business sector, corporatism was significantly more limiting for small firms. Small industrialists were less able to create their own associations outside the corporatist framework: they were encumbered by the standard problems of collective action, discussed throughout this book, and they were not on the receiving end of selective incentives in the form of participation in the "bureaucratic rings." Nor were small firms successful in attaining leadership positions in and control over the official organizations. As one commentator on small business politics in this period has written, within the corporatist organizations "passage to positions of leadership was limited, if not blocked altogether" (Nylen 1992, 113). The combination of small firms' difficulties in creating associations outside of the corporatist framework and inability to commandeer official organizations within the corporatist framework meant that the weaker segment of national industry would not have its own organization in Brazil.

For comparative purposes, it is worth recalling the process by which small manufacturing firms came to control CANACINTRA in Mexico. These firms did not displace large ones. Rather, they gained control over the chamber as large firms abandoned it upon creating separate sector-specific organizations. Business corporatism in Mexico gave official organizations but a single role, that of representation. To the extent that large firms could secure

---

22. Weinstein (1990, 395) argues that the laws governing these programs allowed large firms to create their own in-house training programs, thus mitigating the importance of these organizations. Schneider (forthcoming 2004) indicates that this "design flaw" was one of the many disincentives that discouraged big business from turning organizations such as FIESP into peak organizations of big business.

representation outside the corporatist framework, which they could, and to the extent that the large firms could organize without the benefit of compulsory membership, which they could as well, official organizations such as CANACINTRA served little purpose. Were large firms to have retained an interest in CANACINTRA, positions of leadership would almost certainly have been out of the reach of small firms as well. In Brazil, a very different (and more substantial) role for the corporatist bodies meant that such a process of abandonment was much less feasible. In neither country did the corporatist frameworks call for organizations that were officially dedicated to small industry, but in Brazil, the existence of a pattern of association that did not feature size-based abandonment meant that such an organization was much less likely to emerge. The result was that small firms, less able to create their own organizations outside the corporatist framework, remained comparatively more marginalized within the corporatist framework.[23]

Corporatism, Democracy, and the Seeds of Representation in Contemporary Brazil

In the aftermath of a long period of military rule (1964–85), the late 1980s and early 1990s were a time of renewed political mobilization on the part of Brazilian business (Payne 1994, chapter 5). This period saw a variety of projects that were initiated in an effort to reconstitute patterns of business representation. For example, the Union of Brazilian Businessmen (UBE) was formed as an economy-wide body to lobby the national constituent assembly that was designing the constitution for the "New Republic."[24] In addition, a group of small and medium-size firms in the National Thought of the Business Bases (PNBE) attempted to change the role and orientation of FIESP.[25] And a handful of Brazil's largest and most influential firms attempted to create a new organization, the Institute for Industrial Development Studies (IEDI), which would actively promote a strategy of industrial promotion.[26]

Despite the proliferation of organizational initiatives, scholars of Brazilian business tend to agree that these efforts had minimal impact on

---

23. It should be noted, however, that voting within FIESP is evenly distributed among all the syndicates, regardless of how much they contribute to industrial production. This makes the federation, arguably the most important organization in the industrial sector, less useful for large firms than CONCAMIN or the UIA. Schneider (forthcoming 2004) further develops this contrast.

24. Weyland (1998) and Schneider (1997–98) discuss the UBE.

25. The origins and trajectory of the PNBE are discussed in Nylen 1992; Kingstone 1999; and Schneider 1997–98.

26. In addition to Kingstone 1999 and Schneider 1997–98, see Kingstone 1998.

prevailing arrangements for business representation. Many of the key features of postwar business politics remain in effect. Business-government interaction has continued to be marked by the "combined corporatist" arrangements, featuring a hybrid system with official organizations and voluntary associations operating side by side (Doctor 2003; Schneider forthcoming 2004).

Underscoring continuity in patterns of interaction is continuity in institutional form. A key feature of contemporary Brazilian business politics is the endurance of corporatism. Although the new constitution eliminated some of the more controlling aspects of labor corporatism, most elements of the Vargas-era CLT were preserved in the course of democratization (Power and Doctor forthcoming 2004; Cook 2002). With regard to business, this meant that compulsory membership, the official role of syndicates and federations, and the fairly rigid division of tasks within and among the official and voluntary organizations, have remained important aspects of the institutional environment in Brazil.

One reason for the endurance of Brazilian corporatism remains its distinct institutional design, in that the CLT addresses both capital and labor. Changing business corporatism is more costly in Brazil, for it implies changes to the national labor code and the entire system of industrial relations. Indeed, reforming labor law is a complex and politically charged issue in many developing countries. In Mexico, for example, while the 1941 Chambers Law (the business side of corporatism) was repealed in 1997, the Federal Labor Law of 1929 remained in effect throughout the democratic transition. But the option of changing corporatism in one arena but not in the other is not available in Brazil. Thus, despite occasional initiatives to revise the CLT, both business and labor have been generally reluctant to entertain fundamental changes to Brazilian corporatism, such as compulsory membership (Cook 2002, 22).[27]

The persistence of corporatism has had decidedly mixed implications for small industry representation. Not surprisingly, representation outside official channels remains extraordinarily difficult. A wide range of voluntary associations have emerged throughout civil society in democratic Brazil, and associations of small firms have undeniably been part of this general tendency.[28] The National Movement of Small and Medium Firms (MONAMPE),

---

27. As Power and Doctor (forthcoming 2004) write, support of corporatism on the part of business and labor "becomes the 'default' position whenever an actor feels threatened by change."

28. For discussions of the growth of associational life and CSOs in the New Republic, see Avritzer 2000; and Friedman and Hochstetler 2002. For a discussion of small business *associativismo* in the context of this larger trend, see Nylen 1992.

to provide but one example, has constituted itself throughout most states in Brazil. Yet such organizations are not well integrated into national politics: they can perform advocacy roles, but because they lack legal standing within the fairly rigid corporatist framework, they suffer from lack of access to important policy-making arenas. With sustained collective action being an uphill struggle, these organizations' continued existence depends on the tireless work and the limited resources of a handful of activists.

Likewise, many instances of collective action by small firms within corporatist organizations have continued to sputter. Nylen's (1992) observations regarding the difficult passage to leadership still appears to be accurate. The case of the PNBE's frustrated, unsuccessful effort to capture control of FIESP in the late 1980s and early 1990s certainly provides evidence of the obstacles that small firms confront in securing representation within the corporatist framework. As a consequence of their "insubordination," many PNBE members were removed from their positions within FIESP, and after being beaten back in the federation's 1992 elections, the movement withered away (Nylen 1997; Kingstone 1999; Schneider 1997–98).[29]

Significantly, however, the persistence of corporatism regulations has also had a positive effect on small industry representation in contemporary Brazil. The most successful and enduring movement has emerged *within* the corporatist framework, with the creation in 1990 of an official Syndicate of Micro and Small Industry of the State of São Paulo (SIMPI). Although FIESP, on behalf of the member syndicates, strongly resisted the creation of this new organization, SIMPI challenged the federation in court and eventually prevailed.[30] According to the terms of agreement reached between the federation and the new syndicate, all micro and small industrial firms in the state of São Paulo could choose which syndicate to join—a sectoral-based organization, SIMPI, or both.[31] For the first time, Brazil would have an organization specially dedicated to small firms that operated within the regulations of the CLT.

The contrast between the success of SIMPI and the failure of the effort to create a separate chamber in Mexico for capital goods and metalworking producers (see Chapter 3) reaffirms the importance of collective action in unoccupied versus occupied space. In Brazil, no organization within the

29. PNBE still exists, but more as a citizenship group that focuses on business ethics than as a representative of small industry.

30. At the same time, and largely in response to this challenge, FIESP created an internal body dedicated to small industry, the Chamber for the Development of Micro and Small Industry (CADEMPI).

31. "Termo De Compromiso Amigável Entre A FIESP, Seus Sindicatos, E O SIMPI," 15 April 1994.

corporatist framework had the role of representing small firms. SIMPI was not attempting to displace any existing organization. SIMPI takes some firms away from some existing syndicates, but it does not directly and massively affect any single organization. In Mexico, in contrast, CANACINTRA was already there to represent firms in the capital goods and metalworking sectors, and the emergence of a new chamber in those sectors would have gutted CANACINTRA's membership. In both cases, official organizations attempted to block the initiative, but the motivation and rational for doing so in Mexico were significantly stronger.

As expected, SIMPI's official status has allowed it to overcome many of the difficulties that beleaguered small firm collective action in the New Republic. SIMPI has a vote within FIESP, and official status provides SIMPI with privileged access to government commissions and policy-making boards. Such access, of course, is an incentive that encourages participation. Corporatism also stabilizes the organization's membership base. Although SIMPI's founder and president insists that the organization does not accept the syndicate tax,[32] the obligation to join nevertheless makes SIMPI less vulnerable to oscillations in membership. Stable membership, in turn, makes investment in services more feasible and less risky: SIMPI is less likely to encounter the grave problems that CANACINTRA experienced in the 1990s, when it invested in services at a time of declining membership. Thus, operating within the corporatist framework, over the course of the 1990s SIMPI continued to grow. With thousands of members, the new organization gained an increasingly important role in Brazilian political economy. SIMPI represents small firms on key issues in the state (and city) of São Paulo, and, significantly, it is regularly consulted by policy makers in Brasilia as well.

To be sure, SIMPI's representative capacity is limited in certain vital respects. It lacks genuine national reach, as it remains based almost entirely in São Paulo. It opened similar organizations in other states, bringing them together under a national association (ASIMPI), but in no state has the success of São Paulo been replicated. Even more problematic is that SIMPI is limited to small and micro firms, as its name indicates. Medium-size firms do not have the option of joining SIMPI, and no similar official organization within the corporatist structure has emerged for such firms. These qualifications and limitations notwithstanding, the presence and role of SIMPI—and the trajectory of *increasing* representation—makes Brazil stand out among

32. Interview with Joseph Couri, 17 June 2003, São Paulo.

the three countries examined here. The persistence of corporatism has enhanced the representation of small industry.

An additional example of increased representation in Brazil, at the district level, reinforces the lessons derived from case of SIMPI. In the tiny municipality of São João do Aruaru, in the northern state of Ceará, small producers of wooden furniture formed a local association that gained an important role in local economic governance, helping state officials implement an innovative procurement program and monitoring the performance of the firms that were involved (Tendler 1997, chapter 5). It is notable that the emergence and stability of this association, the Aruaru Association of Furniture Makers, is attributable to the active encouragement and assistance of local government officials. As Tendler explains, local officials extended incentives to help these small firms create this association and thereby build local constituencies for the procurement program. Organized, small firms were then able to be formally included on the state's Industrial Council, for the first time in the state's history (Tendler 1997, 130). Here too, small industry representation increased not in spite of but rather on account of the state.

Democratization, the State, and Small Industry Representation

These brief reviews of patterns of business organization provide support for a number of the arguments developed in this book regarding the challenges of small industry representation. One valuable lesson is that an open and unrestricted pluralist field of interest articulation, whereby firms are free to organize as they wish, is likely to be captured by associations dominated by larger firms that are better prepared to invest resources in establishing and sustaining such organizations. Small firms, in contrast, have more difficulty taking advantage of the new opportunities for interest articulation that emerge in the course of democratization. Pluralism and democratization are as likely to generate fragmentation as they are to engender collective action.

The case studies also demonstrate the importance of the state. Even where the obstacles to collective action are overcome, as appears to be the case in Argentina with APYME, the lack of reliable access to the state can distort these organizations' development by depriving them of incentives to build internal arrangements for coordinating and aggregating members' interests. Significantly, APYME, like ANIT, dedicates more resources toward coalition-building and social protest than toward improving its capacity to represent. Thus, the comparative analysis suggests that Schneider's (forthcoming 2004) observation regarding big business—that lack of state support can produce low levels of organizational development—is relevant for small firms as well.

In contrast to the cases of Argentina and Mexico, which point to the effects of state *neglect,* in Brazil we see how state *attention* can help small firms organize and secure more reliable representation. Producers in both São Paulo and Ceará have benefited from state concessions. Yet the Brazilian case also demonstrates that the form of organizational support need not be corporatism per se. Although small firms in São Paulo benefited from compulsory membership delivered through corporatism, it was a different form of state support that facilitated collective action and organizational development among furniture producers in the district of Aruaru. In this case the selective incentive for collective action was not compulsory membership, but participation in designing and implementing the government's procurement program.

The comparative analysis thus suggests a reevaluation of the political role of the state. To be sure, dependence on the state can distort interest representation, as is what clearly occurred in Mexico in the 1980s and part of the 1990s. But the absence of the state hardly appears to improve representation. Small firms would do well to distinguish between the state as a source of political control and the state as a resource that may allow such firms to overcome some basic political handicaps and be integrated into local and national politics. More generally, the analysis here points to the considerable role of the state in improving the quality of democracy by facilitating collective action and encouraging the development of richer and more substantial associational life.

Small Industry Representation and Latin America's Changing Industrial Demography

Small manufacturers can make important contributions to economic development (Peres and Stumpo 2002). Most obviously, smaller and more labor-intensive firms can serve as an engine of job creation and thus address the serious problems of underemployment. Many economies in Latin America suffer from insufficient job creation, what the Economic Commission on Latin America has labeled the "Achilles' Heel" of the neoliberal reforms (ECLAC 2000). In the context of a growing populations and expanding labor markets, and with investment concentrated in capital-intensive and natural-resource-intensive sectors, even economies that have experienced growth have remained encumbered by persistent underemployment. Smaller, labor-intensive firms can generate jobs.

Under appropriate conditions, small industrial firms can also serve as mechanisms of industrial integration. The extent to which the producers of final goods operating in global markets use locally produced, rather than imported, inputs, has notable developmental implications. Most obviously, import-intensive industrialization, be it under developmentalism or neoliberalism, increases dependence on capital inflows and, subsequently, vulnerability to external financial shocks. In Mexico, for example, the import content of exports is estimated to exceed 70 percent.[33] However, the ability of larger firms to source locally while remaining competitive internationally depends in great part on the availability and quality of local suppliers. We generally might not expect tiny micro-enterprises to fit into larger production chains, but integrated industrial development requires that small and medium-size firms have such capacity.[34] In sum, a development strategy that promotes employment creation and industrial integration requires that attention be paid to small firms, for how such firms adjust to economic competition has wide-ranging implications. To the extent that neoliberalism leads small industrial firms to idle capacity and lay off workers and relegates such firms to simple, nondynamic activities, the consequences are felt in terms of employment (hence poverty and equity) and industrial integration (hence vulnerability to external shocks).

However, the *potential* contributions of small firms to economic development are unlikely to be realized without adequate representation. Understanding the reason why gets to the heart of the themes developed in this book. While responding to the needs of small firms is technically feasible, it involves political trade-offs—engaging in such a response may bring small industrialists into conflict with other actors with different preferences. Assisting and promoting small firms implies budgetary reallocations (in terms of outlays and patterns of government procurement), potentially new taxes, and sometimes even new regulations being imposed on larger firms. Thus, it is essential that we consider the capacity of small industrialists to construct durable, reliable mechanisms of representation that can articulate

33. One factor explaining why the lack of integration is particularly notable in Mexico is geography. U.S. firms, which dominate the export sector, source heavily from home-country suppliers. As of the early 1990s, U.S. exporting firms based in Mexico sourced 51 percent of their inputs from U.S.-based suppliers. In contrast, the global figure for U.S. exporting firms was 13 percent. See Christensen 1993, 46.

34. Amsden 2001; Addis 1999; Lall 1996; Fishlow et al. 1994.

and defend their interests in the public arena. Doing so, critically, reorients analysis of small industry development away from a technocratic discussion of policies and toward, more appropriately, politics.

The importance of representation can be illustrated through a brief consideration of the small business development programs initiated in the 1990s in Latin America. Virtually all governments throughout the region recognize the importance of small firms and have introduced measures with the stated goals of helping small firms adjust to international competition.[35] But with minimal representation from below, it is not surprising that these programs have been aimed more toward correcting market failures, reducing information gaps, and teaching business administration than toward actively promoting industrial integration. That is—in the language of Chapter 5—they have tended to be horizontal-functional programs that provide public goods. Because activist programs divert more resources, they create more political opposition, which suggests that they are less likely to go forward without representation from below. Someone has to demand these policies, not only on the street corner and in the media or even in the hallways of Congress, but also in the rooms and at the tables where economic policies are designed and negotiated.

But the problem with small business development programs in Latin America has been not only the predominance of the nonactivist approach, but also an inability to maximize the possibilities even with the prevailing horizontal-functional measures. That is, contemporary programs have suffered from a chronic lack of resources and lack of commitment on the part of the governments (Peres and Stumpo 2000). Stronger political advocacy—the existence of durable, reliable small business representatives—can protect these programs' resources and monitor results. Representation could break the pattern of new initiatives being introduced, starved of resources, abandoned, and then replaced with yet new initiatives. Again, the case of Ceará is instructive, for the local association of furniture makers played an important role in attempting to protect the resources that were dedicated to the government procurement program (Tendler 1997, chapter 5).

35. Peres and Stumpo (2002) provide an excellent overview of these programs, with detailed analysis of Argentina (Moori-Koenig, Ferraro, and Yoguel 2002), Brazil (Rocha and da Silva 2002; Saboia 2002); Chile, Colombia, Costa Rica, Ecuador, Mexico (C. Garrido 2002); and Nicaragua, Peru, Trinidad and Tobago, Barbados and Santa Lucia, Uruguay, and Venezuela. This publication was conducted under the auspices of the Small and Medium Enterprise Program of the United Nation's Economic Commission on Latin America (CEPAL), the site of the most comprehensive work on small firms in the region. The Inter-American Development Bank (IADB) has also coordinated a significant amount of research in this area, e.g., Lloréns, van der Host, and Isusi (1999).

The discussion of representation and small business policy has particular relevance for contemporary discussions of participatory policy-making and state-societal synergies. Successful cases of market-completing second-generation reforms have featured the creation of national- and local-level networks of state-societal participation (see Snyder 2001; Montero 2002). Whereas those scholars who emphasized the pernicious effects of rent-seeking sought to minimize state-societal interaction, a new development paradigm at the dawn of the twenty-first century has led to the appreciation and valuing of precisely such interaction.[36] Yet the creation of such participatory networks depends not only on the incentives that impel state officials to include "stakeholders," but also on the capacity of social actors to participate. One of the fundamental problems with the current development discourse on participation is that it takes for granted the ability to participate. We need to take seriously the factors that affect actors' ability to collaborate constructively with the state in the making and implementation of policy. It is precisely for this reason that so much emphasis has been placed throughout this book on small industrialists' core characteristics and the effect of state institutions. A key finding of the literature on participatory policy-making, a finding reinforced by the both longitudinal and cross-national comparisons in this book, is that the state can—and at times must—nurture the development of producer organizations.[37]

Finally, the challenges of small industry representation will only be further heightened by Latin America's changing industrial demography. Since the 1980s, the number of tiny microenterprises has expanded significantly throughout the region. In Mexico, for example, whereas firms with fewer than fifteen employees accounted for 84 percent of all manufacturing firms in 1985, they accounted for 93 percent by 1998.[38] A similar phenomenon has occurred in Brazil, where in only five years, from 1994 to 1999, the percentage of industrial firms with fewer then ten employees increased from 75 percent to 80 percent (IBGE 1995, 2002).[39]

---

36. For the paradigmatic statement of the new development thinking, sometimes labeled a "good governance" approach, see the World Bank's (1997) *World Development Report*.

37. Fox 1996; Tendler 1997; Evans 1996; Snyder 2001.

38. The colloquial term for such "firms" in Mexico is *changaro*. One INEGI official, commenting on the census workers' running out of the special forms for such firms, referred to this as the *changarización* of the Mexican economy.

39. In Argentina, firms with one to ten employees accounted for 83.6 percent of industrial firms in 1994, when the last economic census was undertaken (INDEC 1998). More recent census data are not available as of the time of writing.

The proliferation of tiny firms changes the representative challenges for small industry, as the term has been used here, because it changes the nature of small business politics. Although the basic collective action problems of micro firms are even greater than for small and medium-size firms, a variety of factors lead to governments addressing the needs of microenterprises even if they struggle to secure reliable representation. Microenterprises increasingly have external advocates in the form of international institutions, donor governments, and nongovernmental organizations (NGOs), all of which have placed new emphasis on developing and expanding microfinance programs. Microfinance programs are also less likely to conflict with other policy programs that are supported by more powerful actors in society, for the amount of resources necessary to launch such programs is relatively low.[40] Thus, microenterprises may have trouble constructing their own representative agents, but they are less likely to suffer neglect as a consequence of this political weakness. And because such firms appear to provide a solution to underemployment, many countries have allocated resources to developing and expanding microfinance programs.

This trend toward emphasizing *micro*enterprises has important—and potentially problematic—developmental implications. For not only do tiny firms provide less employment, but they have significantly less capacity to make meaningful contributions to industrial integration. Nor do microenterprises have as much potential for skill upgrading. The danger, ultimately, is that microenterprise promotion will allocate scarce public resources in a way that prioritizes "entrepreneurship" over industrial integration.

Thus, the new industrial demography and the accompanying attention being paid to microenterprises make it even more important that small and medium-size industrial firms secure reliable, durable mechanisms of representation. Absent such representation, small and medium-size firms risk being lowered even further on the political totem pole. Policies that might provide small and medium firms with a greater range of adjustment options are essential, but in the emerging environment such firms risk constituting a "forgotten middle" (Batra, Kaufmann, and Stone 2002) between the biggest and the smallest firms. Increasing small industry representation, then, is essential for recapturing small business policy and reorienting it away from entrepreneurialism and poverty alleviation per se and toward industrial transformation and economic development.

---

40. In fact, to the extent that microfinance programs lead to formalization, they can increase overall tax receipts.

APPENDIX: INTERVIEWS

This list of interviews corresponds to the five groupings indicated in the text: (1) Business Associations, (2) Civil Society Organizations, (3) Political Parties, (4) State Agencies, and (5) Firms (Sectors). Within each category the interviews are separated by country.

1. BUSINESS ASSOCIATIONS
    Mexico
        Asociación de Industriales del Estado de México (AIEM; Association of Industrialists of the State of Mexico)
        Asociación Industrial de Iztapalapa* (AII; Industrial Association of Iztapalapa)
        Asociación Industrial de Tlalneplantla* (AIT; Industrial Association of Tlalneplantla)
        Asociación Industrial de Vallejo (AIVAC; Industrial Association of Vallejo)
        Asociación Latinoamericana de la Micro, Pequeña y Mediana Empresa* (ALAMPYME; Latin American Association of Micro, Small and Medium Firms)
        Asociación Nacional de Industriales de Transformación* (ANIT; National Association of Manufacturing Industrialists)
        Asociación Nacional de la Industria Química (ANIQ; National Association of the Chemical Industry)
        Cámara de la Industria de Transformacón de Nuevo León (CAINTRA; Chamber of Manufacturing Industry of Nuevo León)
        Cámara Nacional de la Industria de la Transformación* (CANACINTRA; National Chamber of Manufacturing Industry)
        Cámara Nacional de la Industria del Calzado* (CANAICAL; National Chamber of the Footwear Industry)
        Cámara Nacional de la Industria Textil (CANAINTEX; National Chamber of the Textile Industry)
        Consejo Coordinador Empresarial* (CCE; Business Coordinating Council)

*Multiple interviews

Cámara Nacional de la Industria del Vestido (CNIV; National Chamber of the Apparel Industry)

Consejor Coordinador de Asociaciones Industriales* (COCAI; Coordinating Council of Industrial Associations)

Coordinadora de Organismos Empresariales de Comercio Exterior* (COECE; Coordinator of Foreign Trade Business Organizations)

Consejo Nacional de Comercio Exterior (CONACEX; National Foreign Trade Council)

Confederación Nacional de la Microindustria* (CONAMIN; National Confederation of Microindustries)

Confederación de Cámaras Industriales* (CONCAMIN; Confederation of Industrial Chambers)

Confederación de Cámaras Nacionales de Comercio (CONCANACO; Confederation of Chambers of Commerce)

Confederación Patronal de la República Mexicana* (COPARMEX; Mexican Employers' Confederation)

Instituto Nacional de Autopartes (INA; National Autoparts Institute)

Argentina

Asamblea de Pequeños y Medianos Empresarios* (APYME; Assembly of Small and Medium Business)

Asociación de Industriales Metalúrgicos de la República Argentina (ADIMRA; Argentine Association of Metallurgy Industries)

Asociación Latinoamericana de la Micro, Pequeña y Mediana Empresa* (ALAMPYME; Latin American Association of Micro, Small, and Medium Firms)

Confederación General Económica* (CGE; General Economic Confederation)

Unión Industrial Argentina* (UIA; Argentine Industrial Union)

Brazil

Associação Brasileira de Empresários pela Cidadania* (CIVES; Brazilian Association of Business for Citizenship)

Assoiação Latinoamericana de Pequenos e Médios Emprasários* (ALAMPYME; Latin American Association of Micro, Small, and Medium Firms)

Associação Regional das Pequenas e Médias Empresas Industriais (ARPEMEI; Regional Association of Small and Medium Industrial Firms)

Federação das Indústrias do Estado de São Paulo* (FIESP; Federation of Industries of the State of São Paulo)

Sindicato da Micro e Pequena Indústria do Estado de São Paulo (SIMPI; Syndicate of Micro and Small Industry of the State of São Paulo)

2. CIVIL SOCIETY ORGANIZATIONS
Mexico
Alianza Cívica (Civic Alliance)
Alianza Nacional de Contribuyentes* (National Taxpayers' Alliance)
Causa Ciudadana (Citizen Cause)
Foro Democrático* (Democratic Forum)
Frente Auténtico del Trabajo (FAT; Authentic Labor Front)
Movimiento Ciudadano por la Democracia* (MCD; Citizen Movement for Democracy)
Red Mexicana de Acción Frente al Libre Comercio* (RMALC; Mexican Free Trade Action Network)

3. POLITICAL PARTIES
Mexico
Partido Acción Nacional* (PAN; National Action Party)
Partido de la Revolución Democrática* (PRD; Party of the Democratic Revolution)
Partido Revolucionario Institucional* (PRI; Institutional Revolutionary Party)
Partido Verde Ecologísta de México* (PVEM; Green Party of Mexico)
Argentina
Frente País Solidario (FREPASO; Front for a Country in Solidarity)
Partido Justicialista (PJ; Peronist Party)
Unión Cívica Radical (UCR) (Radical Civic Union)

4. STATE AGENCIES
Mexico
Banco Nacional de Comercio Exterior (BANCOMEXT; National Bank for Foreign Trade)
Nacional Financiera* (NAFIN; National Development Bank)
Secretaría de Comercio y Fomento Industrial* (SECOFI; Secretariat of Trade and Industrial Development)
Secretaría de Economía (SECON; Secretariat of the Economy)
Secretaría de Hacienda y Crédito Público (SHCP; Secretariat of the Treasury)

Argentina
    Secretaría de la Pequeña y Mediana Empresa* (SEPYME; Secretariat
        for Small and Medium Firms)
Brazil
    Servicio Brasileño de Apoyo a las Micro y Pequena Empresas–SP (SEBRAE;
        Brazilian Service of Support to Micro and Small Firms–São Paulo)

5. FIRMS (SECTORS)
    Mexico
        Apparel
        Autoparts*
        Capital goods*
        Food and beverage
        Footwear*
        Metalworking*
        Plastics*
        Textiles
        Toys*

Acuña, Carlos H. 1994. "Politics and Economics in the Argentina of the Nineties." In *Democracy, Markets, and Structural Reform in Latin America: Argentina, Bolivia, Brazil, Chile, and Mexico,* ed. William C. Smith, Carlos Acuña, and Eduardo Gamarra. Coral Gables, Fla.: North-South Center Press.

———. 1995. "Entrepreneurial Interests, Dictatorship, and Democracy in Present Argentina (or Why the Bourgeoisie Abandons Authoritarian Strategies and Opts for Democratic Stability)." In *Business and Democracy in Latin America,* ed. Ernest Bartell and Leigh A. Payne. Pittsburgh: University of Pittsburgh Press.

Addis, Caren. 1999. *Taking the Wheel: Auto Parts Firms and the Political Economy of Industrialization in Brazil.* University Park: Pennsylvania State University Press.

Águilar, Hector. 1982. *Cuando los banqueros se van.* Mexico City: Océano.

Aggarwal, Vinod K. 1996. *Debt Games: Strategic Interaction in International Debt Rescheduling.* Cambridge: Cambridge University Press.

Agüero, Felipe, and Jeffrey Stark. 1998. *Fault Lines of Democracy in Post-transition Latin America.* Coral Gables, Fla.: North-South Center Press.

Alarcón Gonzalez, Diana. 1994. *Changes in the Distribution of Income in Mexico and Trade Liberalization.* Tijuana, Mexico: El Colegio de la Frontera Norte.

Alba Vega, Carlos. 1990. "Las regiones industriales y los empresarios de México." *Revista Mexicana de Sociología,* no. 2:19–41.

———. 1993. "La microindustria ante la liberalización económica y el Tratado de Libre Comercio." *Foro Internacional* 33, no. 3:453–83.

———. 1996a. "La coordinadora de organizaciones empresariales de comercio exterior: Un caso de cooperación entre el sector público y el privado en México." In *Estado, empresarios, instituciones: Estrategias para la transformación productiva,* ed. Oscar Muñoz. Santiago de Chile: CEPAL.

———. 1996b. "Los empresarios y el estado durante el salinismo." *Foro Internacional* 36, no. 1–2:31–79.

———. 1996c. "Las empresas integradoras en México." In *Estado, empresarios, instituciones: Estrategias para la transformación productiva,* ed. Oscar Muñoz. Santiago de Chile: CEPAL.

Alba Vega, Carlos, and Dirk Kruijt. 1988. *Los empresarios y la industria de Guadalajara.* Guadalajara, Mexico: El Colegio de Jalisco.

Alcazar, Marco Antonio. 1970. *Las agrupaciones patronales en México.* Mexico City: El Colegio de México.

Alvarez Uriarte, Miguel. 1991. "Las empresas manufactureras mexicanas en los ochenta." *Comercio Exterior* 41, no. 9:827–37.

Amaro, Santos. 1958. *Cinco artículos de la Cámara Nacional de la Industria de Transformación sobre inversiones extranjeras.* Mexico City: Departamento de Difusión Técnica, Cámara Nacional de la Industria de la Transformación.

Amsden, Alice H. 2001. *The Rise of "The Rest": Challenges to the West from Late-Industrializing Economies.* New York: Oxford University Press.

Amsden, Alice, and Takashi Hikino. 1994. "Staying Behind, Stumbling Back, Sneaking Up and Soaring Ahead: Late Industrialization in Historical Perspective." In *Convergence of Productivity: Cross-national Studies and Historical Evidence,* ed. William Baumol, Richard R. Nelson, and E. Wolff. Oxford: Oxford University Press.

Armijo, Leslie Elliot. 1999. "Mixed Blessing: Expectations About Foreign Capital Flows and Democracy in Emerging Markets." In *Financial Globalization and Democracy in Emerging Markets,* ed. Leslie Elliot Armijo. London: Palgrave.

Arriola, Carlos. 1981. *Las organizaciones empresariales y el Estado.* Mexico City: Fondo de Cultura Económica.

———. 1988. *Los empresarios y el estado, 1970–1982.* Mexico City: Miguel Angel Porrúa.

———. 1994. *Ensayos sobre el PAN.* Mexico City: Miguel Angel Porrúa.

———. 1997. "La ley de cámaras empresariales y sus confederaciones." *Foro Internacional* 37, no. 2:634–60.

Arroyo P., Alberto, and Mario B. Monroy. 1996. *Red Mexicana de Acción Frente al Libre Comercio: 5 años de lucha (1991–1996).* Mexico City: RMALC.

Aspe, Pedro. 1993. *Economic Transformation the Mexican Way.* Cambridge: MIT Press.

Avritzer, Leonardo. 2000. "Democratization and Changes in the Pattern of Association in Brazil." *Journal of Interamerican Studies and World Affairs* 42, no. 3:59–76.

Ayres, Robert L. 1976. "The 'Social Pact' as Anti-inflationary Policy: The Argentine Experience Since 1973." *World Politics* 28, no. 4:473–501.

Bailey, John J. 1988. *Governing Mexico: The Statecraft of Crisis Management.* New York: St. Martin's Press.

Balassa, Bela. 1983. "Trade Policy in Mexico." *World Development* 11, no. 9:795–811.

Barraza, Leticia, and Ilán Bizgerg. 1991. "El Partido Acción Nacional y el régimen político mexicano." *Foro Internacional* 31, no. 3:418–45.

Bates, Robert H. 1990. "Macropolitical Economy in the Field of Development." In *Perspectives on Positive Political Economy,* ed. James E. Alt and Kenneth A. Shepsle. New York: Cambridge University Press.

———. 1997. *Open-Economy Politics: The Political Economy of the World Coffee Trade.* Princeton: Princeton University Press.

Batra, Geeta, Daniel Kaufmann, and Andrew H. W. Stone. 2002. "Voices of the Firms 2000: Investment Climate and Governance Findings of the World Business Environment Survey (WBES)." World Bank Group.

Baumgartner, Frank R. and Beth L. Leech. 1998. *Basic Interests: The Importance of Groups in Politics and in Political Science.* Princeton: Princeton University Press.

Becerra, Ricardo, Pedro Salazar, and José Woldenberg. 1997. *La reforma lectoral de 1996: Una descripción general.* Mexico City: Fondo de Cultura Económica.

Beltrán Mata, José Antonio. 1987. *El empresario mexicano en la política.* Mexico City: Editorial Pax México.

Bennett, Douglas C. and Kenneth E. Sharpe. 1985. *Transnational Corporations Versus the State: The Political Economy of the Mexican Auto Industry.* Princeton: Princeton University Press.

Bensabat Kleinberg, Remonda. 1999. "Strategic Alliances: State-Business Relations in Mexico Under Neo-liberalism and Crisis." *Bulletin of Latin American Research* 18, no. 1:71–87.

Berger, Suzanne. 1981. "Regime and Interest Representation: The French Traditional Middle Classes." In *Organizing Interests in Western Europe: Pluralism, Corporatism, and the Transformation of Politics,* ed. Suzanne D. Berger. Cambridge: Cambridge University Press.

Berry, Albert. 1993. "Small and Medium Enterprise (SME) Under Trade Liberalization: Canadian and Latin American Experiences and Concerns." IDB-ECLAC Working Papers on Trade in the Western Hemisphere 60, Inter-American Development Bank–United Nations Economic Commission for Latin America and the Caribbean.

Biersteker, Thomas J. 1987. *Multinationals, the State, and Control of the Nigerian Economy.* Princeton: Princeton University Press.

Birle, Peter. 1997. *Los empresarios y la democracia en la Argentina.* Buenos Aires: Editorial de Belgrano.

Bloch, Roberto D. 2002. *Las Pequeñas y Medianas Empresas: La Experiencia en Italia y en la Argentina.* Buenos Aires: AD-HOC.

Boschi, Renato. 1978. "National Industrial Elites and the State in Post-1964 Brazil: Institutional Mediations and Political Change." Ph.D. diss., University of Michigan.

Bowman, John R. 1989. *Capitalist Collective Action: Competition, Cooperation, and Conflict in the Coal Industry.* New York: Cambridge University Press.

Brandenburg, Frank R. 1958. "Organized Business in Mexico." *Inter-American Economic Affairs* 12, no. 3:26–50.

———. 1962. "A Contribution to the Theory of Entrepreneurship in the Developing Areas: The Case of Mexico." *Inter-American Economic Affairs* 16, no. 3:3–23.

Bravo Mena, Luis Felipe. 1987. "COPARMEX and Mexican Politics." In *Government and Private Sector in Contemporary Mexico,* ed. Sylvia Maxfield and Ricardo Anzaldúa Montoya. Monograph Series 20. La Jolla, Calif.: Center for U.S.-Mexican Studies, University of California, San Diego.

Brennan, James P. 1998. "Industrialists and *Bolicheros:* Business and the Peronist Populist Alliance, 1943–1976." In *Peronism and Argentina,* ed. James P. Brennan. Wilmington, Del.: SR Books.

Bruhn, Kathleen. 1997a. "The Seven-Month Itch? Neoliberal Politics, Popular Movements, and the Left in Mexico." In *The New Politics of Inequality in Latin America: Rethinking Participation and Representation,* ed. Douglas A. Chalmers et al. New York: Oxford University Press.

———. 1997b. *Taking on Goliath: The Emergence of a New Left Party and the Struggle for Democracy in Mexico.* University Park: Pennsylvania State University Press.

Burgess, Katrina. 1999. "Loyalty Dilemmas and Market Reform: Party-Union Alliances under Stress in Mexico, Spain, and Venezuela." *World Politics* 52, no. 1:105–34.

Caggiano, Roque. 1975. *Notas sobre el desarrollo de la burguesía nacional: La Confederación General de la Industria y la Unión Industrial en el período 1957–1973.* Buenos Aires: Centro de Estudios Urbanos y Regionales.

Calvo, Thomas, and Bernardo Méndez Lugo, eds. 1995. *Micro y pequeña empresa en México: Frente a los retos de la globalización.* Mexico City: Centro de Estudios Mexicanos y Centroamericanos.

Cámara de Senadores. 1986. *Consulta sobre el GATT: Memoria.* Mexico City: Senado de la República.

Cameron, Maxwell A., and Brian W. Tomlin. 2000. *The Making of NAFTA: How the Deal Was Done.* Ithaca: Cornell University Press.

Camp, Roderic A. 1989. *Entrepreneurs and Politics in Twentieth-Century Mexico.* New York: Oxford University Press.

CANACINTRA. 1946. *Pacto Obrero-Industrial: Conmemoración del primer aniversario.* Mexico City: Cámara Nacional de la Industria de la Transformación.

————. 1949. *El desarrollo industrial de México y el Consejo de Comercio Exterior de los Estados Unidos.* Mexico City: Cámara Nacional de la Industria de la Transformación.

————. 1952. *Doctrina Económica Mexicana.* Mexico City: Cámara Nacional de la Industria de la Transformación.

————. 1953. *Memoria y documentos: Carta de los industriales mexicanos de transformación y antecedenes.* Mexico City: Edición y Distribución Ibero Americano de Publicaciones.

————. 1961a. *20 años de lucha, 1941–1961.* Mexico City: Cámara Nacional de la Industria de la Transformación.

————. 1961b. *Discursos pronunciados durante la celebración del vigésimo aniversario de la fundación de la Cámara Nacional de la Industria de Transformación.* Mexico City: Cámara Nacional de la Industria de la Transformación.

————. 1965. *Nueva era.* Mexico City: Cámara Nacional de la Industria de la Transformación.

————. 1966. *La CANACINTRA frente a la problemática del desarrollo económico de México.* Mexico City: Cámara Nacional de la Industria de la Transformación.

————. 1985a. "México 2010: Prospectiva Industrial." Dirección de Estudios Económicos y Políticos.

————. 1985b. "Posición de CANACINTRA en torno al GATT." Dirección de Estudios Económicos y Políticos.

————. 1992. "La Cámara Nacional de la Industria de Transformación ante el proceso de modernización de México." CANACINTRA, Mexico City.

————. 1993b. *Qué es y quiénes forman CANACINTRA.* Mexico City: CANACINTRA.

————. 1994. "Programa de Acción Inmediata." Confidential internal document, CANACINTRA.

Canitrot, Adolfo. 1980. "Discipline as the Central Objective of Economic Policy: An Essay on the Economic Programme of the Argentine Government Since 1976." *World Development* 8, no. 11:913–28.

Cardoso, Fernando Henrique. 1975. *Autoritarismo e democratizaçao.* Rio de Janeiro: Paz e Terra.

CASA. 1998. *El ajuste estructural en México: Las políticas del Banco Mundial (BM), del Fondo Monetario Internacional (FMI) y sus consecuencias.* Mexico City: SIPRO.

Casar, María Amparo. 1996. "Las bases político-institucionales del poder presidencial en México." *Política y Gobierno* 3, no. 1:61–92.

Castañeda, Jorge. 1990. "Salinas's International Relations Gamble." *Journal of International Affairs* 43, no. 2:407–22.

Castell, Pablo. 1985. *Empresariado nacional y cambios sociales: la acción de las entidades de la pequeña y mediana empresa y de las cooperativas frente al privilegio.* Buenos Aires: Editorial Anteo.

CEESP. 1993. *La economía mexicana en 1993: Retos y perspectives.* Mexico City: Centro de Estudios Económicos del Sector Privado.

Centeno, Miguel Angel. 1997. *Democracy Within Reason: Technocratic Revolution in Mexico.* 2d ed. University Park: Pennsylvania State University Press.

Centeno, Miguel Angel, and Sylvia Maxfield. 1992. "The Marriage of Finance and Order: Changes in the Mexican Political Elite." *Journal of Latin American Studies* 24 (February): 57–85.

Cleaves, Peter S. 1987. *Professions and the State: The Mexican Case*. Tucson: University of Arizona Press.

Chand, Vikram. 2001. *Mexico's Political Awakening*. Notre Dame: University of Notre Dame Press.

Chalmers, Douglas A., et al., eds. 1997. *The New Politics of Inequality in Latin America: Rethinking Participation and Representation*. New York: Oxford University Press.

Christensen, Sandra L. 1993. "Is There a Role for Small Business in the North American Free Trade Area?" *Business Forum,* Winter/Spring, 44–46.

Colín, José R. 1948. *Hacia dónde vamos?* Mexico City: Editorial Rostra.

———. 1954. *Hacia dónde vamos? 1954.* Mexico City: Editorial Rostra.

———. 1966. "The Mexican Revolution: R.I.P." In *Is the Mexican Revolution Dead?* ed. Stanley R. Ross. New York: Alfred A. Knopf. [Reproduction of essay published in *Excelsior,* November 21, 1950.]

Collier, David. 1995. "Trajectory of a Concept: 'Corporatism' in the Study of Latin American Politics." In *Latin America in Comparative Perspective: New Approaches to Method and Analysis,* ed. Peter H. Smith. Boulder, Colo.: Westview Press.

Collier, David, and Ruth B. Collier. 1977. "Who Does What, to Whom, and How: Toward a Comparative Analysis of Latin American Corporatism" In *Authoritarianism and Corporatism in Latin America,* ed. James M. Malloy. Pittsburgh: University of Pittsburgh Press.

Collier, Ruth Berins. 1992. *Contradictory Alliance: State-Labor Relations and Regime Change in Mexico*. Berkeley: IAS.

———. 1999. *Paths Toward Democracy: The Working Class and Elites in Western Europe and South America*. New York: Cambridge University Press.

Collier, Ruth Berins, and David Collier. 1979. "Inducements Versus Constraints: Disaggregating 'Corporatism.'" *American Political Science Review* 73, no. 4:967–86.

———. 1991. *Shaping the Political Arena: Critical Junctures, the Labor Movement, and Regime Dynamics in Latin America*. Princeton: Princeton University Press.

Collier, Ruth Berins, and James Mahoney. 1997. "Adding Collective Actors to Collective Outcomes." *Comparative Politics* 29, no. 3:285–303.

Comisión de Patrimonio y Fomento Industrial. 1998a. *Foro acciones legislativas en apoyo al programa de industrialización*. Mexico City: Cámara de Diputados, LVII Legislatura.

———. 1998b. *Programa de trabajo de la Subcomisión de Política Industrial*. Mexico City: Cámara de Diputados, LVII Legislatura.

———. 1999. *Foro de consulta para la elaboración de una iniciativa de Ley para el Fomento de la Pequeña y Mediana Industria*. Mexico City: Cámara de Diputados, LVII Legislatura.

CONCAMIN. 1991a. *Pequeña y mediana industrias: Desafíos y oportunidades*. Reporte Mensual de Análisis de Coyuntura, numero 6. Mexico City: Centro de Estudios Industriales, Subdirección de Análisis, CONCAMIN.

———. 1991b. *Una política industrial para México*. Mexico City: CONCAMIN.

———. 1992. "Conclusiones del Centro de Estudios Industriales de la CONCAMIN sobre los posibles cambios a la Ley de Cámaras." CONCAMIN, Mexico City.

———. 1993. *Directorio*. Mexico City: CONCAMIN.

Concheiro, Elvira, Antonio Gutiérrez, and Juan Manuel Fragosa. 1979. *El poder de la gran burguesía*. Mexico City: Ediciones de Cultura Popular.

Concheiro Bórquez, Elvira. 1996. *El gran acuerdo: Gobierno y empresarios en la modernización salinista*. Mexico City: Ediciones Era.

Cook, Maria Lorena. 1996. *Organizing Dissent: Unions, the State, and the Democratic Teachers' Movement in Mexico.* University Park: Pennsylvania State University Press.

————. 2002. "Labor Reform and Dual Transitions in Brazil and the Southern Cone." *Latin American Politics and Society* 44, no. 1:1–34.

Cordero, Salvador, and Ricardo Tirado, ed. 1984. *Clases dominantes y estado en México.* Mexico City: UNAM.

Córdoba, José. 1991. "Diez lecciones de la reforma económica en México." *Nexos* 14, no. 158:31–48.

Cornelius, Wayne A. 1973. "Nation-Building, Participation, and Distribution: The Politics of Social Reform Under Cardenas" In *Crisis, Choice, and Change: Historical Studies of Political Development,* ed. Gabriel Almond et al. Boston: Little, Brown.

Cross, John C. 1998. *Informal Politics: Street Vendors and the State in Mexico City.* Stanford: Stanford University Press.

Cuneo, Dardo. 1967. *Comportamiento y crisis de la clase empresaria.* Buenos Aires, Editorial Palmear.

Davis, Diane E. 1994. *Urban Leviathan: Mexico City in the Twentieth Century.* Philadelphia: Temple University Press.

de Castro Gomes, Angela. 1976. "O empresário industrial e a implantaçao de legislaçao trabalhista." In *Empresario nacional e estado no Brasil,* ed. Eli Diniz and Renato Boschi. Rio de Janeiro: IUPERJ.

de la Peña, Joaquín. 1951. *Problemas industriales de México: Notas para una planeación industrial.* Mexico City: Edición y Distribución Ibero Americano de Publicaciones.

de María y Campos, Mauricio. 2002. "Pequeñas y medianas industrias y política tecnológica: El caso mexicano de las tres últimas décadas." Serie Desarrollo Productivo 123. Santiago de Chile: CEPAL.

de Murguía, Valdemar. 1986. *Capital Flight and Economic Crisis: Mexican Post-devaluation Exiles in a California Community.* La Jolla, Calif.: Center for U.S.-Mexican Studies, University of California, San Diego.

del Carmen Solórzano, María. 1993. *La Asociación Mexicana de Casas de Bolsa y la reestructuración del sistema financiero mexicano (1980–1992).* Proyecto Organizaciones Empresariales en México, 6. Mexico City: Institute for Social Research, National Autonomous University of Mexico.

delli Sante, Angela M. 1979. "The Private Sector, Business Organizations, and International Influence: A Case Study of Mexico." In *Capitalism and the State in U.S.–Latin American Relations,* ed. Richard R. Fagen. Stanford: Stanford University Press.

Derossi, Flavia. 1971. *The Mexican Entrepreneur.* Paris: Organization for Economic Cooperation and Development.

Devlin, Robert, and Ricardo French-Davis. 1995. "The Great Latin American Debt Crisis: A Decade of Asymmetric Adjustment." In *Poverty, Prosperity, and the World Economy: Essays in Memory of Sidney Dell,* ed. G. Helleiner. New York: St. Martin's Press.

Diamond, Larry, et al., ed. 1997. *Consolidating the Third Wave Democracies: Themes and Perspectives.* Baltimore: Johns Hopkins University Press.

di Palma, Giuseppe. 1990. *To Craft Democracies: An Essay on Democratic Transitions.* Berkeley and Los Angeles: University of California Press.

Diamond, Larry, Jonathan Hartlyn, Juan J. Linz, and Seymour Martin Lipset, eds. 1999. *Democracy in Developing Countries: Latin America.* 2d ed. Boulder, Colo.: Lynne Rienner.

Diniz, Eli. 1989. "The Post-1930 Industrial Elite." In *Modern Brazil: Elites and Masses in Historical Perspective,* ed. Michael L. Conniff and Frank D. McCann. Lincoln: University of Nebraska Press.

Diniz, Eli, and Renato Boschi. 1978. *Empresariado nacional e estado no Brasil.* Rio de Janeiro: Forense-Universitária.

Doctor, Mahrukh. 2003. "Institutional Modernisation and the Legacy of Corporatism: The Case of Port Reform in Brazil." *Journal of Latin American Studies* 35, no. 2:341–65.

Domínguez, Jorge I., and Abraham F. Lowenthal, eds. 1996. *Constructing Democratic Governance: Latin America and the Caribbean in the 1990s.* Baltimore: Johns Hopkins University Press.

Domingo, Pilar. 2000. "Judicial Independence: The Politics of the Supreme Court in Mexico." *Journal of Latin American Studies* 32, no. 3:705–35.

Donato, Vicente Nicolas. 1996. "Incertidumbre ambiental y procesos productivos 'de alta densidad contractual': La dinámica structural del la industria argentina durante el período de la megainflación (1975–1990)." *Desarrollo Económico* 35, no. 140:601–27.

Doner, Richard, and Ben Ross Schneider. 2000. "Business Associations and Development: Why Some Associations Contribute More Than Others." *Business and Politics* 2, no. 3:261–88.

Dornbusch, Rudiger. 1990. "Mexico's Economy at the Crossroads." *Journal of International Affairs* 43, no. 2:313–26.

———. 1991. "Populism and Economic Policy in Mexico, 1970–1982." In *The Macroeconomics of Populism in Latin America,* ed. Rudiger Dornbusch and Sebastian Edwards. Chicago: University of Chicago Press.

Dornbusch, Rudiger, and Sebastian Edwards, eds. 1991. *The Macroeconomics of Populism in Latin America.* Chicago: University of Chicago Press.

Durand, Francisco, and Eduardo Silva, ed. 1998. *Organized Business, Economic Change, and Democracy in Latin America.* Coral Gables, Fla.: North-South Center Press.

Dussel Peters, Enrique. 1997. *La economía de la polarización: Teoría y evolución del cambio estructural de las manufactureras mexicanas (1988–1996).* Mexico City: Editorial Jus.

———. 2000. *Polarizing Mexico. The Impact of Liberalization Strategy.* Boulder, Colo.: Lynne Rienner.

———. ed. 2001. *Claroscuros: Integración exitosa de las pequeñas y medianas empresas en México.* Santiago de Chile: CEPAL.

ECLAC. 2000. *Equity, Development, and Citizenship.* New York: United Nations Economic Commission for Latin America and the Caribbean.

Edwards, Sebastian. 1995. *Crisis and Reform in Latin America: From Despair to Hope.* New York: Oxford University Press.

Elizondo, Carlos. 1992. "Property Rights in Mexico: Government and Business After the 1982 Bank Nationalization." Ph.D. diss., Oxford University.

———. 1993. "The Making of a New Alliance: The Privatization of the Banks in Mexico." Documento de Trabajo 5, Estudios Políticos. CIDE.

———. 1994. "In Search of Revenue: Tax Reform in Mexico Under the Administrations of Echeverría and Salinas." *Journal of Latin American Studies* 26 (February): 159–90.

Erickson, Kenneth Paul. 1977. *The Brazilian Corporative State and Working-Class Politics.* Berkeley and Los Angeles: University of California Press.

Escobar Toledo, Saúl. 1987. "Rifts in the Mexican Power Elite, 1976–1986." In *Government and Private Sector in Contemporary Mexico*, ed. Sylvia Maxfield and Ricardo Anzaldúa Montoya. Monograph Series 20. La Jolla: Center for U.S.-Mexican Studies, University of California, San Diego.

Espinosa Villareal, Óscar. 1993. *El impulso a la micro, pequeña y mediana empresa.* Mexico City: Fondo de Cultura Económica.

Evans, Peter. 1979. *Dependent Development: The Alliance of Multinational, State, and Local Capital in Brazil.* Princeton: Princeton University Press.

———. 1995. *Embedded Autonomy: States and Industrial Transformation.* Princeton: Princeton University Press.

———. 1996. "Government Action, Social Capital, and Development: Reviewing the Evidence on Synergy." *World Development* 24, no. 6:1119–32.

———. 1997a. "The Eclipse of the State? Reflections on Stateness in an Era of Globalization." *World Politics* 50, no. 1:62–87.

———. 1997b. "State Structures, Government-Business Relations, and Economic Transformation." In *Business and the State in Developing Countries,* ed. Ben Ross Schneider and Sylvia Maxfield. Ithaca: Cornell University Press.

Fishlow, Albert, et al., ed. 1994. *Miracle or Design? Lessons from the East Asian Experience.* Washington, D.C.: Overseas Development Council.

Foster, Kenneth W. 2001. "Associations in the Embrace of an Authoritarian State: State Domination of Society?" *Studies in Comparative International Development* 35, no. 4:84–109.

Fouque, Agustín. 1949. *El tratado de comercio mexico-americano (guión para una revisión equitativa).* Mexico City: Edición y Distribución Ibero Americano de Publicaciones.

Foweraker, Joe, and Ann L. Craig, eds. 1990. *Popular Movements and Political Change in Mexico.* Boulder, Colo.: Lynne Rienner.

Fox, Jonathan Fox. 1994. "The Difficult Transition from Clientelism to Citizenship: Lessons from Mexico." *World Politics* 46, no. 2:151–84.

———. 1996. "How Does Civil Society Thicken? The Political Construction of Social Capital in Rural Mexico." *World Development* 24, no. 6:1089–103.

Franco, Teresa. 1980. *Ensayo sobre la historia de la Cámara Nacional de la Industria de Transformación.* Mexico City: Cámara Nacional de la Industria de la Transformación.

Freels, John William. 1968. "Industrial Trade Associations in Argentine Politics." Ph.D. diss., University of California, Riverside.

Frieden, Jeffry A. 1991. *Debt, Development, and Democracy: Modern Political Economy and Latin America, 1965–1985.* Princeton: Princeton University Press.

Friedman, Elisabeth Jay, and Kathryn Hochstetler. 2002. "Assessing the Third Transition in Latin American Democratization: Representational Regimes and Civil Society in Argentina and Brazil." *Comparative Politics* 35, no. 1:21–42.

Fuentes Mares, José. 1976. *Monterrey: Una ciudad creadora y sus capitanes.* Mexico City: Editorial Jus.

Gallardo, Juan. 1994. "La coordinadora de organismos empresariales para el comercio exterior." In *Testimonios sobre el TLC,* ed. Carlos Arriola. Mexico City: Editorial Diana.

García Figuroa, Gabriela. 1992. "La participación política de los empresarios sonorenses, 1982–1988." In *Los empresarios mexicanos, ayer y hoy,* ed. Cristina Puga and Ricardo Tirado. Mexico City: Ediciones el Caballito.

Garrido, Celso. 1992. *La evolución del actor empresarial mexicano en los ochentas.* Proyecto Organizaciones Empresariales en México, 4. Mexico City: Institute for Social Research, National Autonomous University of Mexico.

———. 2002. "Pequeñas y medianas empresas manufactureras en México en los años noventa." In *Las pequeñas y medianas empresas industriales en América Latina y el Caribe,* ed. Wilson Peres and Giovanni Stumpo. México City: CEPAL.

Garrido, Celso, and Cristina Puga. 1990. "Transformaciones recientes del empresariado mexicano." *Revista Mexicana de Sociología,* no. 2:43–61.

Garrido, Luis Javier. 1986. *El partido de la revolución institucionalizada: La formación del nuevo estado, 1928–1945.* Mexico City: Siglo Veintiuno.

———. 1993. *La ruptura: La corriente democrática del PRI.* Mexico City: Editorial Grijalbo.

Garza Mouriño, R.M. 1993. *El águila rumbo al sol: Crónica histórico-periodística de CANACINTRA desde sus orígenes hasta la época actual.* Mexico City: CANACINTRA.

Gereffi, Gary. 1978. "Drug Firms and Dependency in Mexico: The Case of the Steroid Hormone Industry." *International Organization* 32, no. 1:237–86.

———. 1990. "Big Business and the State." In *Manufacturing Miracles: Paths of Industrialization in Latin America and East Asia,* ed. Gary Gereffi and Donald L. Wyman. Princeton: Princeton University Press.

Gereffi, Gary, and Peter Evans. 1981. "Transnational Corporations, Dependent Development, and State Policy in the Semiperiphery: A Comparison of Brazil and Mexico." *Latin American Research Review* 16, no. 3:36–37.

Gereffi, Gary, and Donald L. Wyman, eds. 1990. *Manufacturing Miracles: Paths of Industrialization in Latin America and East Asia.* Princeton: Princeton University Press.

Gerschenkron, Alexander. 1962. *Economic Backwardness in Historical Perspective.* Cambridge: Belknap Press of Harvard University Press.

Gibson, Edward L. 1996. *Class and Conservative Parties: Argentina in Comparative Perspective.* Baltimore: Johns Hopkins University Press.

González Casanova, Pablo. 1970. *Democracy in Mexico.* New York: Oxford University Press.

González Cosío, Arturo. 1961. "Clases y estratos sociales." In *México: Cincuenta años de revolución.* Mexico City: Fondo de la Cultura Económica.

González Marín, María Luisa. 1996. *La industria de bienes de capital en México.* Mexico City: Ediciones el Caballito.

Grasa, Pedro L., and Victoria E. Erossa. 1995. "Los retos tecnológicos de la pequeña y mediana empresa en México." In *Micro y pequeña empresa en México: Frente a los retos de la globalización.,* ed. Thomas Calvo and Bernardo Méndez Lugo. Mexico City: Centro de Estudios Mexicanos y Centroamericanos.

Guzmán Valdivia, Isaac. 1961. "El movimiento patronal." In *México: Cincuenta años de revolución.* Mexico City: Fondo de la Cultura Económica.

Haar, Jerry, Catherine Leroy-Beltrán, and Oscar Beltrán. 2003. "NAFTA and Small Business Competitiveness: The Impacts of Free Trade, Macroeconomic Policy, and Firm Management." North-South Agenda Papers 64, North-South Center, University of Miami.

Haber, Paul Lawrence. 1994. "The Art and Implications of Political Restructuring in Mexico: The Case of Urban Popular Movements." In *The Politics of Economic Restructuring: State-Society Relations and Regime Change in Mexico,* ed. Maria Lorena Cook, Kevin J. Middlebrook, and Juan Molinar Horcasitas. U.S.-Mexico Contemporary Perspectives Series 7. La Jolla: Center for U.S.-Mexican Studies, University of California, San Diego.

Haggard, Stephan, and Robert R. Kaufman. 1995. *The Political Economy of Democratic Transitions*. Princeton: Princeton University Press.

Haggard, Stephan, Sylvia Maxfield, and Ben Ross Schneider. 1997. "Theories of Business and Business-State Relations." In *Business and the State in Developing Countries,* ed. Ben Ross Schneider and Sylvia Maxfield. Ithaca: Cornell University Press.

Hagopian, Frances. 1990. "Democracy by Undemocratic Means? Elites, Political Pacts, and Regime Transition in Brazil." *Comparative Political Studies* 23, no. 2:147–70.

———. 1998. "Democracy and Political Representation in Latin America in the 1990s: Pause, Reorganization, or Decline?" In *Fault Lines of Democracy in Post-transition Latin America,* ed. Felipe Agüero and Jeffrey Stark. Coral Gables, Fla.: North-South Center Press.

Hakim, Peter. 2003. "Dispirited Politics." *Journal of Democracy* 14, no. 2:108–22.

Hamilton, Nora. 1982. *The Limits of State Autonomy: Post-revolutionary Mexico*. Princeton: Princeton University Press.

Hansen, Roger D. 1971. *The Politics of Mexican Development*. Baltimore: Johns Hopkins University Press.

Hardin, Russell. 1982. *Collective Action*. Baltimore: Johns Hopkins University Press.

Haydu, Jeffrey. 1999. "Two Logics of Class Formation? Collective Identities Among Proprietary Employers, 1880–1900." *Politics and Society* 27, no. 4:507–27.

Hazan, Reuven Y., and Gideon Rahat. 2000. "Representation, Electoral Reform, and Democracy: Theoretical and Empirical Lessons from the 1996 Elections in Israel." *Comparative Political Studies* 33, no. 10:1310–36.

Heath, Jonathan E. 1997. "The Impact of Mexico's Liberalization Strategy: Jobs, Productivity, and Structural Change." In *The Post-NAFTA Political Economy: Mexico and the Western Hemisphere,* ed. Carol Wise. University Park: Pennsylvania State University Press.

Heller, Patrick. 2000. "Degrees of Democracy: Some Comparative Lessons from India." *World Politics* 52, no. 4:484–519.

Hellman, Judith Adler. 1980. "Social Control in Mexico." *Comparative Politics* 12, no. 2:225–42.

———. 1988. *Mexico in Crisis*. 2d ed. New York: Holmes & Meier.

Helms, Brigit S. 1985. "Pluralismo limitado en México: Estudio de un caso de consulta sobre la membresía del GATT." *Foro Internacional* 26, no. 2:172–89.

Heredia, Blanca. 1992. "Profits, Politics, and Size: The Political Transformation of Mexican Business." In *The Right and Democracy in Latin America,* ed. Douglas Chalmers et al. New York: Praeger Press.

———. 1995. "Mexican Business and the State: The Political Economy of a Muddled Transition." In *Business and Democracy in Latin America,* ed. Ernest Bartell and Leigh A. Payne. Pittsburgh: University of Pittsburgh Press.

———. 1996. "State-Business Relations in Contemporary Mexico." In *Rebuilding the State: Mexico After Salinas,* ed. Monica Serrano and Victor Bulmer-Thomas. London: Institute for Latin American Studies.

Heredia, Carlos A. 1994. "NAFTA and Democratization in Mexico." *Journal of International Affairs* 48, no. 1:13–38.

Hernández Rodríguez, Rogelio. 1986. "La política y los empresarios después de la nacionalización de la banca." *Foro Internacional* 27, no. 2:247–65.

———. 1987. "Los hombres del presidente de la Madrid." *Foro Internacional* 28, no. 2:5–38.

———. 1990. "La conducta empresarial en el gobierno de Miguel de la Madrid." *Foro Internacional* 30, no. 3:736–64.

———. 1991. "Los problemas de representación en los organismos empresariales." *Foro Internacional* 31, no. 3:446–71.

Hershberg, Eric, 1999. "Democracy and Its Discontents: Constraints on Political Citizenship in Latin America." In *Democracy and Its Limits: Lessons from Asia, Latin America, and the Middle East,* ed. Howard Handelman and Mark Tessler. Notre Dame: University of Notre Dame Press.

Hiernaux Nicolas, Daniel. 1995. "Pobreza y microempresas en el Valle de Chalco: Las estrategias desde abajo." In *Micro y pequeña empresa en México: Frente a los retos de la globalización,* ed. Thomas Calvo and Bernardo Méndez Lugo. Mexico City: Centro de Estudios Mexicanos y Centroamericanos.

Hirschman Albert O. 1958. *The Strategy of Economic Development.* New Haven: Yale University Press.

———. 1968. "The Political Economy of Import-Substituting Industrialization in Latin America." *Quarterly Journal of Economics* 82, no. 1:1–32.

———. 1970. *Exit, Voice, and Loyalty: Responses to Decline in Firms, Organizations, and States.* Cambridge: Harvard University Press.

———. 1981. "Exit, Voice, and the State." In *Essays in Trespassing: Economics to Politics and Beyond.* Cambridge: Cambridge University Press.

Hobbs, Jeremy. 1991. "The Role of Business Organisations in the Transition from an Import Substituting to an Export Orientated Model of Growth in Mexico After 1982." Ph.D. diss., University of Essex.

Hoeckle, Wolfgang. 1993. CANACINTRA: *Análisis de fuerzas y debilidades.* Mexico City: CIMA, Cooperación Industrial México-Alemania.

Hollifield, James Frank, and Calvin C. Jillson, eds. 2000. *Pathways to Democracy: The Political Economy of Democratic Transitions.* New York: Routledge.

Horvath, Jane. 1991. *Small and Medium Scale Manufacturing in Mexican Development, 1954–1989.* New York: Garland.

Huber, Evelyne, Dietrich Rueschemeyer, and John Stephens. 1997. "The Paradoxes of Contemporary Democracy." *Comparative Politics* 29, no. 3:323–42.

Humphrey, John, and Hubert Schmitz. 1995. "Principles for Promoting Clusters and Networks of SMEs." UNIDO Discussion Papers, no. 1.

Hunter, Wendy. 1996. *Eroding Military Influence in Brazil: Politicians Against Soldiers.* Chapel Hill: University of North Carolina Press.

IBGE. 1995. *Censo Cadastro dos Estabelecimentos da Indústria, Comércio e Serviços, 1994.* Rio de Janeiro: Instituto Brasileiro de Geografia e Estatística.

———. 2002. *Estatísticas do Cadastro Central de Empresas, 2000.* Rio de Janeiro: Instituto Brasileiro de Geografia e Estatística.

INDEC. 1998. *Censo Nacional Económico de 1994.* Buenos Aires: Institúto Nacional de Estadística y Censos.

INEGI. 1988. *XI Censo Industrial, 1981 Resumen General.* Aguascalientes, Mexico: Instituto Nacional de Estadística Geografía e Informática.

———. 1989. *XII Censo Industrial 1986. Resumen General. Datos Referentes a 1985.* Aguascalientes, Mexico: Instituto Nacional de Estadística Geografía e Informática.

————. 1992. *XIII Censo Industrial. Industrias Manufactureras. Censos Económicos 1989.* Aguascalientes, Mexico: Instituto Nacional de Estadística Geografía e Informática.

————. 1995. *XIV Censo Industrial. Industrias Manufactureras. Censos Económicos 1994.* Aguascalientes, Mexico: Instituto Nacional de Estadística Geografía e Informática.

————. 1999. *XV Censo Industrial. Industrias Manufactureras. Censos Económicos 1998.* Aguascalientes, Mexico: Instituto Nacional de Estadística Geografía e Informática.

INEGI-STPS. 1998. *Encuesta Nacional de Micronegocios 1998.* Aguascalientes, Mexico: Instituto Nacional de Estadística Geografía e Informática.

Izquierdo, Rafael. 1964. "Protectionism in Mexico." In *Public Policy and Private Enterprise in Mexico,* ed. Raymond Vernon. Cambridge: Harvard University Press.

Jacobs, Eduardo, and Jorge Máttar. 1985. "La industria pequeña y mediana en México." *Economía Mexicana,* no. 7:35–68.

Jenkins, Barbara. 1992. *The Paradox of Continental Production: National Investment Policies in North America.* Ithaca: Cornell University Press.

Johnson Ceva, Kristin. 1998. "Business-Government Relations in Mexico Since 1990: NAFTA, Economic Crisis, and the Reorganization of Business Interests." In *Mexico's Private Sector: Recent History, Future Challenges,* ed. R. Roett. Boulder, Colo.: Lynne Rienner.

Juárez González, Leticia. 1984. "El proyecto económico cardenista y la posición empresarial (1934–1938)." In *Clases dominantes y estado en México,* ed. Salvador H. Cordero and Ricardo Tirado. Mexico City: UNAM.

————. 1991. "Una década en la organización y participación empresarial: 1928–1938." In *Las empresas y los empresarios en el México contemporáneo,* ed. Ricardo Pozas and Matilde Luna. Mexico City: Editorial Grijalbo.

Kait, Samuel. 1997. *Quién es quien en defensa de la industria argentina.* Buenos Aires: Editorial Visual.

Karl, Terry Lynn. 1986. "Petroleum and Political Pacts: The Transition to Democracy in Venezuela." In *Transitions from Authoritarian Rule: Latin America,* ed. Guillermo O'Donnell, Philippe C. Schmitter, and Laurence Whitehead. Baltimore: Johns Hopkins University Press.

Katzenstein, Peter J. 1984. *Corporatism and Change: Austria, Switzerland, and the Politics of Industry.* Ithaca: Cornell University Press.

Kaufman, Robert R. 1977. "Mexico and Latin American Authoritarianism." In *Authoritarianism in Mexico,* ed. José Luis Reyna and Richard S. Weinert. Philadelphia: Institute for the Study of Human Issues.

————. 1988. *The Politics of Debt in Argentina, Brazil, and Mexico: Economic Stabilization in the 1980s.* Berkeley, Calif.: Institute of International Studies.

Kaufman, Robert R., Carlos Bazdresch, and Blanca Heredia. 1994. "Mexico: Radical Reform in a Dominant Party System." In *Voting for Reform: Democracy, Political Liberalization, and Economic Adjustment,* ed. Stephan Haggard and Steven B. Webb. New York: Oxford University Press.

Kenworthy, Eldon. 1972. "Did the 'New Industrialists' Play a Significant Role in the Formation of Perón's Coalition, 1943–1946?" In *New Perspectives on Modern Argentina,* ed. Alberto Ciría et al. Bloomington: Latin American Studies Program, Indiana University.

King, Timothy. 1970. *Mexico: Industrialization and Trade Policies Since 1940.* London: Oxford University Press.

Kingstone, Peter. 1998. "Corporatism, Neoliberalism, and the Failed Revolt of Big Business: Lessons from the Case of IEDI." *Journal of Interamerican Studies and World Affairs* 40, no. 4:73–96.

———. 1999. *Crafting Coalitions for Reform: Business Preferences, Political Institutions, and Neoliberal Reform in Brazil.* University Park: Pennsylvania State University Press.

Klesner, Joseph. 1997a. "Electoral Reform in Mexico's Hegemonic Party System: Perpetuation of Privilege or Democratic Advance?" Paper prepared for the 1997 annual meeting of the American Political Science Association, Washington, D.C., August 28–31.

———. 1997b. "The Mexican Midterm Congressional and Gubernatorial Elections of 1997: End of the Hegemonic Party System." *Electoral Studies* 16, no. 4:567–75.

Kling, Merle. 1961. *A Mexican Interest Group in Action.* Englewood Cliffs, N.J.: Prentice-Hall.

Knight, Alan. 1994. "Cardenismo: Juggernaut or Jalopy?" *Journal of Latin American Studies* 26, no. 1:73–107.

Krueger, Anne. 1974. "The Political Economy of the Rent-Seeking Society." *American Economic Review* 64, no. 3:291–303.

Kurtz, Marcus J. 2002. "Understanding Democracy in the Open Economy: Neoliberalism and Democratic Deepening in Latin America." Paper prepared for the 2002 annual meeting of the American Political Science Association, Boston, August 29–September 1.

———. Forthcoming 2004. *Free Market Democracy and the Chilean and Mexican Countryside.* New York: Cambridge University Press.

Lall, Sanjaya. 1996. *Learning from the Asian Tigers: Studies in Technology and Industrial Policy.* London: Macmillan.

Lavín, José Domingo. 1954. *Inversiones extranjeras: Análisis, experiencias y orientaciones para la conducta mexicana.* Mexico City: Edición y Distribución Ibero Americano de Publicaciones.

———. 1960. *El desarrollo económico de México y la revolución.* Mexico City: CANACINTRA.

Lawson, Chappell. 1997. "Mexico's New Politics: The Elections of 1997." *Journal of Democracy* 8, no. 4:13–27.

Leopoldi, Maria Antonieta P. 1984. "Industrial Associations and Politics in Contemporary Brazil: The Associations of Industrialists, Economic Policy-Making and the State, with Special Reference to the Period 1930–1961." Ph.D. diss., Oxford University.

Lessard, Donald R., and John Williamson. 1987. *Capital Flight and Third World Debt.* Washington, D.C.: Institute for International Economics.

Levitsky, Steven. 2001. "Organization and Labor-Based Party Adaptation: The Transformation of Argentine Peronism in Comparative Perspective." *World Politics* 54, no. 1:27–56.

Levy, Daniel C., and Kathleen Bruhn. 2001. *Mexico: The Struggle for Democratic Development.* Berkeley and Los Angeles: University of California Press.

Lewis, Paul M. 1990. *The Crisis of Argentine Capitalism.* Chapel Hill: University of North Carolina Press

Lichbach, Mark Irving. 1995. *The Rebel's Dilemma.* Ann Arbor: University of Michigan Press.

Lindblom, Charles E. 1977. *Politics and Markets: The World's Political-Economic Systems.* New York: Basic Books.

———. 1982. "The Market as Prison." *Journal of Politics* 44, no. 2:324–36.

Linz, Juan J., Alfred Stepan. 1996. *Problems of Democratic Transition and Consolidation: Southern Europe, South America, and Post-Communist Europe.* Baltimore: Johns Hopkins University Press.

Lloréns, Juan Luis, Robert van der Host, and Iñigo Isusi. 1999. *Compilación de estadísticas de Pymes en 18 países de América Latina y el Caribe.* Grupo Asesor sobre Pequeña y Mediana Empresa. Banco Interamericano de Desarrollo.

Lombardo Toledano, Vicente. 1951. "Anotaciones al libro de Sanford Mosk: 'La revolución industrial en México.'" *Problemas agrícolas e industriales de México* 3, no. 2:289–96.

López Espinosa, Mario. 1994. "El financiamiento de la pequeña y mediana empresa en américa latina: Propuestas de acción a partir de la experiencia de México." Typescript. CEPAL.

———. 1995. "Consideraciones sobre el acceso de la pequeña empresa y el taller artesanal a los mecanismos formales de financiamiento." In *Micro y pequeña empresa en México: Frente a los retos de la globalización,* ed. Thomas Calvo and Bernardo Méndez Lugo. Mexico City: Centro de Estudios Mexicanos y Centroamericanos.

Loveman, Gary, and Werner Sengenberger. 1991. "Introduction: Economic and Social Reorganisation in the Small and Medium-Sized Enterprise Sector." In *The Re-emergence of Small Enterprises: Industrial Restructuring in Industrialized Countries,* ed. Werner Sengenberger, Gary W. Loveman, and Michael J. Piore. Geneva: International Institute for Labour Studies.

Luna, Matilde. 1992a. "Las asociaciones empresariales mexicanas y la apertura externa." Paper presented at the Seventeenth Congress of the Latin American Studies Association, Los Angeles, September 24–27.

———. 1992b. *Los empresarios y el cambio político: México, 1970–1987.* Mexico City: Ediciones Era.

———. 1995a. "La acción organizada del sector privado: Los empresarios pequeños." In *Micro y pequeña empresa en México: Frente a los retos de la globalización,* ed. Thomas Calvo and Bernardo Méndez Lugo. Mexico City: Centro de Estudios Mexicanos y Centroamericanos.

———. 1995b. "Entrepreneurial Interests and Political Action in Mexico: Facing the Demands of Economic Modernization." In *The Challenge of Institutional Reform in Mexico,* ed. Riordan Roett. Boulder, Colo.: Lynne Rienner.

Luna, Matilde, and Ricardo Tirado. 1992. *El Consejo Coordinador Empresarial: Una radiografía.* Proyecto Organizaciones Empresariales en México, 1. Mexico City: Institute for Social Research, National Autonomous University of Mexico.

Luna, Matilde, Ricardo Tirado, and Francisco Valdés. 1987. "Businessmen and Politics in Mexico, 1982–1986." In *Government and Private Sector in Contemporary Mexico,* ed. Sylvia Maxfield and Ricardo Anzaldúa Montoya. Monograph Series 20. La Jolla: Center for U.S.-Mexican Studies, University of California, San Diego.

Lustig, Nora. 1998. *Mexico: The Remaking of an Economy.* 2d ed. Washington, D.C.: Brookings Institution.

Lütke-Entrup, Monika. 2000. "Business, Labour, and the State in Mexican Industrial Development (1938–1946): The Political Economy of Unidad Nacional." Ph.D. diss., St. Antony's College, Oxford University.

Mahon, James. 1996. *Mobile Capital and Latin American Development.* University Park: Pennsylvania State University Press.

Mainwairing, Scott. 1986. "The State and the Industrial Bourgeoisie in Peron's Argentina, 1945–1955." *Studies in Comparative International Development* 21, no. 1 (Fall): 3–31.

Mainwaring, Scott, Guillermo O'Donnell, and J. Samuel Valenzuela. 1992. *Issues in Democratic Consolidation: The New South American Democracies in Comparative Perspective.* Notre Dame: University of Notre Dame Press.

Mainwaring, Scott, and Timothy R. Scully, ed. 1995. *Building Democratic Institutions: Party Systems in Latin America.* Stanford: Stanford University Press.

Malloy, James M., ed. 1977. *Authoritarianism and Corporatism in Latin America.* Pittsburgh: University of Pittsburgh Press.

Manzetti, Luigi. 1993. *Institutions, Parties, and Coalitions in Argentine Politics.* Pittsburgh: University of Pittsburgh Press.

Mares, David R. 1985. "Explaining Choice of Development Strategies: Suggestions from Mexico, 1970–1982." *International Organization* 39, no. 4:667–97.

Martínez Nava, Juan Manuel. 1984. *Conflicto estado empresarios en los gobiernos de Cárdenas, López Mateos y Echeverría.* Mexico City: Editorial Nueva Imagen.

Máttar Márquez, Jorge. 1991. "Fomento a la industria mediana y pequeña en México: 1983–1988." *Economía Mexicana,* no. 9–10 (August): 33–57.

Maxfield, Sylvia. 1989. "International Economic Opening and Government-Business Relations." In *Mexico's Alternative Political Futures,* ed. Wayne A. Cornelius, Judith Gentleman, and Peter H. Smith. Monograph Series 30. La Jolla: Center for U.S.-Mexican Studies, University of California, San Diego.

———. 1990. *Governing Capital: International Finance and Mexican Politics.* Ithaca: Cornell University Press.

———. 1991. "The Domestic Politics of Mexican Trade Policy." In *North American Free Trade: Proceedings of a Conference,* by Federal Reserve Bank of Dallas. Dallas: Federal Reserve Bank of Dallas.

Maxfield, Sylvia, and Ricardo Anzaldúa Montoya, eds. 1987. *Government and Private Sector in Contemporary Mexico.* Monograph Series 20. La Jolla: Center for U.S.-Mexican Studies, University of California, San Diego.

Maxfield, Sylvia, and James H. Nolt. 1990. "Protectionism and the Internationalization of Capital: U.S. Sponsorship of Import Substitution Industrialization in the Philippines, Turkey and Argentina." *International Studies Quarterly* 34, no. 1:49–81.

Maxfield, Sylvia, and Adam Shapiro. 1997. "Assessing the NAFTA Negotiations: U.S.-Mexican Debate and Compromise on Tariff and Nontariff Issues." In *The Post-NAFTA Political Economy: Mexico and the Western Hemisphere,* ed. Carol Wise. University Park: Pennsylvania State University Press.

Mendez Martínez, José Luis. 1996. "Del estado proprietario al estado promotor? La política hacia la micro, pequeña y mediana industria en México 1988–1994," *Foro Internacional* 36, no. 1–2:31–79.

Mendirichaga, Rodrigo. 1989. *La cámara industrial de Nuevo León, 1944–1988.* Monterrey, Mexico: Emediciones.

Mericle, Kenneth Scott. 1974. "Conflict Regulation in the Brazilian Industrial Relations System." Ph.D. diss., University of Wisconsin.

Middlebrook, Kevin J. 1986. "Political Liberalization in an Authoritarian Regime: The Case of Mexico." In *Transitions from Authoritarian Rule: Latin America,* ed. Guillermo O'Donnell, Philippe C. Schmitter, and Laurence Whitehead. Baltimore: Johns Hopkins University Press.

————. 1995. *The Paradox of Revolution: Labor, the State, and Authoritarianism in Mexico.* Baltimore: Johns Hopkins University Press.

Millán, René. 1988. *Los empresarios ante el estado y la sociedad.* Mexico City: Siglo Veintiuno Editores.

Mizrahi, Yemile. 1994. "Rebels Without a Cause? The Politics of Entrepreneurs in Chihuahua." *Journal of Latin American Studies* 26 (February): 137–58.

Molinar, Juan. 1991. *El tiempo de la legitimidad.* Mexico City: Cal y Arena.

Montero, Alfred P. 2002. *Shifting States in Global Markets: Subnational Industrial Policy in Contemporary Brazil and Spain.* University Park: Pennsylvania State University Press.

Montesinos Carrera, Rafael. 1992. "El discurso empresarial en 1985." In *Los empresarios mexicanos, ayer y hoy,* ed. Cristina Puga and Ricardo Tirado. Mexico City: Ediciones el Caballito.

Moore, Mick, and Ladi Hamalai. 1993. "Economic Liberalization, Political Pluralism, and Business Associations in Developing Countries." *World Development* 21, no. 12:1895–912.

Moore, Pete W. 2001. "What Makes Successful Business Lobbies? Business Associations and the Rentier State in Jordan and Kuwait." *Comparative Politics* 33, no. 2:127–46.

Moori-Koenig, Virginia, Carlo Alberto Ferraro, and Gabriel Yoguel. 2002. "Situación y política PYMES en Argentina en los noventa." In *Las pequeñas y medianas empresas industriales en América Latina y el Caribe,* ed. Wilson Peres and Giovanni Stumpo. Mexico City: CEPAL.

Morris, Stephen. 1995. *Political Reformism in Mexico: An Overview of Contemporary Mexican Politics.* Boulder, Colo.: Lynne Rienner.

Mosk, Sanford A. 1950. *Industrial Revolution in Mexico.* Berkeley and Los Angeles: University of California Press.

Munck, Gerardo L. 1998. *Authoritarianism and Democratization: Soldiers and Workers in Argentina, 1976–1983.* University Park: Pennsylvania State University Press.

————. 2001. "The Regime Question: Theory Building in Democracy Studies." *World Politics* 54, no. 1:119–44.

————. 2003. "Democracy Studies: Agendas, Findings, and Challenges." Unpublished manuscript, University of Southern California.

Muñoz, Oscar, ed. 1996a. *Estado, empresarios, instituciones: Estrategias para la transformación productiva.* Santiago de Chile: CEPAL.

————. 1996b. "Los proyectos de fomento productivo." In *Estado, empresarios, instituciones: Estrategias para la transformación productiva,* ed. Oscar Muñoz. Santiago de Chile: CEPAL.

NAFIN-INEGI. 1993. *La micro, pequeña y mediana empresa: Principales características.* Biblioteca de la Micro, Pequeña y Mediana Empresa 7. Mexico City: Nacional Financiera.

NAFIN-ONUDI. 1977. *México: Una estrategia para desarrollar la industria de bienes de capital.* Mexico City: Nacional Financiera, Organización de las Naciones Unidas para el Desarrollo Industrial.

————. 1985. *Mexico: Los bienes de capital en la situación económica presente.* Mexico City: Nacional Financiera, Organización de las Naciones Unidas para el Desarrollo Industrial.

NAFIN-SPP-INEGI. 1988. *Encuesta de la industria mediana y pequeña, 1985.* Mexico City: Nacional Financiera.

Newfarmer, Richard, and Willard Mueller. 1975. *Multinational Corporations in Brazil and Mexico: Structural Sources of Economic and Noneconomic Power. Report to the Subcommittee on Multinational Corporations of the Committee on Foreign Relations.* Washington, D.C.: United States Senate.

Niosi, Jorge. 1974. *Los empresarios y el estado argentino, 1955–1969.* Buenos Aires: Siglo XXI Argentina Editores.

Norden, Deborah L. 1996. *Military Rebellion in Argentina: Between Coups and Consolidation.* Lincoln: University of Nebraska Press.

Nylen, William R. 1992. "Small Business Owners Fight Back: Non-elite Capital Activism in 'Democratizing Brazil' (1978–1990)." Ph.D. diss., Columbia University.

———. 1997. "Small Business and Democratization in Brazil." Paper presented at the 1997 annual meeting of the American Political Science Association, Washington, D.C., August.

O'Brien, Thomas. 1999. *The Century of U.S. Capitalism in Latin America.* Albuquerque: University of New Mexico Press.

O'Donnell, Guillermo A. 1973. *Modernization and Bureaucratic-Authoritarianism: Studies in South American Politics.* Berkeley: Institute of International Studies, University of California.

———. 1977. "Corporatism and the Question of the State." In *Authoritarianism and Corporatism in Latin America,* ed. James M. Malloy. Pittsburgh: University of Pittsburgh Press.

———. 1978. "State and Alliances in Argentina, 1956–1976." *Journal of Development Studies* 15, no. 1:3–33.

———. 1993a. "The Browning of Latin America." *New Perspectives Quarterly* 10, no. 4:50–53.

———. 1993b. "On the State, Democratization, and Some Conceptual Problems: A Latin American View with Glances at Some Postcommunist Countries." *World Development* 21, no. 8:1355–69.

———. 1994. "Delegative Democracy." *Journal of Democracy* 5, no. 1:55–69.

———. 1996. "Illusions About Consolidation." *Journal of Democracy* 7, no. 2:34–51.

———. 1998. "Horizontal Accountability in New Democracies." *Journal of Democracy* 9, no. 3:112–26.

———. 1999. *Counterpoints: Selected Essays on Authoritarianism and Democratization.* Notre Dame: University of Notre Dame Press.

O'Donnell, Guillermo, and Philippe Schmitter. 1986. *Transitions from Authoritarian Rule: Tentative Conclusions About Uncertain Democracies.* Baltimore: Johns Hopkins University Press.

O'Donnell, Guillermo, Philippe C. Schmitter, and Laurence Whitehead, eds. 1986. *Transitions from Authoritarian Rule: Latin America.* Baltimore: Johns Hopkins University Press.

Offe, Claus. 1981. "The Attribution of Public Status to Interest Groups: Observations on the West German Case." In *Organizing Interests in Western Europe: Pluralism, Corporatism, and the Transformation of Politics,* ed. Suzanne D. Berger. Cambridge: Cambridge University Press.

Offe, Claus, and Helmut Wiesenthal. 1980. "Two Logics of Collective Action: Theoretical Notes on Social Class and Organizational Form." *Political Power and Social Theory* 1:67–115.

Olson, Mancur. 1965. *The Logic of Collective Action: Public Goods and the Theory of Groups.* Cambridge: Harvard University Press.

———. 1982. *The Rise and Decline of Nations: Economic Growth, Stagflation, and Social Rigidities.* New Haven: Yale University Press.

Ortíz Muñíz, Gilberto. 1992. "La integración México–Estados Unidos–Canadá: El impacto de la integración sobre las pequeña y mediana industrias." In *La integración comercial de México a Estados Unidos y Canadá: Alternativa o destino?* ed. Benito Rey Romay. 3d ed. Mexico City: Siglo Veintiuno Editores.

Ortíz Rivera, Alicia. 2000. "El consejo mexicano de hombres de negocios: Órgano de acción política de la élite empresarial." Paper presented at Twenty-second International Congress of the Latin American Studies Association, Miami, March.

Ostiguy, Pierre. 1990. *Los capitanes de la industria: Grandes empresarios, política y economía de la Argentina de los años 80.* Buenos Aires: Editorial Legasa.

Oxhorn, Philip D., and Graciela Ducatenzeiler. 1998. *What Kind of Democracy? What Kind of Market? Latin America in the Age of Neoliberalism.* University Park: Pennsylvania State University Press.

Pastor, Manuel, and Carol Wise. 1994. "The Origins and Sustainability of Mexico's Free Trade Policy." *International Organization* 48, no. 3:459–89.

———. 1997. "Mexican-Style Neoliberalism: State Policy and Distributional Stress." In *The Post-NAFTA Political Economy: Mexico and the Western Hemisphere,* ed. Carol Wise. University Park: Pennsylvania State University Press.

———. 1999. "The Politics of Second-Generation Reform." *Journal of Democracy* 10, no. 3:34–48.

Patterson, Dennis. 1994. "Electoral Influence and Economic Policy: Political Origins of Financial Aid to Small Business in Japan." *Comparative Political Studies* 27, no. 3:425–47.

Payne, Leigh A. 1994. *Brazilian Industrialists and Democratic Change.* Baltimore: Johns Hopkins University Press.

Pellicer de Brody. 1972. *México y la revolución cubana.* Mexico City: El Colegio de México.

Peres, Wilson, and Giovani Stumpo. 2000. "Small and Medium-Sized Manufacturing Enterprises in Latin America and the Caribbean Under the New Economic Model." *World Development* 28, no. 9:1643–55.

———, ed. 2002. *Las pequeñas y medianas empresas industriales en América Latina y el Caribe.* Mexico City: CEPAL.

Peschard, Jacqueline, Cristina Puga, and Ricardo Tirado. 1986. "De Ávila Camacho a Miguel Alemán." In *Evolución del estado mexicano: Consolidación, 1940–1983.* Mexico City: Ediciones del Caballito.

Pion-Berlin, David. 1997. *Through Corridors of Power: Institutions and Civil-Military Relations in Argentina.* University Park: Pennsylvania State University Press.

Piore, Michael J., and Charles F. Sabel. 1984. *The Second Industrial Divide: Possibilities for Prosperity.* New York: Basic Books.

Poitras, Guy, and Raymund Robinson. 1994. "The Politics of NAFTA in Mexico." *Journal of Interamerican Studies and World Affairs* 36, no. 1:1–35.

Pontusson, Jonas. 1995. "From Comparative Public Policy to Political Economy: Putting Political Institutions in Their Place and Taking Interests Seriously." *Comparative Political Studies* 28, no. 1:117–47.

Power, Timothy J. 2000. *The Political Right in Postauthoritarian Brazil: Elites, Institutions, and Democratization.* University Park: Pennsylvania State University Press.

Power, Timothy J., and Mahrukh Doctor. Forthcoming 2004. "Beyond the Century of Corporatism? Continuity and Change in Brazilian Corporatist Structures." In *Authoritarianism and Corporatism in Latin America, Revisited,* ed. Howard J. Wiarda. Gainesville: University of Florida Press.

Prebisch, Raul. 1950. *The Economic Development of Latin America and Its Principal Problems.* New York: United Nations.

Presidencia de la Republica. 1992. *Diccionario biografico del gobierno mexicano.* Mexico City: Fondo de la Cultura Económica.

Przeworski, Adam. 1991. *Democracy and the Market: Political and Economic Reforms in Eastern Europe and Latin America.* New York: Cambridge University Press.

Przeworski, Adam, et al. 1995. *Sustainable Democracy.* New York: Cambridge University Press.

Przeworski, Adam, Susan C. Stokes, and Bernard Manin. 1999. *Democracy, Accountability, and Representation.* Cambridge: Cambridge University Press.

Przeworski, Adam, and Michael Wallerstein. 1982. "Structural Dependence of the State on Capital." *American Political Science Review* 82, no. 1:11–31.

Puga, Cristina. 1984. "Los empresarios y la política en México." In *Clases dominantes y estado en México,* ed. Salvador H. Cordero and Ricardo Tirado. Mexico City: UNAM.

———. 1991. "La lucha política en México: El caso de los industriales, 1982–1985." In *Las empresas y los empresarios en el México contemporáneo,* ed. Ricardo Pozas and Matilde Luna. Mexico City: Editorial Grijalbo.

———. 1992. *Empresarios medianos, pequeños y micro: Problemas de organización y representación.* Proyecto Organizaciones Empresariales en México, 3. Mexico City: Institute for Social Research, National Autonomous University of Mexico.

———. 1993a. *Mexico: Empresarios y poder.* Mexico City: Miguel Angel Porrúa.

———. 1993b. "Las Organizaciones Empresariales Mexicanas de Comercio Exterior." In *Organizaciones empresariales y Tratado de Libre Comercio,* ed. Cristina Puga. Proyecto Organizaciones Empresariales en México, 7. Mexico City: Institute for Social Research, National Autonomous University of Mexico.

Purcell, John F. H., and Susan Kaufman Purcell. 1977. "Mexican Business and Public Policy." In *Authoritarianism and Corporatism in Latin America,* ed. James M. Malloy. Pittsburgh: University of Pittsburgh Press.

Purcell, Susan Kaufman. 1975. *The Mexican Profit-Sharing Decision: Politics in an Authoritarian Regime.* Berkeley and Los Angeles: University of California Press.

———. 1981. "Business-Government Relations in Mexico: The Case of the Sugar Industry." *Comparative Politics* 13, no. 2:211–33.

Putnam, Robert D. 1993. *Making Democracy Work: Civic Traditions in Modern Italy.* Princeton: Princeton University Press.

Rangel Flores, Lucía, and Roberto Fuentes Vivar. 1999. "¿Son mejores que los políticos?" *Expansión.* No. 770, July 21.

Reyes Heroles, Jesús. 1951. "A propósito de 'La revolución industrial en México.'" *Problemas agrícolas e industriales de México* 3, no. 2:242–45.

Reyna, José Luis, and Richard Weinert, eds. 1977. *Authoritarianism in Mexico.* Philadelphia: Institute for the Study of Human Issues.

Reynolds, Clark W. 1970. *The Mexican Economy: Twentieth-Century Structure and Growth.* New Haven: Yale University Press.

Riquelme Inda, Julio. 1957. *Cuatro décadas de vida, 1917–1957.* Mexico City: CONCANACO.

Rivera, Adán. 2000. "Desconcentración de la riqueza y del empresariado." In *Un futuro para México: Visiones y propuestas desde la sociedad,* by Causa Ciudadana. Mexico City: Causa Ciudadana.

Red Mexicana de Acción Frente al Libre Comercio. 1997. *Espejismo y realidad: El TLCAN tres años después: Análisis y propuesta desde la sociedad civil.* Mexico City: Red Mexicana de Acción Frente al Libre Comercio.

Roberts, Kenneth M. 1998. *Deepening Democracy? The Modern Left and Social Movements in Chile and Peru.* Stanford: Stanford University Press.

Rocha, Carlos Henrique, and Hélio Eduardo da Silva. 2002. "Estrutura industrial brasileira e políticas de apoio as empresas industriais de pequeno porte." In *Las pequeñas y medianas empresas industriales en América Latina y el Caribe,* ed. Wilson Peres and Giovanni Stumpo.Mexico City: CEPAL.

Ros, Jaime. 1993. "Mexico's Trade and Industrialization Experience Since 1960: A Reconsideration of Past Policies and Assessment of Current Reforms." Working Paper 166, Helen Kellogg Institute for International Studies, University of Notre Dame.

Roxborough, Ian. 1992a. "Inflation and Social Pacts in Brazil and Mexico." *Journal of Latin American Studies* 24, part 3 (October): 639–64.

———. 1992b. "Mexico." In *Latin America Between the Second World War and the Cold War: 1944–1948,* ed. Ian Roxborough and Leslie Bethell. New York: Cambridge University Press.

———. 1997. "Citizenship and Social Movements Under Neoliberalism." In *Politics, Social Change, and Economic Restructuring in Latin America,* ed. William C. Smith and Roberto Patricio Korzeniewicz. Coral Gables, Fla.: North-South Center Press.

Roy, William G., and Rachel Parker-Gwin. 1999. "How Many Logics of Collective Action?" *Theory and Society* 28, no. 2:203–37.

Rubio F., Luís. 1988. "The Changing Role of the Private Sector." In *Mexico in Transition,* ed. Susan Kaufman Purcell. New York: Council on Foreign Relations.

———. 1992. *Cómo va a afectar a México el Tratado de Libre Comercio?* Mexico City: Fondo de la Cultura Económica.

Rubio F., Luís, Cristina Rodriguez D., and Roberto Blum V. 1989. "The Making of Mexico's Trade Policy and the Uruguay Round." In *Domestic Trade Politics and the Uruguay Round,* ed. Henry R. Nau. New York: Columbia University Press.

Rueschemeyer, Dietrich, Evelyne Huber Stephens, and John D. Stephens. 1992. *Capitalist Development and Democracy.* Chicago: University of Chicago Press.

Ruíz Durán, Clemente. 1993. "Mexico: Diagnóstico de la pequeña industria y de las políticas para fortalecer su competitividad y desarrollo." Typescript. Division de Estudios de Posgrado de la Facultad de Economía, UNAM.

———. 1994. "Introducción: Micro, pequeña y mediana empresa en la economía globalizada." In *El papel de la micro, pequeña y mediana empresa en el proceso de globalización de la economía mundial,* ed. Clemente Ruíz Durán. Mexico City: Nacional Financiera.

———. 1995. *Economía de redes: Elementos de una nueva alternativa empresarial.* Mexico City: Division de Estudios de Posgrado de la Facultad de Economía, UNAM.

Ruíz Durán, Clemente, and Mitsuhiro Kagami. 1993. *Potencial tecnológico de la micro y pequeña empresa en México.* Biblioteca de la Micro, Pequeña y Mediana Empresa 5. Mexico City: Nacional Financiera, S.N.C.

Ruíz Durán, Clemente, and Carlos Zubirán Schadtler. 1992. *Cambios en la estructura industrial y el papel de las micro, pequeñas y medianas empresas en México.* Biblioteca de la Micro, Pequeña y Mediana Empresa 2. Mexico City: Nacional Financiera, S.N.C.

Rustow, Dankwart. 1970. "Transitions to Democracy: Toward a Dynamic Model." *Comparative Politics* 2, no. 3:337–63.

Saboia, Joao. 2002. "Pequenas e medias empresas industriais no Brasil a experiencia da última década." In *Las pequeñas y medianas empresas industriales en América Latina y el Caribe,* ed. Wilson Peres and Giovanni Stumpo. Mexico City: CEPAL.

Salamon, Lester M., and John J. Siegfried. 1977. "Economic Power and Political Influence: The Impact of Industry Structure on Public Policy." *American Political Science Review* 71, no. 3:1026–43.

Saragoza, Alex M. 1988. *The Monterrey Elite and the Mexican State, 1880–1940.* Austin: University of Texas Press.

Schedler, Andreas. 1998. "What Is Democratic Consolidation?" *Journal of Democracy* 9, no. 2:91–107.

———. 2001. "Measuring Democratic Consolidation." *Studies in Comparative International Development* 36, no. 1:66–92.

Schmitter, Philippe C. 1971. *Interest Conflict and Political Change in Brazil.* Stanford: Stanford University Press.

———. 1974. "Still the Century of Corporatism?" *Review of Politics* 36, no. 1:85–131.

———. 1982. "Reflections on Where the Theory of Neo-corporatism Has Gone and Where the Praxis of Neo-corporatism May be Going." In *Patterns of Corporatist Policymaking,* ed. G. Lehmbruch and P. Schmitter. London: Sage.

———. 1989. "Corporatism is Dead! Long Live Corporatism!" *Government and Opposition* 24, no. 1:54–73.

———. 1992. "The Consolidation of Democracy and Representation of Social Groups," *American Behavioral Scientist* 35, no. 4–5:422–49.

———. 1995. "The Consolidation of Political Democracies: Processes, Rhythms, Sequences and Types," In *Transitions to Democracy: Comparative Perspectives from Southern Europe, Latin America, and Eastern Europe,* ed. Geoffrey Pridham. Brookfield, Vt.: Dartmouth.

———. 1997. "Intermediaries in the Consolidation of Neo-democracies: The Role of Parties, Associations, and Movements." Institut de Ciències Polìtiques i Socials, WP núm. 130. Barcelona: Universitat Autònoma de Barcelona.

Schmitter, Philippe C., and Wolfgang Streeck. 1981. "The Organization of Business Interests: A Research Design to Study the Associative Action of Business in the Advanced Industrial Societies of Western Europe." Discussion Paper IIM/LPM 81–13. Berlin: Wissenschaftszentrum.

Schneider, Ben Ross. 1997. "Big Business and the Politics of Economic Reform: Confidence and Concertation in Brazil and Mexico." In *Business and the State in Developing Countries,* ed. Ben Ross Schneider and Sylvia Maxfield. Ithaca: Cornell University Press.

———. 1997–98. "Organized Business Politics in Democratic Brazil." *Journal of Interamerican Studies and World Affairs* 39, no. 4:95–127.

———. 1999. "The Desarrollista State in Brazil and Mexico." In *The Developmental State,* ed. Meredith Woo-Cumings. Ithaca: Cornell University Press.

———. 2002. "Why Is Mexican Business So Organized?" *Latin American Research Review* 37, no. 1:77–118.

———. Forthcoming 2004. *Business Politics and the State in Twentieth Century Latin America.*

Schneider, Ben Ross, and Sylvia Maxfield, ed. 1997. *Business and the State in Developing Countries.* Ithaca: Cornell University Press.

SECOFI. 1991. *Programa para la modernización y desarrollo de la industria micro, pequeña y mediana, 1991–1994.* Mexico City: Secretaría de Comercio y Fomento Industrial.

Secretaría de Economía. 1952. *Tercer Censo Industrial de los Estados Unidos Mexicanos, 1940.* Mexico City: Secretaría de Economía.

Sengenberger, Werner, Gary W. Loveman, and Michael J. Piore, ed. 1991. *The Re-emergence of Small Enterprises: Industrial Restructuring in Industrialized Countries.* Geneva: International Institute for Labour Studies.

Senzek, Alva. 1997. "The Entrepreneurs Who Became Radicals." *NACLA Report on the Americas* 30, no. 4:28–29.

Seoane, María. 2003. *El burgés maldito: Los secretos de Gelbard, el ultimo líder del capitalismo nacional.* Buenos Aires: Editorial Sudamericana.

Shadlen, Kenneth C. 1997. "Corporatism and the Organization of Business Interests: Small Industry and the State in Postrevolutionary Mexico." Ph.D. diss., University of California, Berkeley.

———. 1999. "Continuity Amid Change: Democratization, Party Strategies and Economic Policymaking in Mexico." *Government and Opposition* 34, no. 3:397–419.

———. 2000. "Neoliberalism, Corporatism, and Small Business Political Activism in Contemporary Mexico." *Latin American Research Review* 35, no. 2:73–106.

———. 2002. "Orphaned by Democracy: Small Industry in Contemporary Mexico." *Comparative Politics* 35, no. 1:43–62.

Shafer, D. Michael. 1994. *Winners and Losers: How Sectors Shape the Developmental Prospects of States.* Ithaca: Cornell University Press.

Shafer, Robert Jones. 1973. *Mexican Business Organizations: History and Analysis.* Syracuse: Syracuse University Press.

Sheahan, John. 1987. *Patterns of Development in Latin America: Poverty, Repression, and Economic Strategy.* Princeton: Princeton University Press.

Siavelis, Peter. 2000. *The President and Congress in Postauthoritarian Chile: Institutional Constraints to Democratic Consolidation.* University Park: Pennsylvania State University Press.

SIC. 1959. *VI Censo Industrial 1956.* Mexico City: Secretaría de Industria y Comercio.

———. 1965. *VII Censo Industrial 1961. Resumen General.* Mexico City: Secretaría de Industria y Comercio.

———. 1973. *IX Censo Industrial 1971. Tomo I. Resumen General. Información Referente a 1970 por Actividades Industriales.* Mexico City: Secretaría de Industria y Comercio.

SIID. 1996. *Origen y evolución de la Ley de las Cámaras de Comercio y de las Industrias.* Mexico City: Sistema Integral de Información y Documentación, Congreso de la Unión.

Silva, Eduardo. 1996. "From Dictatorship to Democracy: The Business-State Nexus in Chile's Economic Transformation, 1975–1994." *Comparative Politics* 28, no. 3:299–320.

———. 1997. "Business Elites, the State, and Economic Change in Chile." In *Business and the State in Developing Countries,* ed. Ben Ross Schneider and Sylvia Maxfield. Ithaca: Cornell University Press.

Smith, William C. 1985. "Reflections on the Political Economy of Authoritarian Rule and Capitalist Reorganization in Contemporary Argentina." In *Generals in Retreat,* ed. Philip O'Brien and Paul Cammack. Manchester: Manchester University Press.

———. 1991. *Authoritarianism and the Crisis of the Argentine Political Economy.* Stanford: Stanford University Press.

Smith, William C., Carlos H. Acuña, and Eduardo A. Gamarra, eds. 1994. *Latin American Political Economy in the Age of Neoliberal Reform: Theoretical and Comparative Perspectives for the 1990s.* Boulder, Colo.: Lynne Rienner.

Smith, William C., and Roberto Patricio Korzeniewicz, eds. 1997. *Politics, Social Change, and Economic Restructuring in Latin America.* Coral Gables, Fla.: North-South Center Press.

Snyder, Richard. 2001. *Politics After Neoliberalism: Reregulation in Mexico.* New York: Cambridge University Press.

Snyder, Richard, and James Mahoney. 1999. "The Missing Variable." *Comparative Politics* 32, no. 1:103–22.

Solís, Leopoldo. 1979. "Industrial Priorities in Mexico." In *Industrial Priorities in Developing Countries: The Selection Process in Brazil, India, Mexico, Republic of Korea and Turkey,* by UNIDO. New York: United Nations Industrial Development Organization.

Soskice, David. 1999. "Divergent Production Regimes: Coordinated and Uncoordinated Market Economies in the 1980s and 1990s." In *Continuity and Change in Contemporary Capitalism,* ed. Herbert Kitschelt et al. New York: Cambridge University Press.

SPP. 1979. *X Censo Industrial 1976. Resumen General.* Mexico City: Secretaría de Programación y Presupuesto.

———. 1980. *Caracteristicas de la industria de transformacion en Mexico.* Mexico City: Secretaría de Programación y Presupuesto.

Stepan, Alfred. 1978. *The State and Society: Peru in Comparative Perspective.* Princeton: Princeton University Press.

———. 1988. *Rethinking Military Politics: Brazil and the Southern Cone.* Princeton: Princeton University Press.

Stockbridge, G. R. 1954. "Mexico's Cámara Nacional de la Industria de Transformación: Economic Nationalism at Work." Master's thesis, Boston University.

Stokes, Susan. 2001. *Mandates and Democracy: Neoliberalism by Surprise in Latin America.* New York: Cambridge University Press.

Story, Dale. 1982. "Trade Politics in the Third World: A Case Study of the Mexican GATT Decision." *International Organization* 36, no. 4:767–94.

———. 1986. *Industry, the State, and Public Policy in Mexico.* Austin: University of Texas Press.

———. 1987. "The PAN, the Private Sector, and the Future of the Mexican Opposition." In *Mexican Politics in Transition,* ed. Judith Gentleman. Boulder, Colo.: Westview Press.

Streeck, Wolfgang. 1990. "Interest Heterogeneity and Organizing Capacity: Two Class Logics of Collective Action." Estudio/Working Paper 1990/2, Centro de Estudios Avanzados en Ciencias Sociales, Madrid, Spain.

Streeck, Wolfgang, and Philippe C. Schmitter. 1985. "Community, Market, State—and Associations? The Prospective Contribution of Interest Governance to Social Order." In *Private Interest Government: Beyond Market and State,* ed. Wolfgang Streeck and Philippe Schmitter. London: Sage.

Szusterman, Celia. 1993. *Frondizi and the Politics of Developmentalism in Argentina, 1955–1962.* Pittsburgh: University of Pittsburgh Press.

Teichman, Judith. 1981. "Interest Conflict and Entrepreneurial Support for Perón." *Latin American Research Review* 16, no. 1:144–55.

Tello Villagrán, Pedro. 1995. "La pequeña mayoria: Reflexiones acerca de su estado actual." In *Micro y pequeña empresa en México: Frente a los retos de la globalización,* ed. Thomas Calvo and Bernardo Méndez Lugo. Mexico City: Centro de Estudios Mexicanos y Centroamericanos.

Ten Kate, Adriaan. 1992. "Trade Liberalization and Economic Stabilization in Mexico: Lessons of Experience." *World Development* 20, no. 5:659–72.

Tendler, Judith. 1997. *Good Government in the Tropics.* Baltimore: Johns Hopkins University Press.

Terrones López, Victor Manuel, ed. 1994. *Retos y propuestas: Política industrial.* Mexico City: Fundación Mexicana Cambio XXI-Luís Donaldo Colosio.

Thacker, Strom C. 2000. *Big Business, the State, and Free Trade: Constructing Coalitions in Mexico.* Cambridge: Cambridge University Press.

Tirado, Ricardo. 1992a. "Las organizaciones empresariales y el corporativismo empresarial mexicano." In *Relaciones corporativas en un período de transición,* ed. Matilde Luna and Ricardo Pozas H. Mexico City: Instituto de Investigaciones Sociales, UNAM.

———. 1992b. "Asociaciones empresariales cúpulas en México." Paper presented at the Seventeenth Congress of the Latin American Studies Association, Los Angeles, September 24–27.

———. 1998. "Mexico: From the Political Call for Collective Action to a Proposal for Free Market Economic Reform." In *Organized Business, Economic Change, and Democracy in Latin America,* ed. Francisco Durand and Eduardo Silva. Coral Gables, Fla.: North-South Center Press.

Tirado, Ricardo, and Matilde Luna. 1986. "La politización de los empresarios (1970–1982)." In *Grupos económicos y organizaciones empresariales en México,* ed. Julio Labastida. Mexico City: Alianza Editorial Mexicana.

———. 1995. "El Consejo Coordinador Empresarial de México: De la unidad contra el reformismo a la unidad para el TLC (1975–1993). *Revista Mexicana de Sociología* 57, no. 4:27–59.

Traxler, Franz. 1991. "The Logic of Employers' Collective Action." In *Employers' Associations in Europe: Policy and Organisation,* ed. Dieter Sadowski and Otto Jacobi. Baden-Baden, Germany: Nomos Verlagsgesellschaft.

———. 1993. "Business Associations and Labor Unions in Comparison: Theoretical Perspectives and Empirical Findings on Social Class, Collective Action and Associational Organizability." *British Journal of Sociology* 44, no. 4:673–91.

UIA. n.d. *Evolución y situación actual de las pequeñas y medianas industrias argentinas, 1995–2000.* Buenos Aires: Observatorio Permanente de las PyMIs Argentinas.

UNDP. 2002. *Human Development Report 2002: Deepening Democracy in a Fragmented World.* New York: United Nations Development Program.

USITC. 1990. *Review of Trade and Investment Liberalization Measures by Mexico and Prospects for Future United States–Mexico Relations. Phase I: Recent Trade and Investment Reforms Undertaken by Mexico and Implications for the United States.* USITC Publication 2275. Washington, D.C.: United States International Trade Commission.

Valdés Gaxiola, Alfredo. 1994. "Incrementar las interrelaciones entre las grandes y pequeñas empresas para favorecer la competitividad," In *La competitivad de la industria mexicana frente a la concurrencia internacional,* ed. Antonio Argüelles and José Antonio Gómez Mandujano. Mexico City: Fondo de Cultura Económica.

Valdés Ugalde, Francisco. 1994. "From Bank Nationalization to State Reform: Business and the New Mexican Order." In *The Politics of Economic Restructuring: State-Society Relations and Regime Change in Mexico,* ed. Maria Lorena Cook, Kevin J. Middlebrook, and Juan Molinar Horcasitas. U.S.-Mexico Contemporary Perspectives Series 7. La Jolla: Center for U.S.-Mexican Studies, University of California, San Diego.

———. 1996. "The Private Sector and Political Regime Change in Mexico." In *Neo-liberalism Revisited: Economic Restructuring and Mexico's Political Future,* ed. Geraldo Otero. Boulder, Colo.: Westview Press.

———. 1997. *Autonomía y legitimidad: Los empresarios, la política y el estado en México.* Mexico City: Siglo Veintiuno Editores.

van Waarden, Frans. 1991. "Two Logics of Collective Action? Business Associations as Distinct from Trade Unions: The Problems of Associations of Organisations." In *Employers' Associations in Europe: Policy and Organisation,* ed. Dieter Sadowski and Otto Jacobi. Baden-Baden, Germany: Nomos Verlagsgesellschaft.

———. 1992. "Emergence and Development of Business Interest Associations: An Example from The Netherlands." *Organization Studies* 13, no. 4:521–62.

Vera Blanco, Emilio. 1960. "La Industria de Transformación." In *México: Cincuenta años de revolución.* Mexico City: Fondo de la Cultura Económica.

Vernon, Raymond. 1963. *The Dilemma of Mexico's Development: The Roles of the Private and Public Sectors.* Cambridge: Harvard University Press.

Villalobos, Gildardo. 1989. *La industria mediana y pequeña de bienes de capital en México.* Mexico City: Fundación Friedrich Ebert.

Villareal, Juan M. 1987. "Changes in Argentine Society: The Heritage of Dictatorship." In *From Military Rule to Liberal Democracy in Argentina,* ed. Monica Peralta Ramos and Carlos H. Waisman. Boulder, Colo.: Westview Press.

Villareal, René. 1977. "The Policy of Import-Substituting Industrialization, 1929–1975." In *Authoritarianism in Mexico,* ed. José Luis Reyna and Richard S. Weinert. Philadelphia: Institute for the Study of Human Issues.

Villavicencio, Daniel, and Mónica Casalet. 1995. "Desarrollo tecnológico en las pequeñas y medianas empresas." In *Micro y pequeña empresa en México: Frente a los retos de la globalización,* ed. Thomas Calvo and Bernardo Méndez Lugo. Mexico City: Centro de Estudios Mexicanos y Centroamericanos.

Wade, Robert. 1990. *Governing the Market: Economic Theory and the Role of Government in East Asian Industrialization.* Princeton: Princeton University Press.

Wallace, Robert Bruce. 1980. "Policies of Protection in Mexico." In *Protection and Economic Development in Mexico,* ed. Adriaan Ten Kate and Robert Bruce Wallace. New York: St. Martin's Press.

Weinstein, Barbara. 1990. "The Industrialists, the State, and the Issues of Worker Training and Social Services in Brazil, 1930–1950." *Hispanic American Historical Review* 70, no. 3:379–404.

Weiss, Linda. 1988. *Creating Capitalism: The State and Small Business Since 1945.* London: Basil Blackwell.

Weyland, Kurt. 1996. *Democracy Without Equity: Failures of Reform in Brazil.* Pittsburgh: University of Pittsburgh Press.

———. 1998. "The Fragmentation of Business in Brazil." In *Organized Business, Economic Change, and Democracy in Latin America,* ed. Francisco Durand and Eduardo Silva. Coral Gables, Fla.: North-South Center Press.

Whitehead, Laurence. 1989. "Political Change and Economic Stabilization: The 'Economic Solidarity Pact.'" In *Mexico's Alternative Political Futures,* ed. Wayne A. Cornelius, Judith Gentleman, and Peter H. Smith. Monograph Series 30. La Jolla: Center for U.S.-Mexican Studies, University of California, San Diego.

———. 1996. "Comparative Politics: Democratization Studies." In *A New Handbook of Political Science,* ed. Robert E. Goodin and Hans-Dieter Klingemann. Oxford: Oxford University Press.

Whiting, Van. 1992. *The Political Economy of Foreign Investment in Mexico: Nationalism, Liberalism, and Constraints on Choice.* Baltimore: Johns Hopkins University Press.

Williams, Heather L. 1996. *Planting Trouble: The Barzón Debtors' Movement in Mexico.* Current Issue Brief 6. La Jolla, Calif.: Center for U.S.-Mexican Studies, University of California, San Diego.

———. 2001. *Social Movements and Economic Transition: Markets and Distributive Conflict in Mexico.* New York: Cambridge University Press.

Williamson, John. 1990. *The Progress of Policy Reform in Latin America.* Washington, D.C.: Institute for International Economics.

Williamson, Peter J. 1989. *Corporatism in Perspective: An Introductory Guide to Corporatist Theory.* London: Sage.

Winters, Jeffrey A. 1994. "Power and the Control of Capital." *World Politics* 46, no. 3:419–52.

Wionczek, Miguel S. 1964. "Electric Power: The Uneasy Partnership." In *Public Policy and Private Enterprise in Mexico,* ed. Raymond Vernon. Cambridge: Harvard University Press.

Wise, Carol, ed., 1997. *The Post-NAFTA Political Economy: Mexico and the Western Hemisphere.* University Park: Pennsylvania State University Press.

Wood, Elisabeth Jean. 2001. "An Insurgent Path to Democracy: Popular Mobilization, Economic Interests, and Regime Transition in South Africa and El Salvador." *Comparative Political Studies* 34, no. 8:862–88.

World Bank. 1979. *Mexico: Manufacturing Sector: Situation, Prospects, and Policies.* Washington, D.C.: IBRD and World Bank.

———. 1997. *The State in a Changing World: World Development Report, 1997.* Washington, D.C.: World Bank.

Yashar, Deborah J. 1998. "Contesting Citizenship: Indigenous Movements and Democracy in Latin America." *Comparative Politics* 31, no. 1:23–42.

———. 1999. "Democracy, Indigenous Movements, and the Postliberal Challenge in Latin America." *World Politics* 52, no.1:76–104.

Zabludovsky, Gina. 1980. *México: Estado y empresarios*. Serie Cuadernos de Apoyo a La Docencia. Mexico City: Escuela Nacional de Estudios Profesionales Acatlan.

———. 1984. "Antecedentes del Comité México-Norteamericano de Hombres de Negocios." In *Clases dominantes y estado en México,* ed. Salvador H. Cordero and Ricardo Tirado. Mexico City: UNAM.

Zabludovsky, Jaime. 1990. "Trade Liberalization and Macroeconomic Adjustment." In *Mexico's Search for a New Development Strategy,* ed. Dwight S. Brothers and Adele E. Wick. Boulder, Colo.: Westview Press.

INDEX

Note: Page numbers in *italics* refer to figures and tables.